"Parents and other primary caregivers raising children with intense emotions will benefit from this book, which is the result of a unique collaboration between a seasoned clinician and the parent of a child with emotion dysregulation. Parents will learn critical skills and strategies and receive practical advice on how to help their children. As these parents acquire new skills and learn to look at their challenges in a different way, they will become more effective and witness positive results. Ultimately, they will feel better about their lives."

—Celia Serkin, executive director of the Montgomery County Federation of Families for Children's Mental Health

"Intensely emotional children engage in behavior that is intensely trying to parents. In this important work, Pat Harvey and Jeanine Penzo have provided both a frame of reference by which to understand the basis of those emotions and behaviors in children and a treasure trove of practical interventions that equip parents to respond in helpful and constructive ways. This important work will prove invaluable for parents and for clinicians working with parents, children, and families."

—Robert Ciottone, Ph.D., ABPP, professor of psychology at Clark University and adjunct faculty at University of Massachusetts Medical School

D0950600

"*Parenting a Child Who Has Intense* ... arents and professionals who live and work with children who are often described as overreactive. The authors break down highly charged interactions in thoughtful, useful ways that explain how parents can defuse the most intense scenarios. The outlined skills serve to assist parents, educators, and all who work with children in everyday interactions that may become unpredictable without notice. This book helps everyone take a deep breath."

—Jill G. Aubry, former special educator and school director at Falls Church City, VA public schools

"This book will be an excellent resource for parents and other caregivers of children and adolescents with mental health issues and challenging behaviors. I think it will be on many a parent's bedside table."

—Emily Novick, MPP, child and adolescent program coordinator at the National Alliance on Mental Illness, Montgomery County

"Harvey and Penzo have written a book that is first and foremost a guide to understanding and developing specific strategies for addressing their child's intense emotions. That the book attends to the deep feelings that parents themselves experience along the journey to emotional and behavioral stability sets it apart from other books in this genre. *Parenting a Child Who Has Intense Emotions* takes the parent step-by-step through a process of healing and growing that will resonate immediately with those who have struggled to provide what their children need. Parents will feel better for having read this book, as it will allow them to address things that have been troublesome for years."

—Terry Landon, LICSW, clinician/consultant with Wediko Children's Services

"This book provides communication skills and strategies that are easy for parents to use with all types of children. Wonderful to have as a resource to help raise a happier child."

—Gina Shawl, RN

"Our child's highly emotional behaviors really strained our marriage. We did not know how to change our family dynamic and break the cycle of pain and frustration. Harvey and Penzo gave us a quintessential bible of principles and techniques that dramatically changed how we all interacted. It is a must-read in order to help you and your child be more effective."

—Minna and Robert Golden

Parenting a Child Who Has Intense Emotions

Dialectical Behavior Therapy
Skills to Help Your Child
Regulate Emotional Outbursts
& Aggressive Behaviors

PAT HARVEY, LCSW-C
JEANINE A. PENZO, LICSW

New Harbinger Publications, Inc.

Publisher's Note

This publication is designed to provide accurate and authoritative information in regard to the subject matter covered. It is sold with the understanding that the publisher is not engaged in rendering psychological, financial, legal, or other professional services. If expert assistance or counseling is needed, the services of a competent professional should be sought.

Distributed in Canada by Raincoast Books

Copyright © 2009 by Pat Harvey and Jeanine A. Penzo
New Harbinger Publications, Inc.
5674 Shattuck Avenue
Oakland, CA 94609
www.newharbinger.com

FSC
Mixed Sources
Product group from well-managed
forests and other controlled sources

Cert no. SW-COC-002283
www.fsc.org
© 1996 Forest Stewardship Council

Acquired by Tesilya Hanauer; Cover design by Amy Shoup; Edited by Carole Honeychurch; Text design by Tracy Marie Carlson

Library of Congress Cataloging-in-Publication Data

Harvey, Pat.
   Parenting a child who has intense emotions : dialectical behavior therapy skills to help your child regulate emotional outbursts and aggressive behaviors / Pat Harvey and Jeanine A. Penzo.
      p. cm.
   Includes bibliographical references.
   ISBN-13: 978-1-57224-649-2 (pbk. : alk. paper)
   ISBN-10: 1-57224-649-9 (pbk. : alk. paper)   1. Emotional problems of children. 2. Behavior disorders in children. 3. Child psychotherapy--Parent participation. 4. Child rearing. I. Penzo, Jeanine A. II. Title.
   BF723.E598H37 2009
   649'.154--dc22

                                        2009023489

11 10 09
10 9 8 7 6 5 4 3 2 1   First printing

To Danielle,
For bringing us together as friends and colleagues. Your perseverance against life's challenges is an inspiration to us all.

—JP and PH

To all the parents who trusted me with their stories: your courage, insights, and willingness to learn taught me more than you can imagine

—PH

Contents

Acknowledgments

This book is the culmination of a long journey. I started my social work career as I was just stepping out of adolescence, and as my career advanced I got married, had children, and continued to learn and grow in both my personal and my professional life. As a clinician who always focused on families, it was natural that when I was introduced to DBT (dialectical behavior therapy) at the Bridge of Central Massachusetts I would find a way to use it to benefit parents. This book is the result of all that I've learned along the way.

I want to thank my earliest teachers of cognitive behavioral techniques and much more, Paul Rosen and Larry Peterson. Your lessons are included in many ways. I also want to thank Steve Murphy at the Bridge, the originator of the term "the story of emotion." Steve hired me as a division director and gave me the opportunity to learn, practice, and understand DBT and was the first one to suggest I write a book about parents and DBT. I want to thank Christy (Clark) Matta, who was my first teacher in all things DBT and to whom I owe a tremendous token of gratitude. It was while at the Bridge that I met Jeanine, who provided the inspiration for this book and who is always available to remind me what skills help me the most. I am grateful for her trust and her friendship.

When I moved from Massachusetts to Maryland, I was lucky to be introduced to parents and professionals who were interested in learning about DBT. I am most grateful to Diane Sterenbuch, who led me to the National Alliance on Mental Illness (NAMI) and whose shared interest in borderline personality disorder and dialectical behavior therapy opened many doors for me. I want to acknowledge all the parents I have worked with in Maryland who have taught me so much. Of these, I am most grateful to Gina Shawl, who, as I developed this book, showed me that effective parenting using DBT skills could help very young children manage intense emotions.

Along my journey, I was often guided by Bob Ciottone, psychologist extraordinaire. Bob taught me that "change brings opportunities," and his belief in me enabled me to take advantage of many new possibilities. My "family of friends" in Massachusetts has been a major support throughout, and their cheerleading of this project often kept me going. I am so grateful to have you all in my life. And to the most important people in my life, my children and my husband, I send a very special thank-you for your love and for making everything in my life worthwhile. To Jennifer and Sarah, thank you for letting me practice DBT skills as I parented you and for letting me share our stories as examples for others. I am so proud of the adults you have grown up to be. And I'm grateful to my husband, Brad, whose strength and love made the entire journey possible. Thank you for helping me become the person that I am. Thank you all.

—*Pat Harvey*

I was first introduced to DBT skills in 2003, when my daughter with emotion dysregulation moved to a DBT group home for young adults. There, my husband and I participated in the DBT skills group for parents. At that time, I had no idea what an impact the lessons I learned there would have on my life. Pat Harvey was the gifted teacher who shared with us the new skills and strategies that would help us parent our daughter more effectively and allow us to begin looking toward the future with renewed hope. As I later began to teach DBT skills to other parents, patients, and families, Pat was and still remains my mentor. I'm grateful to her for all that she has taught me personally and professionally. More importantly, I am thankful for her friendship and inspiration.

I want to express my appreciation to my daughter's first treatment team: Jeannie Marcus, MD; Renee Brant, MD; and Roberta Sacks, Ed.D. They showed us unwavering support and encouragement as my husband and I raised our three children while struggling to negotiate the health care system of the 1990s in search of answers and effective treatment options for our oldest daughter. In addition, the personal and professional support I continue to receive from Revan Miles, LICSW, is invaluable as I continue to strive to move forward and balance it all.

The "Manville Moms," Donna Burke, Eileen D'Entremont, Deb Chamberlain, and Betty Needham, will always hold a special place in my heart. When our children moved on and we no longer attended our formal weekly support group, our personal support network kept me going when life seemed to spin out of control.

Last but certainly not least: without the love of my family, this project would not have been possible for me. I am very grateful to my husband, Mike, and to my children, Danielle, Katharine, and Michael, for your patience and support. Your help has enabled me to coauthor this book. I also want you all to know how proud I am of your commitment and impassioned involvement in mental health advocacy and education—something that has become a family endeavor.

This book for parents is the fulfillment of a goal I have had for several years: sharing with parents living in similar circumstances the valuable lessons I have learned about parenting a child with intense emotions. The support I received from all those mentioned above has allowed me to fulfill my dream. Thank you.

—*Jeanine Penzo*

We would both like to thank all the friends and colleagues who read this book along the way and provided ongoing support and advice. A special thank-you to Emily Novick, Rowena Abadi, Gina Shawl, Jill Aubry, Terry Landon, and Revan Miles. And a very special thank-you to Dr. Murray Claytor and Dr. Robert Ciottone, who read the whole manuscript and provided us with invaluable feedback and ideas. We couldn't have done this without all of your help.

We would also like to thank the folks at New Harbinger for giving us the opportunity to write this book. We are grateful to Tesilya Hanauer for believing in this project and for giving two unknown authors the chance to publish this book. We also appreciate all the invaluable editorial guidance we received from Jess Beebe and everyone else at New Harbinger who worked on this project. And we would like to thank our editor, Carole Honeychurch, for working with us collaboratively to bring additional clarity to our message.

—*PH and JP*

Introduction

As you pick up this book, are you wondering whether *your* child has intense emotions? Is it your child screaming in the grocery store because he can't have something you told him in advance he couldn't have? Is your child the one who keeps crying when everyone else seems to be having a good time? Does your child look at you with anger in his eyes when you tell him he can't do something he wants to do? Does he have a tantrum when you have simply asked him to get ready for bed? Is homework a nightmare? Do you dread telling your child no?

If you answered yes to any of these questions, this book is for you. While the behaviors mentioned in the questions above may differ, they are all signs that a child suffers from some degree of what is called *emotion dysregulation*. A child who is emotionally dysregulated reacts intensely and immediately to situations or circumstances that others may not react to and has a hard time returning to her initial emotional state. You might describe this child as going from zero to 100 in seconds. The behaviors that are so overwhelming and disconcerting to you are your child's responses to emotions that she cannot manage in other ways.

Marsha Linehan developed dialectical behavior therapy (DBT) to help people whose inability to manage their emotions affects their ability to regulate the resulting behaviors (1993a). The goals of DBT treatment include teaching people (1) new, more effective behaviors to replace dangerous and problematic behaviors and (2) how to think dialectically in order to accept that different perspectives that may seem contradictory can be true. These new skills, as we discuss them throughout the book, help people manage the way they think, feel, and behave more effectively.

In 2001, I (Pat Harvey) began to teach DBT skills to the parents of adolescents and young adults living in DBT residential group homes in Massachusetts. My goal was to enhance the kids' clinical treatment by teaching the parents the DBT skills their kids were learning in the program. There I met my coauthor, Jeanine. As the parent of a child with emotion dysregulation, Jeanine showed me how helpful these skills could be for parents. As I taught Jeanine the skills, she taught me to be sensitive to the stories of the parents whose lives are dominated by their child's intense emotionality. I learned about the overwhelming emotions parents feel when their children suffer from emotion dysregulation, emotions that are often ignored or dismissed by others. As the parents learned skills to help their children, it became clear that these skills were helping them manage many aspects of their own very difficult lives as well.

Parents of children whose behaviors often spiral out of control tell me they have a difficult time getting effective guidance and help. Everyone seems to have advice which is often different and contradictory. Parents may be told, "Don't worry, it's just a phase," or "Don't be so hard on your child," or the reverse, "Your child needs more discipline." Parents searching for direction, guidance, and practical advice continue to feel overwhelmed and confused. With anger, sadness, and sometimes guilt, these parents also report being blamed for their children's behaviors by family members, school personnel, and some mental health professionals. My hope is that this book will validate the feelings you have been unable to share with others and will help you see that you're not alone.

This book is not about blame or fault. It is about learning, change, and hope. It encourages you to see that you and your child can learn to do things differently. This will not be easy and will require patience and persistence. With insight, awareness, and new strategies and techniques, ineffective and maladaptive behaviors *can* be replaced by new, more effective and adaptive behaviors. The automatic, troublesome patterns you and your child have developed over time *can* be replaced by calmer and more positive interactions.

Parenting a Child Who Has Intense Emotions has been written in response to all the parents I continue to work with who say, "I wish I had known these skills when my child was younger." Though this book has been designed as part of a series for parents of children who are ages five through twelve, I've found over the years that the skills and guidance in this book help parents regardless of the age of their child. Many of the questions I'm asked by parents of children of all ages are answered in the following chapters. In addition, these skills make it possible for parents to feel more hopeful about helping their child, are effective whether or not the child is involved formally in DBT or any other kind of treatment, and are helpful to teachers and other individuals who work with children and parents. Since I began teaching DBT skills, the parents I work with have reported that the skills help them understand, accept, and calm children whose behaviors once seemed unmanageable. Whether your child has periodic outbursts, behaves aggressively, withdraws, or has a diagnosed emotional disorder, these skills will be helpful to you.

As you read this book, you will learn about the dialectic of acceptance and change that Linehan identified as one of the core DBT principles (1993a). In the context of parenting, this means that you—and your child—are doing (and have done) the best you can, *and* you can both learn new skills to even better. In this book you will see that this understanding will help you accept your child for who he is and, at the same time, help him work to improve those behaviors that are a challenge for him and for you. You will not only learn DBT assumptions (or statements) that will help you become more accepting of your child, you will also learn to use these assumptions to become more accepting and less judgmental of yourself, as well. You may eventually look back and wish you had done things differently. There will be days when you are unable to use the skills from this book or forget to use them in the midst of your parenting. Times like these are when it's important for you, the parent, to let go of your own negative judgments and blame. We encourage you to accept yourself and your actions by telling yourself, "I did the best I could. I am doing the best I can." If you are reading this book, you're trying to help your child and also striving to do things better yourself. It takes strength and courage to learn to parent more effectively. You can feel good about your desire to do so.

Through my clinical experiences and Jeanine's personal experiences, we know that having a child who has intense emotions affects the entire family. I have heard of marriages that disintegrated over disagreements about whether a child needed more discipline or more love. I have heard healthier siblings describe themselves as feeling invisible and acknowledging that they just didn't know how to develop their own identity separate from the child whose behaviors dominated the family. I have listened as parents describe how it feels to be negatively judged by friends, family, and strangers who all feel they know how to be a better parent to the child who has intense emotions. This book will provide ways for you to respond to others as well as ways to manage your own feelings about what's happening to your child and your family.

This book is the result of the collaboration between Jeanine and me. It brings together my clinical understanding of what is most helpful for parents whose children have intense emotions and the insights Jeanine provides about the roller coaster of emotions and behaviors experienced by parents of these children. Together we have weathered the ups and downs in our professional and personal lives, using these skills to manage difficulties and to be effective more often. We continue to learn about the benefits of DBT as we work to understand the dilemmas and needs of parents and children whose lives are dominated by intense emotions.

These skills now form the backbone of everything I do professionally. For Jeanine, these skills have helped her parent her own child with emotion dysregulation more effectively while also moving on with her life. While Jeanine now uses DBT skills professionally, working in the VA with spinal-cord injured veterans and their families, I continue to find that they enhance my personal life, my relationships with my own children, and my interactions with others as well. Both Jeanine and I have richer and more balanced lives because of these skills. Using these skills has allowed us both to learn how to be aware, accepting, and appreciative of what we have while we continue striving to make things better. We hope that the skills described in this book will help you do the same.

HOW TO USE THIS BOOK

This book has four parts: The first part (chapters 1 and 2) provides the foundation and background for all the skills that follow; the second part (chapters 3, 4, and 5) focuses on emotions, providing understanding about how they develop and specific, step-by-step skills that you and your child can use to calm disruptive and disquieting emotions; the third part (chapters 6, 7, 8, and 9) uses similar skills to help you reduce the occurrence of behavioral outbursts and to manage already escalated behaviors; and the fourth part (chapters 10 and 11) addresses your emotional needs and those of other family members. After you read the first part, you can read the remaining chapters in order or move through the sections that seem most relevant. If you are feeling overwhelmed by the information, you can advance to chapter 11 and learn how to take care of yourself. Our hope is that, by reading this book, you will find the practical advice and strategies you have been looking for.

Many skills are repeated throughout the book. Repetition helps learning. In DBT, you learn through practice, and this book provides a variety of exercises, examples, and suggestions for using the skills. For shorter exercises and questions, you can write directly in the book. For those that are longer, you will write down your answers in a dedicated DBT notebook that is always handy. Or, if you prefer, you can use a computer folder that you have easy access to. Try different DBT skills and see what works. Be patient with yourself and with your child. Parents report that it takes a long time to understand and consistently practice these skills; this has been our experience as well. I can assure you, however, that when the skills are practiced over time, parents report how helpful they are. The parents I've worked with say that DBT skills enable them to become more effective parents, develop a more positive relationship with their child, and feel better about themselves, their child, and their lives.

—Pat Harvey

PART 1

You, Your Child, and Emotional Intensity

CHAPTER 1

Emotional Intensity and Your Child's Feelings

Does your child show displeasure by pouting, complaining, or throwing herself on the floor? Does your child whimper, cry for a minute, or scream for hours when hurt? Are your child's demands so relentless that you feel you have to give in? Do you wonder why your child seems so emotional, why she tends to react so intensely to situations that other children seem to ignore, or why it takes her so long to get over things?

Children, like adults, have emotions. These emotions are real and not easily dismissed. How you feel affects all you do, how you do it, and your overall sense of yourself. Therefore, understanding emotions is central to understanding your child's intense behavioral responses, as they result from emotions that she cannot manage. This chapter will help you understand what drives your child's behaviors, as well as your own reactions to your child. This foundation will help you begin to use the skills discussed throughout this book to help your child manage her emotions and the resulting behaviors.

PRIMARY AND SECONDARY EMOTIONS

Everyone has both primary and secondary emotions. *Primary emotions* are biologically based and virtually automatic, while *secondary emotions* are created when we react to our own primary emotion (Lazarus and Folkman

1984). We have less control over primary emotions, while we have quite a bit of control over the development and perpetuation of our secondary emotions. Secondary emotions tend to last longer and cause more maladaptive behavioral responses.

Primary Emotions Happen

Primary emotions (such as fear) are usually hardwired. They are your initial reaction, or the first emotion you feel, to situations that affect you. They are experienced physiologically within your body. Usually these emotions come and go, much as waves come and go on the shore (Linehan 1993b).

To help you to understand primary emotions, let's look at a situation that might cause you to experience one.

EXERCISE: Primary Emotions

Imagine that you've just been called to the principal's office at your child's school. You know only that your child has been involved in a fight. You think about this as you drive to the school. List the feelings that you might experience as you drive:

_____

_____

_____

_____

Secondary Emotions Are Created

Let's continue with our example of being called to the office of your child's principal. You listed some of the initial, or primary, emotions in the preceding exercise. Your primary emotions may have been alarm, fear, or anger, especially if your child has been guilty of starting fights in the past. When you get to the principal's office, she tells you that your child was hit by another child and was not the instigator. Now you begin to think about your initial anger and the erroneous conclusion that you jumped to. These thoughts create the secondary emotion of guilt.

Secondary emotions are reactions to your primary emotions and result from beliefs and assumptions that you've learned throughout your life. For example, if your parents often showed disapproval when you were angry as a child, you may continue to experience guilt whenever you feel anger, especially when the anger is not justified by someone else's actions. It's possible to have several secondary emotions as responses to one primary emotion. In fact, you or your child may have so many secondary emotions that you cannot remember the primary emotion that triggered them.

THE CONTINUUM OF CHILDHOOD EMOTIONS

Just as all children look different, so their emotional responses differ as well. Emotions vary in their intensity, in how long they last, and in the behavioral responses they motivate.

Some children will cry for a long time over an incident that another child might not cry about at all. Some children love the thrill and terror of roller coasters, while others are fearful and attempt only rides that seem safer to them. Some children seem to adapt easily to situations, while others have a difficult time with changes. For most children, these characteristics fall along a continuum. Different situations may cause the same child to respond with more or less intensity; different children may respond to the same situation with different levels of emotional intensity. Look at Table 1.1 (on the next page) and notice the ways different children might initially react to falling off a bike (under "Initial Reaction").

Table 1.1: Emotional and Behavioral Continuum

		Initial Reaction	**Delayed Reaction**
Less intense	Child A	• Gets up • Gets back on bike	• Talks to parents about the incident
	Child B	• Gets up, looks around • Whimpers • Gets back on bike	• Shares with friends and family what happened
	Child C	• Gets up • Kicks his bike • Walks away with his head down	• Does not discuss what happened • Yells at his parents
More intense	Child D	• Stays on ground • Cries • Waits for someone to help • Will not get back on bike	• Responds to comfort and calms down • Later talks about what happened
	Child E	• Gets up crying • Goes running and screaming for help • Will not get back on bike	• Cannot be comforted • Continues to cry • Is angry at his parents and unable to explain why

What assumptions might you make from the behaviors of these children? How would you judge each child according to the behaviors you've witnessed? Do you assume that Child A is brave or unafraid? Do you assume that Child B is fearful, even though she confronts her fears to return to the bike activity? Would you characterize Child C as "angry"? Is Child D overly dependent because she waits for help from someone else? Do you think Child E is anxious and stubborn in her unwillingness to get back on the bike? What is your reaction to each of these responses? Do you judge these children as strong or weak?

Our reactions to children's behaviors are shaped by assumptions we make about their behaviors. Your assumptions or judgments (the way in which you think about your child) will affect how you feel about and how you respond to your child. The danger in jumping to conclusions is that you will act as if something is true when it may not be. For instance, some parents may assume that the child who whimpers and looks around is seeking attention and is fine when, in actuality, she may be momentarily scared. Parents who assume their child is seeking attention may choose to ignore her very real need. We will discuss this later in this chapter when we address the links between thoughts, feelings, and behaviors.

Events sometimes cause a delayed behavioral reaction in children. Parents may become aware that something has happened to their child only later, when their child behaves in an unexpected way. This is illustrated in the column under "Delayed Reaction" in the chart above. See if one of these children behaves like yours.

As you can see, this incident and the feelings that have evolved from it continue to have an impact on the behavior of each child. You may see your child (1) yelling later in the evening, (2) being quiet and uncommunicative, (3) readily sharing what happened, or (4) refusing to get back on a bike in the days to come.

Asking why your child is behaving as she is may do little to help you understand. Depending on the nature of your child, she may easily forget this incident or remember it for quite some time. You may feel confused by the behaviors you see. Try not to blame your child if her behavior confuses you. She may need help figuring out and sharing what has happened and how she feels.

Recognizing Worrisome Responses and Behaviors

How can you differentiate responses and behaviors that are typical of children your child's age from behaviors that might require some additional help or consultation? The answer to that question lies not simply in looking at the behavior you see. It also lies in looking at (1) the intensity of the response; (2) how long the response lasts before your child is able to return to a state of calm; (3) whether the emotional response generalizes and transfers to other, similar situations; and (4) whether or not your child begins to respond in a similar way to a wider variety of contexts and situations. In other words, there are several determining factors that require observation and consideration over a period of time (Werner 1948; Ciottone 2008).

Let's return to the example in which your child has fallen from her bike. We've already discussed different responses ranging from your child showing no reaction at all to your child not being able to move on from the incident. Her reactions may indicate whether you have reason to worry, as you will see below.

What would it mean if your child, after falling off her bike, is no longer willing to go play outside? The anxiety and fears that result from falling off the bike have now generalized to any outside activity. Your child isn't able to differentiate between riding her bike and other outside activities. This lack of differentiation might be cause for worry.

What if your child feels that the reason she fell off her bike is that you weren't there to keep her safe? She might become less independent and want to stay by your side, feeling anxious when she is away from you. This would be a regression to a more dependent state for your child, which might also be cause for concern.

Focus on your child's behaviors as you consider the questions below. Your answers to the questions will help you determine whether or not your child might benefit from additional help. You can simply think about the answers or write down your thoughts in your notebook.

- Does your child have a tantrum with her whole body as she might have done at a younger age? If she returns to an earlier stage of coping, how long does she stay there?

- Does your child respond to emotional situations in the same way she did when she was younger?

- How long does it take your child to calm down? Is she still upset when other children have already recovered and moved on?

- Does your child respond with the same level of interest, intensity, and reactivity to all environmental or emotional stimuli? Is she able to differentiate and prioritize among them?

- Do you often think of your child as going from zero to 100 in seconds?

The answers to these questions will help you relate the next section to your child.

When to Get Help for Your Child

You might want to seek help for your child by consulting with a professional when you observe that she:

- Is unable to differentiate between situations, responses, causes, and effects

- Responds to events in an extreme way

- Reaches a high level of intensity very quickly

- Has trouble prioritizing what is important and is overwhelmed by choices

- Takes a long time to return to a calm state after an upsetting incident

You may find it helpful to get additional feedback from people who have received training about child development and who also see your child's interactions with others. Talk to your child's primary care physician/pediatrician, day care provider, or teacher. Don't hesitate to share your concerns about your child. Always be clear and descriptive about your child's behaviors. If you and/or the professional continue to be worried, it might be time to make an appointment with a mental health professional, preferably one who specializes in work with children.

If your child does have seriously intense emotional reactions, the sooner she receives help, the better the outcome will be. Remember, however, that one incident or situation is usually not indicative of a problem. All children have emotionally intense reactions at times. In addition, all children have periods of time when they remain emotional for longer than you would expect. The key to understanding when your child might need professional help is to review the bullets above and look at *how often and consistently* these responses occur.

There are many possible ways that a child can react to a situation, but some responses may become consistent patterns. You may change a particular way you respond to your child's behaviors when you learn that responses can be triggers for an emotional outburst. You and your child are teaching each other, even as you begin to wonder why your child reacts the way she does.

RESPONDING EMOTIONALLY, REASONABLY, AND WISELY

Marsha Linehan describes three states of mind that are useful in describing how people respond to life's experiences: emotion mind, reasonable mind, and wise mind (1993a). In some people, one state of mind may dominate. Others will vacillate between one state of mind and another, depending on the situation. These terms are a way to understand and acknowledge that people think, act, and make decisions in different ways. The goal of DBT is to learn to think wisely. Many DBT skills help you learn how to do that (Linehan 1993a).

Responding Emotionally

According to Linehan, some people are governed primarily by their emotions (1993a). Their interpretations and responses are dictated by how they feel at that moment. Their perceptions of reality may even become distorted, so they see the facts of the situation in a way that coincides with what they are feeling. They then make decisions based on those distortions. If others describe you as highly emotional, you probably operate often in *emotion mind*.

If you parent primarily with frustration and anger, with a short temper and a lot of yelling, you're most likely responding emotionally. When you are emotional, it's more difficult for you to problem solve, and you may find that developing plans of any kind (even as simple as what to make for dinner) seems very difficult.

Your child is responding emotionally when she is whining, yelling, demanding, or constantly crying. When she's emotional, your child may not be able to get tasks done and may change the facts of a situation to fit her mood. You may think she is lying when she is justifying her actions in a way that is dictated by her emotions. You may be frustrated by your "emotional child" and find it difficult to comfort her, although you may want very much to do so.

Responding Reasonably

There are people who think primarily in a rational, logical way and who are said to be governed by what Linehan terms *reasonable mind* (1993a). Someone who responds in a reasonable manner most of the time may not understand why emotions affect others. A person whose responses are most often reasonable doesn't allow emotions to be involved in her decision making.

When you are responding reasonably, you may feel calm and seemingly unaffected by the emotionality that surrounds you. You may find resolutions for most conflicts and be very comfortable fixing problems. However, you may feel uncomfortable with emotions and unable to understand them in your child or in other family members. Problems without ready solutions will cause you great distress. The calm of a parent who operates reasonably and calmly often frustrates a parent who operates more emotionally, and vice versa. Learning that each parent functions differently can help parents find ways to support rather than be angry with each other.

If your child usually responds reasonably to situations, she may do a lot of thinking, be disciplined, and tend to be very focused on tasks and expectations. This child may be described as a "little adult" or a "serious child."

Responding Wisely

If you view reasonable and emotion minds as opposite ends of a continuum, you will understand the need to integrate the two. A person who thinks emotionally will not usually think reasonably or logically. Likewise, a person who thinks reasonably will have difficulty bringing feelings into her decisions or behaviors or recognizing them in others.

In Linehan's DBT framework, the integration and overlap of emotion and reasonable thinking is called *wise mind*, which describes a path to thinking wisely (1993a). When you make decisions wisely, you will decide intuitively, seeing the whole situation clearly and incorporating both feelings and logic. Wise mind will help you feel calmer and more comfortable with your decisions. Thinking wisely will help you make necessary changes in your responses to your child.

When your child is thinking wisely, she can make reasonable choices and will be comfortable with the way she resolves problems. For instance, a child who is thinking wisely comes home from school and goes immediately to complete her homework efficiently and without complaint when she knows that she can't play with her friends until her work is done. She will be able to feel good about herself and her efforts.

If your child has intense emotions or reacts emotionally most of the time, it will be very important for *you* to think wisely as often as possible. Wise mind will allow you to respond clearly, calmly, and intuitively to your child's emotionality.

We will be examining wise mind in much greater detail later in the book, and you will learn skills to help you operate in wise mind more often.

THE NATURE/NURTURE CONFLICT

As you learn about the states of mind, you may be wondering about your own child and how she has come to be in emotion mind so often. You may wonder why your child seems so out of control and why it is so hard to calm her. You may have wondered if you're doing something wrong or if something is wrong with your child. These thoughts can lead you to question whether your child is the product of her genetics (her inborn temperament or nature) or a product of her environment (how she is nurtured). This brings us to the question of nature versus nurture and how your child has developed intense emotions.

This question of nature (genetics and biology) versus nurture (environment) does not have an either/or answer. The answer involves a combination of both. Every child is born with a unique and distinctive temperament. According to research that was done in the 1950s (Chess, Thomas, and Birch 1959) and is still quoted today (Fox and Calkins 2003), certain characteristic qualities of a child (level of distractibility, intensity, risk taking, responses to change or to new situations, and so on) are present at birth and may continue to influence the way that child responds or adjusts to the world for the rest of her life. These inborn childhood characteristics exist along a continuum and can affect and be affected by the environment in which the child lives.

Emotion Dysregulation

You may wonder why your own children are different from one another and why your parenting strategies can work effectively with one child and seem ineffective with another. Marsha Linehan developed what is called a *biosocial* theory as a way to understand pervasive emotional dysregulation (1993a). According to Linehan, some children are born with a predisposition to emotion dysregulation (1993a). These children react immediately and intensely to emotional situations and have a hard time calming down and returning to how they were before the situation occurred. A child with emotion dysregulation is then unable to modulate her behavioral responses to the intense emotions that she experiences as overwhelming. Her behaviors mirror her overwhelming feelings, so that you see a child whose behaviors are out of control.

Does this sound like your child? Are your child's problems entirely caused by this biological predisposition to emotional intensity? Are your child's behaviors totally inborn? Basically, the answer is no. Next we will discuss what else is involved.

The Interaction Between Your Child's Responses and Yours

A child who has intense reactions may overwhelm parents who don't know how to respond to her. Even generally supportive parents may become confused by the intensity of their child's reactions and may be tempted to question or dismiss them. This is simply one way of trying to cope with behaviors in your child that you don't fully understand. Parents may attempt to help their child feel better and minimize their own discomfort without realizing that they are inadvertently trivializing their child's feelings. Parents' attempts to help their children manage internal feelings that the parents themselves don't actually understand may miss the mark. How often might a parent say, "Don't worry, honey. You'll feel better later"? Although the parent means it to be helpful, this kind of statement might make a child believe that her feelings don't matter. A highly reactive child can cause a parent to react in a dismissive manner, causing the child to feel more distraught. This is an interactive process in which *no one* is to blame.

Unintentional Invalidation

It's difficult for any parent to see his child upset, and you, as any parent, will try very hard to make your child feel better. As you try to soothe her by saying, "You'll feel better soon," "It isn't a big deal," or "Don't worry," you're actually, without realizing it, *invalidating* or not acknowledging your child's experience (Linehan 1993a). As you seek to reassure her, you may be unintentionally minimizing an issue that is of great concern to her. For some children, this doesn't cause future difficulties. They are able to rebound and recover quickly, no matter how upset they might have been. For other children, recovery is not so easy.

If a child has a predisposition for being intensely emotional, a lack of acknowledgement or invalidation by those around her leaves her feeling bewildered and even more upset. She doesn't know how she's supposed to feel or why you don't understand. This can become a family dynamic. Take a look at the following illustration to see how this dynamic can play out.

Figure 1.1: The Dynamic of Emotional Invalidation

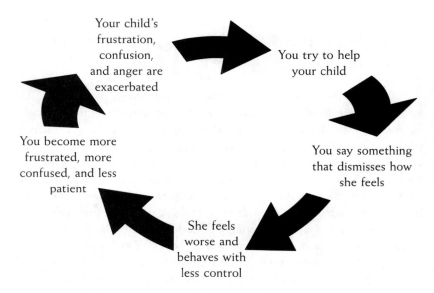

The cycle of confusion, frustration, and dysregulation often continues and feeds on itself. Extreme, intense emotions and the inability to appropriately control the ensuing behavioral responses occur more and more often and seem to take over your family. In chapter 2 we will discuss how to acknowledge your child's feelings in order to interrupt this common dynamic.

THOUGHTS, FEELINGS, AND BEHAVIORS

It's important to remember that emotions do not develop or occur in isolation. They are the result of physiological reactions and/or cognitive processes. Something internal (a thought) or external (an event) causes you to experience an emotion. Sometimes you experience the emotion so quickly that you may be unaware of what actually caused it.

Thoughts Lead to Feelings, Which Lead to Behaviors

What a person feels is directly related to what she is thinking about something, which then leads to certain behavioral responses (Beck 1972; Peterson and Gerson 1975).

The triangle below provides a way to visualize this dynamic. *Thoughts* are internal phrases, attitudes, beliefs, or even images that you say to yourself. Some of these thoughts may occur so automatically that you might not be aware of their existence. However, feelings are almost always caused by thoughts. *Feelings* are the physiological reactions in your body that shape your ongoing experience. *Behaviors* are the result of these thoughts and feelings; they are the way you respond and act as a result of what you're feeling.

Figure 1.2: The Dynamic of Thoughts, Feelings, and Behaviors

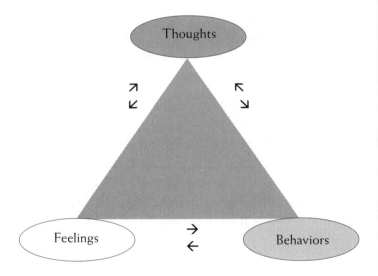

Obviously, you can't see what your child is thinking or feeling. You can see only her behaviors, which are the direct result of her thoughts and feelings. Because you don't know for sure what thoughts and feelings are behind the behaviors you witness, you're likely to make certain interpretations or assumptions. Depending on several factors, your interpretation may be more or less accurate. There may be a difference between your assumptions and your child's reality. Much to your frustration or confusion, your child may not be able to explain *what* she feels or *why* she's feeling it. We will talk about this more in chapter 3, when you will learn how to help your child tell you what she's feeling.

In order to understand how thoughts lead to feelings, look at the situation we describe below and notice how different thoughts about the same event lead to different feelings and behaviors.

> Your child is not doing what you want her to do (event). You think: "Why doesn't she ever listen to me? Why must we go through this every time I ask her to do something?" You might become angry (your feeling) and yell at her (your behavior).
> **Or**
> "Okay. She's having a hard day. I'll let this slide today." In that case, you may be relieved (your feeling) and move on (your behavior).

In this example, what you said to yourself about the event (your thoughts) affected how you felt and what you did in response. Learning to be aware of your thoughts will give you the skills you need to change your emotional and behavioral responses to situations.

Your child also responds to her thoughts, whether or not she (or you) is aware of them. In the example below, you can see how a different thought leads to a different emotional and behavioral response in your child.

> Your child sees a girl she knows (event).
> Your child thinks, "That girl is ignoring me" (thought). She will be sad (emotion) and withdraw from the situation (behavior).
> **Or**
> Your child thinks, "That girl is my friend" (thought). She may feel happy (emotion) and will approach the child to play (behavior).

As you can see, what you think about a situation affects how you feel about and behave in that instance.

Your Child Is Not Her Behavior

Behaviors can be changed. Children's behavioral responses are learned and not ingrained in their personalities. Understanding and helping your child depends on learning to separate your child from her behaviors. *Your child is not her behaviors.* Her behaviors are what she *does,* not who she *is.* Your child may behave in an angry way, she may even scream and yell, but that doesn't make her an "angry child." It makes your child someone who yells or screams when she is angry. Likewise, you don't have a "disobedient child," but a child who does not follow directions.

Why is this distinction important? You don't want your child to grow up feeling that she is inherently damaged, has a flawed character, or should be ashamed of herself. You want her to learn that she is not her behaviors. You want your child to feel accepted and loved regardless of her feelings and behaviors. For your child to grow up with a positive self-image, she must learn that her behaviors define what she does, not who she is.

THE STORY OF EMOTION

We have examined the links between thoughts, feelings, and behaviors. We've also discussed that our emotions do not *just happen* but are related to events, to thoughts, and to physiological responses in our bodies. Based on DBT, the story of emotion is another way to view the steps that lead from an event to an emotion and from that emotion to its behavioral outcome (Linehan 1993b). Knowing the steps in the story will help you to have more control over *your* emotions and your behavioral responses, and it will provide a way to help your child gain more control over hers.

A Parent's Story of Emotion

Consider Jane's story and see how her emotions develop.

Jane has two daughters, four-year-old Emma and eight-year-old Jackie. Jane was up most of the night with Emma, who is running a fever and feels sick to her stomach. It's now 7:30 a.m., and Jane is trying to get Jackie up, ready for school, and off to the school bus. Jane is also watching the clock, waiting for the pediatrician's office to open so she can make an appointment for Emma, who continues to whine and wants her mother to stay with her. As the minutes tick away, Jackie doesn't get out of bed. Jane begins to think, "Here we go again. This will be one of those days when Jackie won't get ready for school by herself." She begins to yell for her to get up. Jackie gets up and says that she needs help in the bathroom. Jane says she doesn't have time and wonders, "Why can't she just do this by herself like she did yesterday?" Jane begins to think that Jackie is doing this on purpose because Jackie knows that Jane is tired this morning and because her sister is sick. Jane's neck muscles begin to tighten, and she feels her heart beating faster. She gets angrier and yells more. She begins to worry that Jackie will miss the bus, but she still refuses to help her in the bathroom. By the time Jackie runs to catch the school bus, Jane is exhausted and frustrated with Jackie and with herself. After she takes Emma to the doctor and is able to relax, she feels guilty about how she reacted to Jackie.

The Components of the Story

Does this story sound at all familiar? In it, you can see each of the components of the story of emotion: vulnerabilities or contributing factors (how someone is already feeling), the prompting event or trigger (what happened), the thoughts and beliefs about the event, body sensations and physical reactions (how the person's body feels), the emotion itself (the word that describes how the person feels), and the actions or behaviors that follow (what the person actually does), which is the outcome of the story (Linehan 1993b). Let's go through the scenario above, looking at each of the components in turn.

VULNERABILITIES AND RISK FACTORS

These are circumstances or feelings that exist prior to an event and that might cause a person to be at risk to feel negatively. In other words, if you are tired or hungry, have had a bad day at work, or are worried about other situations, you'll be less able to manage a situation that you might otherwise be capable of handling with ease.

> **Jane's Vulnerabilities**
>
> - Jane has not had enough sleep and is tired.
> - Jane is worried about Emma.
> - Jane is anxious to call the doctor.

PROMPTING EVENT OR TRIGGER

This is the situation that you're reacting to in the moment and that may be occurring internally or in the environment. For example, a prompting event may be a headache (internal) or someone telling you to do something you don't want to do (external).

> **Jane's Trigger**
>
> - Jackie doesn't get out of bed when her mother asks her to and requests help in the bathroom.

THOUGHTS AND BELIEFS ABOUT THE EVENT

These are the statements that you make to yourself about the situation or prompting event. That is, what do you think about the event? Sometimes these thoughts are so automatic that you don't even recognize them as thoughts.

> **Jane's Thoughts and Beliefs About the Event**
>
> - "Here we go again. This will be one of those days when Jackie won't get ready for school by herself."
> - "Why can't she just do this by herself like she did yesterday?"
> - "She is doing this on purpose."

BODY SENSATIONS OR RESPONSES

This is the way you begin to feel in your body. This may include tension through your neck or shoulders, your heart beginning to race, and/or your stomach beginning to twist and turn.

Jane's Body Sensations or Responses
- Jane's neck muscles begin to tighten.
- She feels her heart rate quicken.

THE EMOTION OR EMOTIONS

This component is where you give your emotion a name in order to communicate to yourself and others what you are feeling. All of the previous steps in the story of emotion have led to this point. Your ability to communicate your emotion by naming it can't occur without the previous steps, even if you're unaware that they've occurred.

Jane's Emotions
- Anger
- Frustration
- Anxiety

BEHAVIORS AND ACTIONS: THE OUTCOME OF THE STORY

These are what you actually *do* with your feelings. Every emotion has an embedded action urge. When you're sad, you want to cry; when you're angry, you want to yell or punch something. Whether or not you follow through on your urge to act is up to you. The behavior you choose will have its own consequences and will affect which emotions you feel afterward (your secondary emotions).

Jane's Behaviors/Actions
- Jane yells.
- She refuses to help Jackie.
- Eventually, she feels guilty about her behaviors (secondary emotion).

Changing the Outcome of the Story

By looking at every step of the story, you can develop awareness about how your emotions develop and behaviors follow. Once you're aware of these steps, you can choose to make changes in one or more of them. Each change that you make affects or changes the outcome of the story and can lead to more effective behaviors. Each step of the story provides an opportunity for change.

KNOWING WHEN YOU'RE VULNERABLE

When you are aware of your vulnerabilities, you can take actions that keep you out of stressful situations or make stressful situations easier for you. In this instance, Jane was tired and worried about her ill daughter. However, despite these vulnerabilities, she still had to get Jackie up and ready for school. If she were aware of the fact that she was at risk for negative emotions, she might have made a decision to help Jackie in the bathroom. She could have made a game of getting ready rather than expecting Jackie to do it by herself. A child has an uncanny ability to know when parents are stressed, and then she may become stressed herself. If you find a way to remain calm, there is a higher possibility of cooperation and a lower probability of feeling guilty.

CHANGING THOUGHTS

You can consciously change the thoughts that lead to negative emotions. Just as some thoughts can lead to emotions such as anger and frustration, other thoughts can lead to tenderness and optimism. If Jane had thought, "Okay, Jackie needs some help. If I help her, she'll get ready faster," Jane might have been less angry. Or, if she hadn't said to herself, "Here we go again" (a common thought of parents) and instead thought, "How can we make this easier for all of us?" she might not have yelled at her daughter or felt guilty later in the day.

BEING AWARE OF YOUR BODY'S RESPONSES

There are times when you might not be aware of your vulnerabilities or your thoughts. Your only cue that something is going on may be your body's reactions. You may begin to feel your body responding to your thoughts about the triggering event and sense a tightening in your chest, butterflies in your stomach, or your heart starting to race. Even if you're unaware of *why* you feel this way, you can still change your emotional state and the outcome of your story. It may take only a few seconds to take some deep breaths, count to ten, or consciously relax your hands or shoulders—anything that allows your body to slow down. These actions can give you a moment to find a behavioral response that is more effective and feels better to you and to your child.

CHANGING BEHAVIORS

The last chance that you have to change the outcome of the story is to behave in a different way, finding responses to the situation that will feel better. If Jane had recognized that yelling wasn't going to help and that refusing to help Jackie was only going to prolong the process, she might have decided to help her or to talk to her more calmly. By changing these behaviors, the outcome of the story might have felt better to Jane and to her daughter.

You can learn something new from each story of emotion. Every event is an opportunity to change different parts of the story until the outcome is one that you feel good about and that is most helpful to your child.

EXERCISE: A Story of Emotion

Now we will walk you through your own story of emotion. Your first task is to think of a recent situation that triggered a negative emotion. Write a brief description of the situation at the top of a page in your notebook.

Next, consider each of the questions below and write the answers in your notebook. As you do so, notice where you might have made changes. We'll be teaching you skills that will help you change your responses to situations like this one. For now, developing awareness is important. Your stories may change as you learn skills throughout the book.

VULNERABILITIES and RISK FACTORS

How did you feel before the event happened?

TRIGGER

What happened?

THOUGHTS AND BELIEFS ABOUT THE EVENT

What did you think about what happened? What words came to your mind after the event?

BODY SENSATIONS AND RESPONSES

How did your body feel?

NAME YOUR EMOTION

What is the name that describes what you were feeling?

BEHAVIORS AND ACTIONS

How did you act because of your feeling? What would have been a more helpful response?

Understanding your own story of emotion is an important step toward self-awareness and changing the way you interact with your child. Your child has her own unique stories of emotion that affect how she feels and behaves. We'll discuss your child's stories in chapter 3.

SUMMARY

This chapter provides the foundation for the rest of this book by providing ways to:

- Begin to understand your child's emotions

- See that each child has an established temperament at birth that contributes to the way she feels and behaves

- Understand that your child's temperament and subsequent emotional reactions may be different from yours or even from your other children's

- Understand how differences in your child may cause you to be less accepting and supportive than you might otherwise be

- Understand how your child's emotions lead to her behaviors

- Change behavioral outcomes to intense emotions

Throughout this book, we will continue to emphasize that (1) there is no blame and no fault in the fact that your child has intense emotions and behavioral difficulties, and (2) there is hope for change in the future.

CHAPTER 2

Effective Parenting

What does it mean to parent effectively? It means interacting and/or responding to your child in ways that enable you to achieve your parenting goal: to help your child grow with self-esteem, values, and a belief in himself. When you parent in an effective way, you respond wisely and keep your goals for your child clear, consistent, and realistic. Your responses to your child are based on understanding, validation, and doing what works best (Linehan 1993a).

Throughout this book, you will learn ways to parent in a more effective manner. However, the fact that you can benefit from learning new skills doesn't mean that you have been a "bad" parent. As you read this book, and as you parent your child, do so without blaming or judging yourself. Given your unique situation in life at this time and the skills and knowledge that you have, you've been doing the best you can.

In DBT you are asked to accept two facts that may seem contradictory: that *you are doing the best you can* and that *you can do better* (Linehan 1993a). This is a no-fault, no-blame framework for change. One of the intentions of DBT is to help you develop the awareness you need to accept that you have done, and are doing, the best you can while providing skills and knowledge that can help you be more effective in meeting your goals.

Learning to accept yourself may be one of the hardest skills you'll learn, and it's also a crucial lesson. A lack of self-acceptance often leads to parenting choices based on emotions such as guilt, which may make you feel better in the moment but aren't necessarily effective in the long run. When you can be more accepting of yourself, you will have more patience with yourself and your child and be better able to make your parenting decisions wisely. So give yourself credit for having done the best you could at any point in time.

THE DBT ASSUMPTIONS

To guide the therapeutic work in DBT, Linehan delineated several assumptions (below) with the expectation that they would be accepted as fact (1993a). Several of these assumptions, as well as those developed by Miller for adolescents and their families, are especially relevant for parents of children with intense emotions (2001). These are assumptions we're asking you to accept as an important part of the DBT learning process. They are:

- Your child is doing the best he can

- Your child needs to do better, try harder, and be more motivated to change

- Your child wants to do things differently and make things better

- Your child must learn new behaviors in all important situations in his life

- Family members should take things in a well-meaning way and not assume the worst

- There is no absolute truth

Let's look at each of these assumptions in more detail.

Your Child Is Doing the Best He Can

This is one of the most important assumptions you can learn. It means that your child is doing the best he can at this particular moment in time. There might have been times in the past when your child was able to manage better, and there might be times in the future when your child will do better. *Now,* in this moment, your child is doing his best.

In order to understand this assumption, think about being a parent when you're not feeling well. You still get up to feed the kids, and then you turn on the TV. On another day, you might have read your children a story instead of letting them watch television, but today your throat hurts. You sit down with your children in the family room and answer their questions, and though you usually like to initiate conversations with the kids, today you're quieter. *You are doing the best you can,* given how you feel at the time.

Your child may feel better or worse on certain days or in certain circumstances. He may not have slept well and wakes up cranky and irritable. He may accept hugs on some days and may push you away on others. On each day, your child is doing the best he can.

Accepting and reminding yourself that your child is doing the best he can helps you feel less angry, less disappointed, and less frustrated with your child. In turn, your child is less angry, less frustrated, and more able to hear what you say to him. Remembering the assumption that your child is doing the best he can will prove quite helpful when your child has intense emotions.

Your Child Needs to Do Better

The next assumption, that your child needs to do better, try harder, and be more motivated to change, is usually one of the easier ones for parents to accept. You probably already believe that your child needs to do better and try harder. However, this assumption must be partnered with the first one in order to have any benefit, as we explain below.

Accepting that your child has to make changes doesn't mean that he's been unacceptable, bad, or otherwise to blame for what has occurred in the past. Your child will be more willing and better able to accept feedback and guidance if he doesn't feel he's being blamed or judged. To parent effectively, balance acceptance of your child in the moment with expecting and helping him to do things better in the future.

If you are confused by trying to accept your child as he is at the same time that you're asking him to change, you are not alone. Most parents are confused by this at first. It often helps to believe that your child is doing the best he can *at this moment in time,* which allows you to help him move toward change in the future.

Your Child Wants to Do Better

The third assumption is that your child wants to do things differently and make things better. At times, it may seem that your child likes things the way they are, no matter how many consequences you give him or how miserable he might be. You may think your child controls the household and is able to do everything the way *he* wants. It may be hard to believe that he might actually want things to improve.

Children seek their parents' approval, regardless of how they behave or what they say. Your child would much rather live in a house that is free of tension and anger, even if that anger begins with him. *No* child likes to be constantly at odds with others, either as the antagonist or as the victim.

The angry, explosive, aggressive behaviors you may see are ways that your child has learned to manage his feelings. It doesn't mean that he *likes* behaving this way—only that this is the most effective way he knows to manage his feelings. Change may be very difficult for him. However, given the opportunity, he would want things to be different.

Your Child Must Learn Behaviors for All Situations

The fourth assumption is that your child needs to learn new behaviors in all important situations in his life. It's not surprising that children may behave better in certain circumstances than in others. Your child may be able to manage within the structure of school and then fall apart when he comes home, where he feels safer and more comfortable. Sometimes the opposite may be true—your child has difficulty with the structure at school and manages to control behaviors more effectively at home, where the structure is different. Your child may fight nonstop with siblings but get along well with friends. These inconsistencies in your child's behavior often lead others to blame you for not being able to manage your child (a topic we'll discuss in chapter 10). Or, they may cause you to believe your child is choosing to behave or not behave in each circumstance. The assumption that a child *should know* how to behave in all circumstances is an unrealistic expectation with negative consequences for everyone.

Different situations require different competencies. The assumption that your child should know how to behave effectively in one situation because he knows how to behave in others is inaccurate. Nor is it helpful to believe that your child chooses to behave better in certain situations or with certain people. Your child must be *taught* new skills for different situations until he is able to use skills in all situations.

Family Members Should Not Assume the Worst

The assumption that family members should take things in a well-meaning way and not assume the worst was developed specifically for families. Members of families often jump to conclusions about other family members, believing these conclusions to be true regardless of unknown or contradictory information. You may think your child is behaving in a certain way in an effort to get your attention; your child may think that you won't let him have candy before dinner because you're mad at him. These assumptions often cause unnecessary anger, disappointment, and confusion within the family.

The intent of a behavior (which is often unknown) is often confused with the impact of a behavior (which is experienced by others). For example, your child may believe that his brother's intent was to make him feel bad when he is not asked to play with his brother's friends. In reality, his brother may have simply forgotten to ask him and had no intention to hurt his feelings. Your child's intent may not be to make you angry, even if this is how you feel.

There may be many reasons why someone is behaving as he is, some of which may have nothing to do with anyone else in the family. When family members ask questions and learn to check the facts, there are more opportunities to accept one another.

There Is No Absolute Truth

The truth of any situation is based on the perspective of each person and is therefore relative and changeable. When you accept that someone's point of view, memory, or understanding may be different from your own, you will no longer feel the need to prove that you are right or the other person is wrong. Calmly agreeing to disagree tends to prevent fights, arguments, and parent–child power struggles.

How often do you and your child argue over the truth? You tell your child that he can't have a friend visit this weekend, and he complains, "You never let me do anything fun." You know this statement doesn't represent the truth as *you* know it. So, you now have a choice. You can dispute what your child said and argue about whose truth is right, or you can choose not to respond to his statement. Accepting your child's truth for that moment does not negate your own. It also doesn't override the limit that you set, which can still be enforced. You will, however, avoid a battle over truth, an argument that can't really be won by either side and that makes losers of everyone.

As the parent, you'll often be the one who will be able to understand that there can be more than one truth. A child's tendency to think concretely (without being able to abstract meaning or look at the bigger picture) can make it hard for him to see this subtlety. That's why it's important for you, the parent, to accept that your child has his own point of view that feels very real to him. You don't need to defend your point of view, nor do you need to dismiss his; you need only to accept that they are different.

Learning to Believe the Assumptions

You may be thinking that you do not and cannot believe the assumptions above. They challenge parents in different ways. Some assumptions might seem believable, while others may not feel comfortable to you at all. While some of these statements will be difficult to accept, behaving *as though* they are true is actually necessary so that you can accept, change, and feel better about yourself and your child.

If you feel that you simply can't accept some of the statements, you're not alone. This is true for most parents we work with, so try not to worry. All change occurs over time, which is why one of the key elements of DBT is that you need to practice in order to learn. You can practice the following steps with any of the assumptions that you may be having difficulty with or any assumption that you think would be effective if only you believed it. We have provided examples of some assumptions you might want to think about.

- Repeat a challenging assumption to yourself, even if you don't fully believe it. ("Even though my child is not cooperating with me, *he is doing the best he can.*")

- At times when it seems relevant and/or when you're having a difficult time, think about a helpful assumption. ("Even though my child doesn't want to go to therapy, *he still wants to make things better.*")

- Repeat the words of the challenging assumption to yourself. ("*My child is doing the best he can.*")

- Remind yourself what the assumption means whenever it seems appropriate. ("He is doing what he can despite his many difficulties; *right now, he is doing the best he can.*")

As we've seen, changing thoughts actually leads to changes in feelings and beliefs. Over time, you will begin to feel a little differently. As you practice believing them, the assumptions will feel true.

EXERCISE: Practicing the Assumptions

Take another look at the DBT assumptions and think about how treating them as facts might change how you think, feel, and behave. Answer the following questions in your notebook:

- Which assumption do you think will help you the most?

- Which assumption challenges you the most? Why?

Think about one situation in which believing an assumption would change what you would do or how you would feel toward your son or daughter. Use the points below to help you clarify your thoughts:

1. Describe the situation. (What was your child doing? What were you feeling?)

2. Write down the assumption you would use.

3. Describe a possible new response. (For instance, "I decided to walk away rather than argue.")

4. Describe what you think would be the outcome of the new response. (For example, "Less yelling, more calm.")

FINDING WISE RESPONSES

In the preceding chapter, we introduced the idea of wise mind and responding wisely (Linehan 1993a). You already know that if your child has intense emotions, it is most effective to respond wisely and make choices and decisions based on a larger context and not on emotions.

Using the DBT assumptions is one way you can begin to respond to your child more wisely. To further help you learn to respond wisely, DBT teaches several skills that involve learning to step back from a situation and to see things with new eyes and a different point of view (Linehan 1993a). These skills also involve learning to focus, to think in a nonjudgmental way, and to do what works (what is effective).

Skills to Help You See with New Eyes

The purpose of these skills is to help you learn to participate actively and with awareness in your life (Linehan 1993a). People often go "mindlessly" or automatically through the motions of their lives, paying little attention to what is happening in the present moment. In order to learn new skills and change ineffective patterns, you must bring your full attention to what you're doing in the moment.

Many people find it helpful to put a bit of distance between an event and their response to it. There are skills that allow you to mentally step back and fully attend to the moment, responding in a thoughtful way. Try these steps to help you respond more wisely to a challenging event or situation:

1. Stand back and look at what is happening. Observe the situation.

2. Put words to the situation or experience, describing it so that you can separate the reality of the situation from your assessment of or feelings about it. For example, a person who is yelling (the description) may not be, as you are thinking, angry at you (your assessment of the situation).

3. Attend to the situation with full awareness. Be actively and fully involved in whatever you are doing in the present moment. For example, the next time you're doing the dishes, fully attend to the actions you're performing. Most of us do many tasks mindlessly, simply performing the familiar actions while thinking of other things. When you actively concentrate on a task that is difficult, you can find more effective ways to manage it. The same is true even for challenging times with your child.

Mindfulness Exercise to Focus and Notice

Mindfulness exercises are used to help people become aware of the present, focused in the moment, and fully aware of their actions and/or their surroundings. Mindfulness exercises can be used at any time to focus and free your mind of distractions.

Mindfulness Exercise

Try writing your name *very slowly*. Notice how:

- You pick up the pen and rotate it into position in your hand

- You hold the pen

- Your other hand is positioned

- You move your hand

_____

_____

See how differently your name looks when you slow down and notice what you're doing. How hard or easy was it for you to change this behavior? Notice that when you slow down your responses and focus with more awareness, you change an otherwise automatic response.

Skills to Guide Wise Responses

DBT provides invaluable skills to help you see with new eyes and develop wise ways of thinking, communicating, and behaving (Linehan 1993a). These new skills involve thinking in a nonevaluative way, doing what works, and focusing all of your energy on one thing in the moment. We have already mentioned several of these skills, and we will review them in more detail now.

Think in a Nonevaluative Manner

The Buddhist quality of DBT philosophy encourages thinking in terms that do not evaluate (Linehan 1993a). Being nonevaluative doesn't mean that you think only positively, because every positive has a corresponding negative. Thinking in a nonevaluative way means that you don't think in terms that judge at all. For example, let's say that your son comes home from school and has gotten an A on an exam. You respond happily and say, "You're such a good student!" What happens when your son later comes home with a C? Because you've previously framed the situation in terms of "good" when he got an A, he'll now be tempted to see his performance as "bad." Evaluative language invites comparisons and judgments that can create difficulty in the future.

Instead of evaluating, try to simply describe. For example, instead of using evaluative language, simply say something like, "I see that you're studying for many hours," and do not label or judge at all. To move from evaluative language: (1) describe the behavior just as you see it, and (2) describe the consequence of that behavior. For instance, you might say to your child, (A) "You're being so good (evaluative statement) and making me proud right now," or (B) "You're spending a lot of time on your homework (nonevaluative and describing), and it makes me feel good when you do that (focus on consequences)."

Statement A labels and judges; your child will likely feel you're talking about *him* rather than his behavior. The child doesn't know exactly what he is doing to make you proud or what he needs to do in the future. Statement B describes what your child is *doing* in a way that is clear to him and can be repeated in the future. Effective parenting enables your child to understand that it is his *behaviors* (which are changeable) and not *him* that you are describing.

In Table 2.1 we have listed some judgmental phrases that are used often. Next to them are ways of describing what your child is doing in ways that do not evaluate. Notice that the nonjudgmental phrases (those that describe) provide more ways to help your child do things differently.

Table 2.1: Phrases That Judge vs. Phrases That Describe

Phrases That Judge	Phrases That Describe
• "That is not appropriate behavior."	• "Your behavior is ineffective and will not help you get what you want."
• "You are such a good boy."	• "Thank you for doing what I asked."
• "My child is so manipulative."	• "My child asks her father after I already said no."
• "He's very disruptive."	• "He interrupts his siblings when they're doing their homework."
• "I wish he wasn't so difficult."	• "He breaks the rules at home and appears not to listen to me."
• "You are so lazy."	• "It would make me happy if you got your chores done when I ask."
• "You're terrific."	• "I really like that you share things with me and listen when I ask you to do something."

It's very hard to think in terms that do not evaluate. We've all learned to label and judge what we see rather than describe it. It takes practice to be nonevaluative. It is, however, a very important skill to learn. As we have seen, how you think affects how you feel and how you act. Children who are labeled or judged don't separate labels from facts and do not feel separate from their behaviors. Your child's sense of who he is and his self-esteem are affected by the way you think about him and the honest, descriptive words you use in talking to him. The more you are able to use descriptive rather than judgmental language, the better your child will be able to know himself and understand the connection between his behaviors, your reactions, and how he feels about himself.

EXERCISE: Describing Your Child in Nonevaluative Terms

Now try using descriptive rather than judgmental language. To do this, picture your child standing in front of you. Now ask yourself the following questions and write your thoughts in the spaces below or in your notebook:

• What does your child look like? How tall is he? What color is his hair? (Note: While words like fat or skinny are not factually evaluative, they are often perceived in evaluative ways.)

_____

_____

• What does your child enjoy? What foods does he like? What hobbies does he have? What is his favorite game?

_____

_____

• How does your child spend his day? What grade is he in? What subject does he like? Does he play sports? What sports team does he root for?

_____

_____

• Does he have a talent for art, performing, or playing an instrument?

_____

_____

There is much more about your child to describe than you usually think about. You may be so overwhelmed by your child's emotional intensity that you think of little else. This exercise allows you to see your child with new eyes and in new ways.

Do What Works

Parents often ask how to teach a child who reacts so intensely how to behave or how to recognize the impact of his behavior on others. You may be concerned that if you accept your child and don't judge him you will be unable to teach him values and morals.

Learning adaptive behaviors, according to DBT, requires that you evaluate what you are currently doing to see if your behaviors are helping or hurting your efforts to achieve your ultimate goals (Linehan 1993a). Ask yourself or your child, "Is this working?"

If you want to teach your child new behaviors, focus on describing the current behavior and helping your child evaluate the consequences of that behavior. Is he getting what he wants? If he wants to have more friends but fights with them when they visit, does his behavior lead to having more friends? Likewise, you can ask yourself whether your responses to your child are having the outcome you're looking for. Ask yourself, "Does this response or action help me to accomplish what I'm trying to do? Is it working?" Doing what works means responding wisely. It means eliminating "shoulds" and evaluations such as right and wrong or fair and unfair.

Think about how you respond to your child when he's upset and slams the door. Slamming the door is against the rules in your home, and you would like to give him a consequence for this behavior. You tell him that, because he slammed the door, he can't listen to music for a half hour. However, your child uses music to soothe himself when he's upset. Is your response effective? How will your child calm down when he isn't able to use something that soothes him?

A more effective response would be to have him stay in his room for a half hour without the TV and allow him to listen to music. This will help him settle down and may also teach him a new way to manage his emotions the next time he's upset (taking some time alone with music).

Focusing on One Thing with Full Attention

Another Buddhist aspect of DBT encourages people to focus in the present moment (Linehan 1993a). Therefore, the last skill to guide wise responses involves learning how to give one activity your full attention, with full awareness and total involvement, and without being distracted by other things. This is the opposite of multitasking. Many of us try to use time as effectively as possible by doing as many things as possible. Actually, when we multitask, we are less effective in what we're doing. To get the best result in a situation and to be able to respond most wisely, bring your full attention to each task by doing them one at a time with full awareness.

Focusing on One Thing with Full Attention

Think about what happens when you are helping your child with his homework while you talk to a friend on the phone. While you're looking at your child's homework, you miss something that your friend says and ask her to repeat it. Or, you are listening to your friend and are unable to see a mistake your child made. Your child and your friend may each feel a little left out and unimportant. You may be too distracted to effectively help your child, and you're not able to be fully present for your friend. Neither your friend nor your child is fully helped by your multiple efforts.

For this exercise, pick an activity that you do often and try doing it with your full attention and without distractions. Or choose an activity from the list below:

- Eat something very slowly. Pay attention to how it feels in your mouth and how it tastes.

- Spend time with your child without answering the phone or talking to anyone else. Hear what your child is saying and see if you can repeat it to yourself.

- Look at something in your purse or pocket that you look at quite often. See if you can find out something new about it.

Responding vs. Reacting

When your interactions with your child are based on your emotions, you are *reacting* to your child. Your emotions will dictate what you say and how you say it. When you begin to think wisely, you will *respond* to your child in a well-planned and reasonable way (Linehan 1993b). You will take your child's feelings into consideration and respond in a way that is thoughtful and effective. When you interact with your child, ask yourself if you are reacting emotionally or responding wisely. You will want your answer to be the latter.

VALIDATION

Validation refers to the act of letting someone know that you understand, acknowledge, empathize with, and accept his thoughts, feelings, and behaviors in the context of his own life experiences (Linehan 1993a). This is a very important concept in DBT that we mentioned earlier and will now look at in more detail.

In our groups, parents have reported that validation is the most important skill they learn. As we noted in chapter 1, when your child feels that you are not listening or do not understand, he feels invalidated. As a result, his emotions and behaviors can become more intense as he tries to get you to understand what he's trying to communicate. Validation skills help you let your child know that you're listening and taking him seriously, that you can understand his behavior within the context of his life circumstances, and that you accept him. When your child feels validated, he may be less intense and more willing to discuss his feelings.

Validation can take many forms. These can include:

- Sitting quietly and listening

- Actually telling someone you are listening carefully

- Expressing an acknowledgment of someone's feelings

- Trying to understand what someone is feeling or telling you

Whatever form you use to validate your child has to be acceptable *to him*. If your child feels that you can't understand him, do not validate him by saying "I understand." If your child responds favorably when you sit quietly and listen, that may be an effective form of validation for him. Sometimes it takes trial and error to find the most effective way to validate your child. Do not give up; the benefits of validation are immeasurable.

Letting someone know that you accept his feelings may not be an easy thing to do. It is especially hard for parents when the behaviors resulting from those emotions seem strange, out of control, or dangerous or they are aimed at you. It helps to remember that validating your child's feelings or behaviors *does not mean* that you agree with those feelings or behaviors or that you like them. It only means that you are listening to your child and trying to understand from his point of view.

The Importance of Validation

Of all the parenting skills, this one may be the most difficult for parents to learn—and the most important. Validation helps you to:

- De-escalate emotional situations

- Communicate effectively with your child

- Listen in a way that allows your child to talk more, share more, and listen more

- Enable family members to feel more positive about each other (Fruzetti 2005)

Validation also helps you to remain calm in the face of your child's emotionality. Validation is the first line of defense in chaotic situations.

Acceptance and Change

A person must feel accepted before he can change (Linehan 1993a). A person must feel heard in order to hear. Think about when someone ignores your feelings about a situation and instead tries to tell you how to fix it. You might feel that the person doesn't understand you or isn't listening. Without acceptance, it becomes more difficult for you to listen or take the subsequent advice seriously.

The same is true for your child. In order for him to hear what you have to say, he wants to know that you are listening as well. For him to accept advice, he has to feel that he is acceptable first so that he can change without feeling like something was wrong with him to begin with.

You will know if your validation is effective by the response you receive from your child. Does he calm down or begin to share more? Do not give up if this doesn't work the first time. Keep trying. Your child will need time to learn new responses to your new behaviors.

Learning to Make Validating Statements

Below are the steps you will take to practice validating your child and others. Read them a few times and come back to them when you know you may be facing a challenging situation or wish to review an interaction you feel you could have handled more effectively. Remember, as with any new skill, practice is essential.

STEP 1: FIND A WAY TO ACT WISELY

The first step in this process is to stop, step back, observe, and think about the situation.

- Take a moment before responding.

- Observe the situation.

- What do you need to do for yourself to slow down your response time? (Try taking a few deep breaths, close your eyes for a second, unclench your fists.)

- Determine your goal.

- Respond wisely and try not to react emotionally.

STEP 2: LOOK AT YOUR CHILD WITH NEW EYES

The next step is to be aware of old patterns and to develop new ways of thinking.

- Remember, your child is doing the best he can under the circumstances. You might even say this to yourself as a reminder.

- Try to determine what emotion your child is feeling. If you don't know, can you ask?

- Consider what may be leading to the present behavior.

- Think about what is going on for your child. Is this situation bringing up difficult memories for him?

STEP 3: EXPLORE WHAT MAY BE GETTING IN THE WAY

Next, consider what circumstances may be impeding your validation of your child.

- Think about the vulnerabilities or concerns you bring to the situation. What is this situation bringing up for you?

- Be aware of your thoughts and feelings about the situation.

- Consider whether the event has triggered old memories or old feelings in you.

- Determine whether you're judging your child or yourself in this moment.

STEP 4: MAKE A VALIDATING STATEMENT

Practice making statements that calm you and your child and that show your understanding and acceptance of him. You may miss the mark at first, and you may need to keep practicing to find ways to validate your child that work for him. Make sure that your attempts are genuine, and your child will begin to feel validated.

Practice Is Essential

Remember that in learning all of these skills, it's necessary to practice, practice, and practice. Learning anything new requires openness and repetition until it feels like second nature.

Let's take a look at an example to see how thinking about validation can change a response to a child and lead to a better outcome.

Sheila's seven-year-old son, Keith, is having problems getting to bed at a reasonable time. One of the problems is that Keith is complaining about his pajamas. Sheila doesn't understand the problem—Keith has never complained about this before. Sheila knows that her son has very aggressive temper tantrums when he's overtired and frustrated. Although she also knows that it won't help the situation if she begins to yell at Keith, she's becoming increasingly frustrated herself.

Sheila is beginning to worry that if she can't get Keith to bed at a reasonable time, he won't be able to get up for school the next day. Sheila tells her son, "Please, just put on the pajamas and go to bed." Keith refuses and a verbal struggle ensues. The next day, Sheila looks at the Validation Worksheet for alternative responses to her son. Let's look at her Validation Worksheet for this situation.

This is what my child is doing:
(Observe and describe the situation.)

"Keith is not following his bedtime routine. He's being slow in getting into his pajamas and is complaining that they feel 'scratchy.' He has worn these pajamas before without incident."

My thoughts and feelings about what my child is doing:

"Why does he have to make such a fuss about this? Why can't he just get into these pajamas and get to bed?"

[Note: If you voice these feelings to him and say, "No, they aren't scratchy, you picked them out yourself…" you will be invalidating his experience and feelings. See the next statement for an effective answer.]

I can accept my child when I remember that he's doing the best he can. I can let him know that I am hearing him by saying:

"I see that these pajamas feel scratchy to you tonight. Do you think that we can find another pair of softer pajamas that feel more comfortable to you? It's time to get to bed, and I want you to feel okay in your pajamas. We can buy new pajamas tomorrow."

The outcome of this situation is:
(Include your feelings and how your child responded.)

"I feel like I heard my son and we resolved this situation without dismissing his feelings or diminishing him. He went right to bed after we changed his pajamas."

To help you become more familiar with developing validating responses, we've created a way for you to practice the steps that will lead to a validating response. To practice, think about a situation that you wish you had handled more effectively or consider situations that may arise in the future. As Sheila did above, follow the directions in each example and write your responses in your notebook.

Validation Practice Worksheet

This is what my child is doing:
(Observe and describe the situation.)

My thoughts and feelings about what my child is doing:

I can accept my child when I remember that he's doing the best he can. I can let him know that I am hearing him by saying:

The outcome of this situation is:

I feel:

My child responds by:

PARENTING ROLES, GOALS, AND EXPECTATIONS

As you know, your role and your goals as a parent include loving your child, nurturing him, keeping him safe, teaching him moral values, and helping him become an independent and stable member of society. What happens when your child's emotional intensity makes it feel impossible to fulfill your role? Do your goals shift? Do you prioritize your goals and try first to meet those that seem most important? How do you manage your own feelings about your child while still trying to parent as effectively as possible?

It's difficult to parent a child who reacts with emotional intensity to rules, expectations, and the limits you need to place on his behaviors. However, it's not impossible. The way you parent may need to shift somewhat. You may have to adjust and have fewer priorities while you do your best to raise your child with values and a respect for expectations. In this section and the chapters that follow, we will provide you with strategies and techniques to help you fulfill your responsibilities as a parent despite your child's intense emotionality.

Interacting and Communicating in Ways that Work

In order to interact and communicate with your child in ways that work, think about how you can effectively get your point across and teach your child new behaviors. Once again, you may have to put aside your feelings and think wisely. Throughout your interactions with your child, ask yourself, "Is this working? Am I meeting my goals?"

For example, imagine a situation in which your child appears upset when he comes home from school. He doesn't want to talk to you about it, but he seems angry and is taking his anger out on you. You feel hurt and tell him that he's not being fair to you (this response is emotionally based). He begins to yell even louder. He begins to use language that isn't acceptable. How could you have initially responded more wisely? (Hint: validate his feelings.) Now, how do you disengage from this situation without letting him think that his behavior is acceptable?

When your child is responding with intense emotionality, he isn't able to hear or think reasonably or rationally. This is because the part of his brain that's active when he's emotional blocks out the part of his brain that lets him think rationally. You can continue to talk, but he probably won't hear what you're telling him or the lessons you are trying to teach him. He will not be able to listen and learn until he begins to calm down. Validate his feelings first. Calming your child, or waiting until he is calm, is your first step. Making sure you are calm is important too. Then you will be ready to:

1. Assess your goals

2. Develop priorities

3. Feel effective

ASSESSING YOUR GOALS

To manage difficult situations effectively, you have to remember what you're trying to accomplish and what goals are most important. You may ask yourself some of the following questions and think about the possible answers beneath each one.

What do I want to accomplish now? You may want:

- Your child to stop yelling

- To make sure your child knows what are acceptable and unacceptable behaviors

- To understand what is upsetting him so that you can help him feel better

What is the most important goal I have? In the long term, you want:

- To have a relationship with your child that is based on caring, understanding, and mutual acceptance

- Your home to be a calmer place

How do I want both of us to feel when this is over? You will want:

- Your child to feel better about himself

- To feel that you handled the situation well

- To feel that you focused on your goals and didn't get distracted

DEVELOPING PRIORITIES

Prioritizing your goals and developing a strategy for moving forward effectively will necessitate using the skills and principles we've already discussed.

If you are afraid of your child or afraid that limits will trigger him to become violent or aggressive, your first priority always needs to be safety for your child, yourself, and the rest of your family. You must make sure that nobody will be harmed. Parenting a child when you are afraid is difficult and, while safety is always the first goal, fear shouldn't override your responsibilities as a parent. You will still need to set limits or your child will believe that his anger can control other people and that threats are an effective way of getting what he wants. We will talk more about safety in chapter 8.

Reestablishing a calm and safe environment is your first priority. Once your child is calm, either because he has accepted your validation or because you have left him alone to calm down, you will then decide on your next priority. Ask yourself the following questions and evaluate the answers.

Do you want to set limits or give your child a consequence for his behavior? This might be your priority if your goal is to teach more effective behaviors to a child who is often out of control.

Do you want to find out what was upsetting your child in the first place? This is your priority if your child's difficulties are primarily emotional and he is generally able to manage his behaviors. This may *not* be your priority if your child becomes more frustrated talking about feelings. In this case, calming him may be enough.

Do you want to talk to him about more effective ways of expressing his feelings? This may be your priority if you are trying to teach your child more effective skills for managing his emotions.

Below are a number of strategies to help you make these situations into learning opportunities for your child:

Don't be afraid that your child may respond to your limits with anger. Sometimes you will need to set limits, even if it leads to your child being angry. As much as you would like to have a positive relationship with your child, there are times that you and he will not see eye to eye. It's still your role to teach effective and moral behaviors. When you set limits:

- Focus on your child's behaviors (not on his character)

- Focus on the consequences of his behaviors

- Be nonevaluative in your language

Your child will not stay angry forever, and neither will you.

Stay focused on the situation at hand. Sometimes it's easy to get distracted by new information. If your child calms down and begins to talk about his day at school, you may be glad that he's sharing and want to let go of his previous behavior. Choosing among talking about your child's feelings, sharing his day, and taking the opportunity to teach lessons about effective behaviors is often hard. Balancing all of them is important.

There may be times when one issue demands immediate attention due to circumstances (for instance, a family situation arises that needs attention or a particular problem is getting in the way of daily life). However, you also want to take advantage of opportunities to set limits on ineffective and unacceptable behaviors. Try not to be distracted by other situations when this is the priority. As we discussed above, choose the priority that seems most relevant but also be willing to eventually follow through on the other issues as well.

When it's over, let it go. Once you and your child have spoken about the situation, it's important that you let it go and move on. Even if your child remains angry or feels that you have been unfair or that you don't understand, it's important that you, as the parent, be able to hear your child and not react emotionally. You are the model of effective behavior for your child. If you're able to let go of your anger, your child will learn how to do this too.

FEELING EFFECTIVE

How you feel at the end of an interaction with your child will help you to determine how you've handled the situation. This is similar to evaluating the outcome of the story of emotion. Do you feel like you responded wisely or that you reacted emotionally? Were you able to remain calm? Were you able to stay focused? Do you feel like you accomplished what you set out to do? Parents often judge their own behaviors in harsh ways. Try to be fair with yourself. Look at your behaviors and avoid judging yourself too harshly. Nobody is perfect, and nobody handles every situation effectively.

We caution you not to judge the effectiveness of your behavior by your child's response. You can only control what *you* do; you can't control your child's responses to you. You may sense, for example, that your child is upset and calmly say, "It looks like something is bothering you." He may respond by screaming, "You don't know everything, even if you think you do!" Despite your attempt at validation, your child became angry. Don't judge yourself negatively because of your child's response. If you are able to (1) say what you want to say, (2) validate your child, and (3) respond wisely even as your child continues to respond emotionally, you are most likely doing the best that you can under the circumstances.

BALANCED PARENTING

Taking a balanced approach to your parenting means that you don't make extreme decisions, that you can weigh options before responding, and that you are able to be flexible and do what works. It means that you can be gentle *and* firm. You can allow your child to make some decisions and choices while maintaining the ability to set rules, limits, and expectations. Balancing your approach means that you can change your mind or do something differently when there is new information, and it also means compromising with your child and hearing his perspective while not ignoring your own.

Why is it important to take a balanced approach to parenting?

- Extreme responses are rarely effective. They are usually made when feeling emotional (setting limits based on fear or anger, for example) and do little to teach your child effective ways of managing his life.

- Extreme responses tend to confuse your child, especially if you vacillate between different extreme responses.

- When your thinking is rigid and you believe that there is one right way to do things, you will miss opportunities to see other options, and your ability to learn or teach new behaviors will be limited.

Dialectics: Thinking in a Balanced Way

Dialectical thinking enables a person to (1) view behaviors within a whole context, (2) entertain different perspectives in others and within himself, (3) recognize that two things that seem like opposites can both be true, and (4) find less extreme and more effective ways to think (Linehan 1993a). When parents are able to accept, incorporate, and synthesize other, conflicting points of view, they become less rigid, become more balanced, and are able to develop entirely new ways of thinking (Miller et al. 2007).

Thinking in a balanced way requires some new skills (Miller et al. 2007). These include:

- Using phrases like "sometimes" and "some people" and avoiding extreme words such as "always," "never," "everyone," and "all the time"

- Thinking in terms of both/and instead of either/or, such as "I am angry, *and* I still love you," and "This is hard for me *and* I'm going to do the best I can"

- Reminding yourself that other opinions can be legitimate even if you don't agree with them

- Describing situations by making "I feel _____" rather than "You are _____" statements

- Asking questions to clarify what others want and telling people what you want them to know

Examples of Balanced Thinking

Remember the seemingly contradictory assumptions that your child is doing the best he can *and* that he has to do better? Many parents are initially confused by trying to accept two seemingly opposite statements but find that it's very valuable when they're able to do so. The world of parenting is full of paradox and confusion. Practicing balanced thinking helps to negotiate life's seeming contradictions. Below we will discuss a number of examples of balanced thinking that are especially relevant for parents of children with intense emotions.

ACCEPTANCE AND HOPE

Sometimes parents struggle with the idea of acceptance because they worry that they are giving up on their child or, worse, losing hope. They worry that acceptance is an acknowledgment that their child will never change. The synthesis here is that you accept your child as he is at this moment and keep on hoping for change in the future. This hope enables you to continue to strive to do things more effectively and allows for a vision of a better future. Acceptance does not mean that parents are resigned to the situation as it currently is—only that they accept it in the moment while finding the strength and motivation to work for change in the future.

INDEPENDENCE AND ASSISTANCE

You want your child to learn some independence *and* to know that you will be there if needed. For example, you drop your child off at a birthday party and, for the first time, you turn to leave. You know your child is anxious and unsure. He is beginning to whine and cling. You calmly acknowledge his concerns (validation) and tell him that you will call him in a little while to see if he's okay (move toward change). You turn him over to another parent and you leave. After a little time has passed, you check in, letting him know that you have confidence in him *and* that you are available if needed. You acknowledge his anxiety and encourage his independence. You are both firm and reassuring.

CHOICES AND LIMITS

You can give your child choices and still be ultimately responsible for setting limits and expectations. In this case, you may negotiate within certain parameters and not negotiate others (giving your child some extra TV time but not until after his homework is done). You set limits *and* allow choices; your child learns to be assertive and accept limits. Learning to negotiate is a valuable skill for you and your child.

GIVING IN AND CHOOSING PRIORITIES

You may question whether you are being an effective parent if you "give in" and let your child have what he wants when you disagree with his choice. You may feel that you have to put your foot down so that your child knows that you're in control. This is an example of rigid thinking. You don't have to *always* be in control to have control. A balanced approach allows you to see that there are times when the issue is not important enough to argue over, and you can let it go. You can let your child win some of the battles without feeling like he's winning the war or that he's controlling the household. You are able to be in control *and* let go of control, depending on the particular situation and what will work best at this particular time.

The Impact of Unbalanced Thinking and Behaviors

Extreme thinking and behavior increases conflict and tension. The more a parent exercises absolute control (such as demanding that a child eat everything on his plate before leaving the table), the more a child will rebel against it. The more extreme a consequence for a behavior, the less likely the child will be to follow or learn from it. Extreme consequences are rarely effective.

A person who takes an extreme point of view or who responds in an extreme way tends to become rigid in defense of that particular point of view. Likewise, a parent who is convinced that his way is the right way will view other possibilities as "wrong" and may not attempt more effective responses. Unbalanced thinking leads to an unwillingness or inability to assess alternative responses that may be more effective. New learning will not occur.

Examples of Unbalanced Thinking

There are some patterns of unbalanced thinking that can describe the problems that some parents experience (Miller et al. 2007). They include:

- Ignoring behaviors that are problematic versus worrying about behaviors that are more developmentally appropriate

- Not allowing independence versus giving your child more freedom and autonomy than he is ready for

- Being excessively lenient versus parenting with authoritarian control

UNDERSTANDING PARENT RESPONSES

Parents respond in unbalanced ways for a number of reasons, most of them emotional. If your child is often intensely emotional, you may:

- Want to ignore certain problematic behaviors or excuse them because you think everyone is doing it

- Deny that your child has emotional problems (providing short-term relief)

- Find it exhausting to set limits and consequently set fewer of them (appearing very lenient)

- Find it very difficult to differentiate between developmentally appropriate behaviors and worrisome behaviors

- Be so afraid of your child's impulsivity and poor judgment that you may not want to give him any freedom or responsibility

- Be excessively controlling because of your fear of what might happen to your child

To gain more balance, it's important to ask yourself if you are making decisions or choices wisely or emotionally. It's up to you, the parent, to assess the effectiveness of your responses and to determine if a more balanced approach would help lessen the tension and conflict in your family.

Changing Patterns

Self-observation may make you aware that you have developed automatic responses to your child's extreme behaviors based on thoughts like "Here we go again" or "This shouldn't be happening." Every parent can recognize and acknowledge ineffective patterns when he starts to look for them. However, it may be very hard to break out of these familiar family patterns or "dances."

Let's look at an example of eight-year-old Justin's interaction with his mother, Julie, to see how their pattern plays out. Then we'll look at how Julie might have interrupted and changed the pattern in this instance.

> When Julie asks Justin to go straighten up his room, he scowls and ignores her request. This is a common reaction for Justin, and Julie struggles to deal with it effectively. Julie is instantly angry at Justin's reaction. In a loud voice she tells him that he is being disrespectful and should not treat her this way. Justin then becomes angry at his mother and begins to scream and yell. Even angrier now, Julie begins to yell back at him. Within minutes, Justin's behavior has escalated out of control.

Imagine yourself in Julie's place. What would you do in this situation? To change this interactive dance you could:

- Stand back and observe what is happening, then find a wise response (see earlier in this chapter)

- Ask yourself if your response is effective or helpful

- Slow down your automatic response

- Look at your child's behavior from his point of view and try validating him

- Evaluate possible alternative responses

- Balance your thinking to be less confrontational, less rigid, and more effective

In our example of Julie and Justin's interaction, Julie will be more effective if she slows down her reaction to him. Pausing in her reaction may give her time to acknowledge and accept that her son doesn't like being told what to do. She can then realize that reacting angrily to her son's scowl leads to an even greater battle, which she would rather avoid. This realization may enable her to ignore his scowl and give him some more time to get his chore completed. Another reminder may be necessary later. If Julie is able to let go of her automatic reaction to her son, he may not escalate out of control. Then the dance will change.

Finding Balance

Finding balance and responding wisely means thinking in a holistic way that integrates emotion and reason. Regardless of whether your comfort is in emotional or reasonable responses, what works best is balancing the two over time and over situations—doing what is needed when it's needed. Balanced and effective parenting requires flexibility and the ability to see what will work best.

When one parent thinks and acts emotionally and the other parent thinks and acts reasonably, it helps for each parent to accept and not judge the other. Try to understand each other and the consequences of your differences. Does how you handle your differences help your child or confuse him? Your child may go from one parent to the other in search of the answer he's looking for without really knowing what is expected. Despite your differences, it's important that your child get a consistent set of responses.

Be mindful that there is never one right answer when you are exploring ways to resolve situations. When each parent believes that only he or she knows the right way to handle things, arguments and disagreements are sure to follow. More than likely, some compromise is going to be the most effective response. Neither parent should try to win an argument over effective parenting. The issue is about finding what works best for the family. If you keep in mind what works for your child, compromises may come more easily. When each parent listens and is respectful of the other's point of view, more balanced parenting is possible.

Loving a Child with Intense Emotions

You may wrestle with your own feelings toward your child. You know you love him and there may be some days, especially when your child appears to be out of control or when his anger is directed at you, when you don't like your child very much. There may be days when you question your love for your child, and this can lead to feelings of guilt and shame. Again, think in terms of balance. You can, indeed, have mixed feelings for your child. You can also have different emotions on different days. Not liking your child at times does not negate your love for your child; you can hold two different truths at the same time. You can love your child *and* be angry at your child. You can love your child and want your child to disappear at times. You can want to be with your child and not like being with him. Accepting that you can have different emotions at different times—or even at the same time—will make it easier for you to parent and to love your child.

Accepting Yourself

Balance will help you to accept yourself as a parent. You don't have to accomplish all of your goals or fulfill all of your responsibilities to be effective. Situations may change, and so may your abilities. Your priorities may shift, and what is effective may be different at different times. Sometimes listening is all you need to do, while at other times talking is important. Be flexible. Be realistic. Accept that you're doing the best you can.

If you feel that you could have handled a situation better, acknowledge that and don't judge yourself. Learning from each situation is helpful. If you regret that you reacted emotionally, you can apologize to your child. You and your child will share an important lesson—that everyone makes mistakes. You do the best you can, *and* you can learn to do it better. Modeling this lesson for your child empowers you both.

Planting Seeds

You don't need to feel that you've won every battle. Parenting is a marathon, not a sprint. Your child may storm off and dismiss everything you say. That doesn't mean that you don't say it or that he didn't hear it. We talk to parents about "planting seeds." You never know when they will germinate. It may take years before your child understands the meaning of your words. The lessons you teach today make take hold tomorrow. Seeds take time to germinate. Parents who are patient are often surprised and pleased to see what grows.

SUMMARY

In this chapter we focused on strategies and techniques for parenting in ways that will help you accomplish your goals and have calmer interactions with your child. These skills for effective parenting include learning to:

- Believe a set of assumptions that will help you feel less angry and frustrated with your child

- Change automatic patterns into new responses by standing back, observing, and thinking calmly about possible alternative responses

- Develop wise responses by bringing your full awareness to a situation, not evaluating it, and figuring out what will work best

- Validate your child by showing him that you're listening and trying to understand, even if you don't agree with him

- Assess goals, set priorities, and stay focused on what is most important at the time

This chapter has provided guidance in making balanced and effective parenting decisions and choices. In our next chapter we'll be focusing on understanding and reacting to your child's world of emotion and helping your child to express emotion more effectively.

PART 2

Responding to Your Child's Feelings

CHAPTER 3

Understanding What Your Child Is Telling You

Do you sometimes feel frustrated when you recognize that something is bothering your child and she is unable to tell you what she is feeling or what is bothering her? Back when she was an infant you were able to figure out her needs through her cries or behavioral cues. You may have noticed that she relaxed her fingers when she was calm and balled her hands into fists when stressed or angry. When she got a little older, you learned that she wanted to be picked up when she raised her arms; she may have whimpered and pointed at something until you figured out what she wanted. As she got older, you expected her to use words to tell you what she wanted. Now when you want to understand your child, it's easier for her to identify what she wants when something is concrete (like a toy or something to eat). It's much harder for her to identify feelings that are more abstract.

Your young child cannot differentiate what she's experiencing because she is feeling it throughout her entire body. Feelings like "sad," "mad," "upset," and "hurt" all feel the same, and your child cannot differentiate them. While it may be frustrating for you, her response that she doesn't know how she's feeling may be accurate for her. So, you may wonder, how can you effectively help your child with her overwhelming emotions if you don't know what she's feeling or what's bothering her? You may also be wondering how you can help your child express some of what she's feeling in ways that you can understand. These are the issues we will address in this chapter.

YOUR CHILD'S STORY OF EMOTION

In chapter 1 we discussed the story of emotion, which describes how an emotion develops until it is expressed verbally and behaviorally (Linehan 1993b). Understanding the steps in your child's story of emotion will help you understand your child's feelings with acceptance and without judgment. Knowing the steps in her story will enable you to intervene before your child has escalated to the point of uncontrollable behaviors. As you've already seen with your own story, each step below will provide an opportunity to change the outcome of the story.

Your Child's Vulnerabilities or Risk Factors

Knowing when your child is vulnerable to negative emotions enables you to help her prepare for or avoid difficult or stressful situations until she is better able to manage them. If you're aware that your child is vulnerable, you can implement wise decision making and/or advance preparations to help minimize the possibility that she will react with an emotional outburst.

How do you know when your child is vulnerable? Think about how your child behaves when she hasn't had her nap or when her schedule is disrupted. Is she cranky or more easily frustrated? Your child may not say that she's tired because she missed her nap (few children will actually know or admit this) but *you* can:

- Hypothesize why your child's emotions seem more intense at this time

- Figure out what makes this day different from another

- Begin to discern patterns

When your child misses her nap is she more emotional? Are there more outbursts? Is she harder to put to bed at night? Over time, you will learn to maintain routines for your child and keep other demands to a minimum when she is tired or otherwise vulnerable.

As your child gets older, you will notice other patterns. How does your child behave when she returns from school, for example? If you ask her about her day, does she respond angrily and go off to her room? If you sit with her quietly, does she begin to share? Your child's responses are indicative of her vulnerabilities and can teach you what her needs are. Watch closely over time, and your child will let you know how she feels and what she needs.

When your child feels very strong and intense emotions, being sensitive to her vulnerabilities may help you avoid saying or doing something that will trigger an outburst.

Your child comes home from a friend's house and responds in an angry manner when you ask her if she had a good time. When you ask what's wrong, she yells, "Nothing!" She responds sarcastically to whatever you ask, and you feel like you can't say anything that will not lead to a nasty response. You ask your daughter to set the table, and she begins to scream at you. When you ask again if something is wrong, she goes running to her room. She has returned home vulnerable and is easily overcome by negative reactions to ordinarily simple requests.

What Do You Do Next?

- As long as she is safe in her room and is not breaking things, let your child have some time alone. Don't take her silence personally.

- Despite your desire to understand, don't ask your child again what is wrong. She's already telling you, verbally and nonverbally, that she doesn't want to talk about it.

- When she seems calmer, acknowledge that she seems upset about something. Tell her that you will be there to listen *when she is ready to talk.*

- If she denies being upset, accept her response.

- *Remain calm.* Do not get defensive or argue your point of view.

- Do not put pressure on your child at this point to do anything.

Let her calm down. When your child is vulnerable, she will not be able to complete tasks, listen to you, or participate in activities until she has moved on. There will be time for expectations later.

POSSIBLE RISK FACTORS FOR CHILDREN

There are a number of factors that can make your child vulnerable to intense emotionality. These include:

- Lack of sleep

- Not feeling well

- A change in routine

- Tension in the house (even tension about positive events)

- New people or situations

- Stress from playmates, friends (even in young children), or siblings; being picked on or teased

- A perceived sense of having done something wrong or having upset a loved one

- Difficulty in school or in completing homework

This is by no means an exhaustive list. Each child will be sensitive to situations that are unique to her. Be aware of your child's moods and try to understand the circumstances that preceded them.

To help you think about what makes your child vulnerable, write in your notebook or in the lines below situations that have made your child vulnerable to intense emotions in the past.

_____

_____

Your Child's Triggers

The trigger for your child is anything that causes or leads to an intense emotional response. No behavior occurs in isolation. The trigger may be something in the environment, or it may be something going on inside your child, like a thought or a feeling. Because it will be hard to recognize internal triggers, it's easier to help her when *she* can identify and tell you what she is thinking and/or feeling.

As your awareness of your child's reactions grows, you will begin to recognize those situations that trigger intense reactions. It may be something as common as bedtime or as uncommon as a vacation. Even when you're aware of a trigger, it may be hard to avoid the struggle. If your child has a hard time leaving the house you may still have the urge to hurry her, despite the fact that this increases her resistance and can lead to an outburst. If asking your child to do something is a trigger, does that mean that you don't ask anything of her? Your child's reactivity causes parenting dilemmas. How do you balance your needs and her feelings? Some triggers can't be avoided. We will discuss how to help your child handle these expectations in chapter 7.

RECOGNIZING TRIGGERS

The list of triggers for each child is unique and can be quite varied. Triggers for children might include:

- **Limits**: Not allowing your child to do something she wants to or saying no to her

- **Separation from a Parent**: A parent leaving the house or leaving the child at school; the separation itself is the trigger

- **Change**: Adjusting to change in routine or circumstance, even if the change is one she wants

- **Losing in Competitive Activities:** Not winning in competitive sports or games with other children or not getting as much attention as other children in these situations

In order to recognize triggers, look at patterns and determine if a specific situation or a particular kind of situation consistently leads to an emotional reaction. If it does, it's most likely a trigger. Following an emotional outburst, you can also look back at the circumstances that occurred right before it with attention to all aspects of the environment and interactions.

List your child's most frequent triggers below or in your notebook.

Your Feelings as Triggers

At times, the anticipation of a struggle becomes a trigger for *your* emotions. Your emotions can then trigger your child. For example, if you know that your child has trouble getting dressed in the morning and you have an early morning appointment, you may become tense *in anticipation* of your child's response in this situation. As you approach your child, your tension may become a trigger for her reactivity. Your child, like most children, is very sensitive to your moods and feelings, even those that you are trying to hide from her. Use this knowledge to keep yourself calm and to keep your expectations simple. A little time to calm yourself in advance will save time spent battling your child later.

Siblings as Triggers

Your child's sibling may be a trigger for emotional outbursts for any number of reasons (jealousy; a perception that you're spending too much time with the sibling; being teased or left out, whether or not this is truly happening or is simply your child's perception). This presents a dilemma for parents, and each parent must find his or her own most effective way to resolve it. Even while you try to avoid triggers for one child and try to keep her calm, your other child(ren)'s needs and feelings, even if they are triggers, need to be acknowledged and validated as well. We will discuss siblings further in chapter 10.

Minimizing Your Child's Reactions to a World Full of Triggers

You cannot create a world that is safe from triggers for your child. However, there may be steps you can take to minimize their impact on her. You can:

- Try to avoid or lessen problematic situations that are not necessary. For example, if your child becomes more aggressive after watching cartoons, you may lessen her access to certain cartoons and increase her access to calmer TV.

- Make certain accommodations to minimize your child's reaction to necessary expectations. For example, if your child spends a long time getting ready for school, wake her earlier to give her the time she needs.

You can also prepare your child for something that may be a trigger by:

- Discussing it in advance

- Asking her what will make it easier for her

- Trying to find ways to minimize stress and anxiety

- Validating her feelings and remaining calm and nonjudgmental when in the situation

Your Child's Belief System and Concrete Thinking

Your child's belief system and the way that she interprets events are based on a concrete, literal way of thinking. Her understanding is based on her experiences in the world, and she cannot generalize or abstract meaning from those experiences. Children tend to feel that they control more than they do. They often feel responsible for things that they have had no impact on, and they make very literal connections (Piaget 1926, 1928). If your child was mad and yelled, she might think it's her fault when you and your spouse have a fight soon afterward. A child whose grandparent died in a hospital might come to blame the hospital for the death and be afraid to visit a doctor in the hospital. She might become very afraid if a parent has to be hospitalized for any reason. Your child may not respond to explanations that contradict her beliefs. While her reaction may seem inexplicable to you, you may need to think about past events to understand your child's anxiety in the present. Remember that your child's abstract reasoning develops as she gets older, and until she can think abstractly, she will feel responsible for things she couldn't have caused and will make connections you may not understand.

Remember that your child's reality and imagination are very real to her. To understand your child's story of emotion, keep in mind that her belief system is quite different from your own. Let go of your more abstract way of understanding and try to see things more the way your child does.

Body Sensations

Recognizing your child's body sensations, which occur prior to the outburst, provides you with another opportunity to help her change the behavioral outcome of her story.

You are probably aware of the physical signs that your child is becoming distressed. She may:

- Look as though she's going to cry

- Speak louder or faster

- Not look directly at you

- Become more active or even jumpy

Knowing your child's signals will help you respond effectively to her and provides you with opportunities to calm her down before her emotions escalate.

Take the opportunity here or in your notebook to list the physical signs you have recognized in your child that show when she's becoming intensely emotional.

_____

_____

_____

Communicating Feelings

As you become more familiar with your child's risk factors, triggers, and body sensations, it becomes a little easier to understand what your child is feeling. Giving a name to an emotion is a way to gain some control over it as well as a way to reduce negative emotions (Linehan 1993b). Thus, the more your child can name and talk about what she's feeling, the more she'll be able to manage and modulate her emotions. Learning to give names to what you and your child are feeling will make it easier to communicate, support, and help one another.

Some of the primary emotions listed by Marsha Linehan (1993b) include:

- Anger

- Fear

- Joy

- Love

- Sadness

- Shame

Other emotion names derive from these with increasing subtlety and sensitivity in describing what a person feels. As your child gets older, she will be able to differentiate and communicate various emotions, such as feeling hurt or disappointed instead of just sad. The older your child gets, the more specific she will be in naming her emotions.

It is less threatening for your child to begin to hear about emotions when you're not directly talking about *her* emotions. For example: Imagine that your child's kindergarten teacher tells you that some of the other kids picked on your child during the day. You can help your child to express feelings she may have difficulty with by making connections for her and suggesting possible feelings in a way that your child might find easier to accept. You might say, "I heard that some kids bothered you in school today. Some kids feel angry or sad when other kids bother them."

You can find mood charts that you can hang on your refrigerator or in the playroom. (See Web resources in the appendix.) If your child is able to identify with a picture of a mood, it will help her to name how she is feeling. Some families use the charts as a way to monitor mood on a daily basis. Your goal is to give your child a way to communicate her feelings.

Behaviors and Actions: The Outcome of the Story

As we discussed in chapter 1, the outcome of every story of emotion is a behavior. Your child will be able to change the outcome of the story by making different behavioral choices when she learns new behaviors that have more positive consequences.

In DBT, behaviors are seen as ways to manage difficult emotions (Linehan 1993a). Your child learns ways to help her feel better. The stronger her negative feelings, the more she will search for ways to get rid of those feelings and the more intense her behavioral response will be. Yelling, for example, may release *some* emotion, but if her emotions are very strong, hurting herself (or someone else) may be the only way she can find to feel better. Ironically, her attempts at feeling better may become more destructive as the intensity of her emotions increases.

TEACHING ALTERNATIVE BEHAVIORS

In most situations, it is the behavior, not the emotion itself that has negative consequences for your child. If your child is angry and hits someone, she will face a negative consequence. If she is angry and talks about it without physical aggression, chances are that there will be no negative consequences. As we will discuss more in chapter 6, part of the job for parents is to teach the child alternative and adaptive behaviors that replace those that are less effective. The goal is to teach your child behaviors that will lead to more positive consequences. These can include:

- Telling someone what has happened

- Taking some time or space alone

- Hugging a stuffed animal

- Pounding on clay or a soft cushion

In your notebook, or on the lines below, write down some alternative behaviors that will work for your child.

_____

_____

_____

Katie and Samantha's story helps illustrate.

Katie is a five-year-old who has an eight-year-old sister, Samantha. Katie is often frustrated by her sister's behavior and has begun to retaliate by hitting her. Since Katie is younger than Samantha, she feels that hitting is the only way she can handle her frustration. Katie's mother wants to validate Katie's feelings of frustration. She doesn't want Katie to learn to be aggressive as a way to manage her feelings, and she knows that Katie does need a way to express her frustration. Katie's mom searches for an alternative behavior for Katie that will be acceptable and effective. Katie and her mom choose a stuffed bear that Katie will use when she is angry. She is told that she can go to her room and hit her stuffed bear. She *can't* hit her sister. Katie has learned two things: (1) to walk away from her sister and (2) to find an alternative way of handling frustration. Eventually, all Katie will need to do is to go to her room and take some time away from Samantha in order to feel better.

Additional considerations about alternative behaviors. Some children become more aggressive when they are allowed to be aggressive in any way. Watching wrestling, getting a punching bag, or even hitting a stuffed animal may not be the best strategy for children who are unable to turn off the aggression switch once it has been turned on. For these children, a more effective alternative response may be to do a physical activity or to learn to take deep breaths, as we discuss in chapter 6.

Every child is unique, and not every child will benefit from the same alternative behaviors. Work with your child to find the best alternative behaviors to help her manage her feelings. These behaviors can then become alternative responses to negative emotions.

Certain alternative behaviors are effective in certain situations and not in others. Your child may be allowed to scream in her room but not in other areas of the house where it will disturb others. In that case, if your child is upset, allow her to leave the area (despite the activity the family is engaged in) and manage her emotions in a way that has less impact on the whole family. As you teach your child to choose alternative behaviors, also teach her that different situations call for different behaviors—a very important life lesson.

The earlier in the story that you encourage your child to use an alternative behavior, the easier it will be for your child to follow through by using that behavior. By the time your child's emotions have escalated, it will have become harder to change the behavioral response. Help your child to use the earlier steps in the story to minimize her reaction and increase the likelihood of a positive outcome.

An alternative behavior is not a punishment. An alternative behavior is used by your child *instead of* a more dangerous, less adaptive one. It is a positive outcome. As such, an alternative behavior should not be confused with a punishment, which is the negative consequence that occurs *after* a less effective behavior.

Teaching your child to take space (a behavioral response that means going somewhere to calm down) gives her a way to regulate her feelings and behaviors by taking herself out of stressful situations. Remind your child that going to her room for quiet time *before she escalates* is not a punishment, and she is not in trouble. In fact, you will praise her for this choice. She will be much more willing to use this strategy if she sees it as an effective alternative and not a punishment.

Modeling Effective Behaviors

When you help your child calm down, she will be aware of and learning from your behaviors. If you remain calm, it will be easier for her to do so; if you become emotionally reactive, her emotionality will increase as well. If you slam your hand against something when you're angry or frustrated, this is the behavior that your child will learn. On the other hand, if you tell your child that you are going to your room to calm down, she will learn this behavior instead. Because your child's emotional intensity may cause her reactions to be more intense than yours, it's even more important to model and teach her effective behaviors.

SHAME AND APOLOGIES

Some children are overwhelmed by shame when they do something "wrong." These children may project their shame onto others as anger. Helping your child to understand that everyone makes mistakes may minimize her shame. Apologizing when you make a mistake reinforces this lesson. It also models for your child an alternative behavior to replace the angry outburst that might otherwise occur when she has made a mistake.

ONE CHILD'S STORY OF EMOTION

You can look at the following example of a child's story which illustrates the components of the story and how the outcome can be changed through understanding and awareness.

Ricki, age ten, returns home from school. She seems quiet and brooding and doesn't respond to any of her mother's questions. Her mother, Penny, thinks, "She's refusing to talk to me." What Penny doesn't know is that Ricki found out that a girl in her class was having a sleepover and she wasn't invited. She has spent most of the day thinking that nobody likes her and that she will never have any friends. Ricki finally blurts out that she is a "loser" and tells Penny that nobody, even her mother, understands her. Penny doesn't know what to do. She tells Ricki that she is not a loser in the hope that Ricki will begin to feel better. Instead, Ricki begins to shout at Penny and goes running to her room and slams the door. Penny hears things being thrown in Ricki's room. Penny tries to talk to Ricki, who only yells louder and begins to swear at her. Penny responds by telling Ricki not to talk to her that way. It takes several hours for Ricki to calm down. Even then, she and Penny refuse to speak to each other.

The Components of the Story

As you can see, Ricki is already at risk when she returns home from school. She is feeling ashamed and left out (*risk factors*). Her quietness upsets her mother, and the interaction (*trigger*) begins. Ricki and Penny trigger thoughts and emotions in one another. Penny thinks her daughter is disrespectful and should be better behaved (*parent thoughts*). Ricki believes that nobody understands her (*child thoughts*). These thoughts cause both Penny and Ricki to be angry (*identifying the emotion name*). Ricki responds to her anger by yelling, slamming her door, and throwing things (*child behaviors/ actions*). Penny responds to Ricki by admonishing her to speak to her differently and then refusing to talk to her (*parent behaviors/actions*).

Now, using Ricki's story, look at the Story of Emotion worksheet below with the actual steps written in the A section and the alternative steps written in the B section. You can see how alternative responses might have led to a different outcome. Think about how this worksheet can guide your own responses to your child's story.

Story of Emotion

Vulnerabilities/Risk Factors

A. Ricki returns home feeling ashamed and left out. She is quiet and brooding, and her mother is upset when Ricki does not answer her questions.

B. *Penny notices that when Ricki comes home, she is quiet and she looks like she is about to cry. Penny knows that Ricki is bothered by something. Penny is very calm, makes no demands on her, and is available when and if Ricki decides to talk to her.*

Triggers

A. Ricki did not get invited to a sleepover with other girls in her class. This made her vulnerable. Her mother's questions are a prompting event for her to get angry at her mother.

B. *If Penny is able to remain quiet and make fewer demands, Ricki may be able to handle her emotions without further escalation.*

Thoughts/Beliefs About the Event

A. Ricki believes that she is a "loser" and will *never* have any friends. She also believes that *nobody* understands her, including her mother. Penny has thoughts about how Ricki should behave, increasing her negative feelings about Ricki's behavior.

B. *If Ricki changed her thoughts to accept that not being invited to one party did* not *make her a "loser" and did not mean that she would "never" have friends, she might be less vulnerable. If she thinks that her mother is able to understand her, she might be less reactive to her. When Penny understands that her daughter is hurt and is not attacking her, she can let go of her "shoulds," validate Ricki's feelings, and help Ricki feel less alone.*

Body Sensations or Responses

A. Ricki is quiet and brooding. She seems tense inside. Internally, she is on the verge of tears and then becomes agitated by her mother. Penny begins to feel agitated when Ricki doesn't answer her questions.

B. *Penny would be helped by taking a few deep breaths. Then she might give Ricki some space to calm down or help her do something that she feels good about (see chapter 4). In this case, they will both feel less agitated.*

Identifying Emotions

A. Ricki is feeling sad, lonely, and depressed. She later feels angry. Penny is confused and agitated.

B. *Penny can validate that Ricki is sad and give her an opportunity to talk about her feelings when she is ready to do so. Penny may feel sad about what her daughter is going through and also may feel competent if she is able to help her.*

Behaviors/Actions

A. Ricki initially doesn't respond to her mother and then is angry, yelling and swearing. Eventually, she runs from the room, slams the door, and becomes destructive. Penny dismisses her feelings and tries to talk to her.

B. *Ricki expresses her thoughts that nobody likes her. She may feel better when her mother validates her feelings of sadness. She will feel more understood and less angry. She may be able to use a calming activity (see chapter 4) to help her distract herself from her sadness. Penny's understanding and validation of Ricki's feelings encourage additional nonjudgmental and helpful behaviors.*

Let's take a closer look at one of the events in the story. When Penny tells Ricki that she is not a loser, she is dismissing how Ricki feels about herself and inadvertently invalidating her (chapter 1). Even though Penny is trying to be helpful in saying this, Ricki feels that one more person does not understand her, triggering a more negative response. A validating response such as "It must feel really awful when your friends leave you out of things. I can imagine how this might make you feel about yourself," might lead to a more positive response from Ricki. Listening to and validating your child actually helps her feel better about herself.

The story of emotion for parents and children is often intertwined. The manner in which a parent responds to a child can either help minimize *or* trigger an intense response, especially in a child with intense emotions. The outcome of one story often leads directly to a new story. Monitoring your thoughts and behaviors and responding wisely increases the likelihood that the next story will be more positive.

FINDING YOUR CHILD'S TRUTH

There is no easy way to figure out what your child is trying to tell you. There will be trial and error involved in the process. Keep an open mind and do not make assumptions. Listen to your child with an open mind, a nonjudgmental attitude, an accepting manner, and eyes that reflect your child, not yourself. The following sections might provide some guidance.

Know Your Child

Your child is an individual with her own vulnerabilities, triggers, and feelings. Accept her uniqueness and do not compare her to other children or assume that she feels as they do. Ask your child what makes her scared, angry, worried, or happy. Listen to her and don't dismiss or minimize what she is trying to say. Ask questions and focus on her answers with your full attention. Let her teach you what she needs and how you can help her. Listen without judgment or assumptions, and eventually you will learn her truth.

Write here or in your notebook what your child has taught you about herself.

Accept Your Child's Truth

Your child's truth is real to her. If your child responds to stressful situations with somatic complaints ("My tummy hurts," "My finger hurts"), *what is your child saying*? She is telling you that *something* is bothering her. The specifics are not as important as her reality that something hurts. You can comfort your child and validate her feelings, even if you don't know specifically what the problem is. You can say something like, "I see that you are upset," or "It seems like something is bothering you," and provide your child with your physical presence and comfort. Do not deny her feelings. This will only cause her to find other, possibly more intense ways to let you know how she feels. When you validate your child's unspoken feelings, she is more likely to share more of the story. Think about responding to the "music" and not to the "lyrics."

Are you wondering how to respond when your child tells you something you know not to be true? What do you say when your child says she has nothing to do and you are aware of all the activities and toys available to her? *What is your child saying*? She is probably telling you that, right now, nothing interests her and she is feeling bored. If you can validate her truth by saying, "It seems like you can't find anything to do," you and she will be better able to problem solve and find an activity that will engage her.

Sometimes the specific words your child is saying are ineffective ways she has found to express herself. Your child may be yelling at you that you love her sibling more. If these words are a trigger for you because you feel they are unfair, your first instinct may be to defend yourself. However, the truth is in the feelings behind the words, not in the words themselves. Your child is angry at you, and you can acknowledge that. You can disagree with all that your child is saying while still validating the feelings behind the words.

If you can let go of the truth of the words, you will be much better able to recognize and respond to your child's feelings effectively.

Acknowledge When Something Is Important to Your Child

Your child might perceive a situation to have more importance than you think it warrants. If your child talks about hating her best friend, acknowledge her feelings. Your attentiveness and validation may encourage her to tell you more. She may tell you about a situation that seems quite minor to you, and you might not understand the intensity of her response.

Do not minimize her feelings; don't judge her or try to "fix" the situation by telling her what to do. Validate that it is important to her, and the next day, when her friend is her best friend again, do not remind her of the situation the day before. If she has moved on, you should too.

HELPING YOUR CHILD EXPRESS WHAT SHE IS FEELING

The most effective way to teach your child how to express what she is feeling is to spend time when she is calm talking to her about her feelings and her behaviors. When your life seems dominated by "putting out fires," you may not notice times of calm and may miss opportunities to talk to your child. "Fire prevention" is, however, necessary. The importance of teaching your child how to effectively express her feelings cannot be minimized and is well worth the time it takes.

We outline the keys to helping your child express her feelings in the sections below.

Create a Validating Home Environment

A child will be more willing to share her feelings effectively in an environment in which emotions expressed in words are not ignored, dismissed, or negatively judged. How, then, do you assure your child that her home is a safe environment to express her feelings? No family talks about feelings all the time, but your child may be a keen observer who notices how and when other family members choose to share their feelings and how those feelings are received by others. Welcome honest expression of *all* feelings. Encourage understanding, acceptance, and validation. When your child sees that feelings expressed by family members are accepted and that the consequences are positive, she will feel safe expressing hers. A validating home environment provides many opportunities for your child to learn to express her feelings.

Talk About Your Own Feelings

As a parent, you don't want to burden your child with all of the issues and concerns that you face. This does not mean that you can't share some of your feelings with your child. Through your modeling, your child will find other opportunities to learn how to express her emotions. If you feel sad because you just heard sad news, you can share this with your child without overwhelming her. If you share feelings of happiness or joy or anger, your child will learn that people have a full range of emotions, all of which are acceptable. The more you express your emotions in an honest, straightforward way, the more comfortable your child will be expressing hers.

If you are overwhelmed by your emotions or if you're having a hard time expressing them effectively, you may not want to show your child your reactivity. Instead, tell your child the name of the emotion you're feeling ("I'm feeling angry," for example), and find a private place to calm yourself. You do *not* want to overwhelm your child or model less than adaptive behaviors. You *do* want to teach your child that dealing with feelings privately and in a safe place can be a useful and effective skill.

Acknowledge Positive and Negative Emotions in Others

Pointing out emotions in others is often less threatening than pointing them out in your child. When you see someone expressing emotions, use the opportunity to talk to your child about emotion names as well as effective and less effective ways to manage feelings. Your child can learn ways to acknowledge her own emotions by recognizing responses in others.

Share Positive Activities

When your child demonstrates intense emotionality, you may look forward to times she is calm as opportunities to engage in pleasant activities alone or with friends or other family members. When you do this, however, your child learns that you are most available to her when she is having a difficult time and less available when she is calm and pleasantly engaged. This increases the likelihood that your child will have intense negative reactivity because she knows this is when she has your attention. When you spend time with your child sharing pleasant activities, she will learn that she doesn't have to express negative emotions in order to feel connected and that you are not only available when she "needs" you. She learns, instead, that expressions of pleasant feelings are attended to as well, increasing the likelihood that they may continue and decreasing her overall vulnerability to negative emotions.

List some positive activities here or in your notebook that you and your child can enjoy when she is calm.

_____

_____

_____

SUMMARY

Each child is unique and has her own needs, wants, feelings, and ways to express herself. Too often parents have predetermined ways they expect their child to feel and express those feelings. Your child, however, has her own story and is experiencing a life different from the one you expected her to have. Look at your child with wide-open eyes and see her for the individual that she is. Your acceptance of your child will go a long way toward encouraging her to express a full range of emotions and to see herself in an accepting way.

In this chapter, we discussed skills you can use to discern, understand, and validate your child's emotions and help her learn to communicate and express them in adaptive and healthy ways. The skills discussed in this chapter are:

- Using your child's story of emotion to understand your child

- Helping your child find alternative behaviors

- Finding your child's truth

- Using yourself and others to model effective communication of feelings

In the next chapter, you will learn additional skills for helping your child lessen her emotional intensity by changing her environment. You will also learn to use her story of emotion to help her de-escalate her emotional responses.

CHAPTER 4

Responding When Your Child Is Overwhelmed by Emotions

Do you feel as if you're always on edge, waiting for the next explosion? Do you wonder what you can do to lessen the outbursts that seem to occur frequently and without apparent warning? Do you feel like you have little control? When your child reacts with intense emotions, you may feel as if life is a minefield and you and the rest of your family try to avoid saying or doing anything that will trigger an explosion. This is an exhausting and stressful way to live. You have already seen that knowing your child's story of emotion can give you some control. In this chapter, we'll offer more guidance about lessening the possibility of emotionally intense reactions and some hints about what you can do to de-escalate situations once they occur.

LESSENING THE POSSIBILITY OF EMOTIONAL OUTBURSTS

In the last chapter we discussed that knowing your child, recognizing his vulnerabilities, and acknowledging his triggers can help you minimize the possibility that he will become intensely emotional. While it's impossible to create a life without stress or pain for your child, there are steps you can take to create a home that is as structured, consistent, and calm as possible.

Parents often react emotionally with their children and ride an emotional roller coaster with them. However, when parents maintain balanced emotions despite the dysregulation of their child, they will be less reactive and calmer. The calmer the parent, the calmer the home, and the calmer all the children in that home will be.

If your child is overwhelmed by intense emotions, he may feel more comfortable when his life is predictable and routine. You won't be able to prevent some unexpected situations from occurring, and you can't protect your child from all situations that he cannot control. You can, however, do your best to minimize surprises in your child's life, prepare him for new situations, and give him control as often as possible. In addition, the lessons of DBT (Linehan 1993a) encourage parents to provide opportunities for (1) pleasant activities, (2) activities in which your child feels competent, and (3) activities that calm and distract him.

Create a Home with Routines and Predictability

In a society in which children have many after school activities, sports year-round, and playdates and other social activities, and in which parents work and have their own activities, home life can be chaotic under the most stable circumstances. When you have a child with intense emotions, everyday chaos feels more out of control and exacerbates the reactivity of your child. You may have to make accommodations that will enable him to manage his emotions and minimize times when he is overwhelmed by them.

The following steps can help you provide a calmer environment in which emotions can be more effectively managed.

CREATE ROUTINES

Your child will be less susceptible to emotional outbursts if he knows what is expected of him and can count on some predictability. Here are some tips:

- Have dinner at about the same time each night.

- Have a specific bedtime that doesn't change from day to day.

- Encourage an uninterrupted quiet time for your child when he is too old for naps.

- Allow your child time for activities that soothe and calm him as often as possible.

- If your child has a chore, give him the time of day by which it has to be completed and make it a regular part of your household routine.

- Do not change the routine too much on weekends, although it will deviate to some degree. As often as possible, try to keep your child on the same sleep schedule on weekends.

When you recognize that your child is becoming overwhelmed, look at your schedule and see what you can adjust. Is your child involved in too many activities? Is he getting enough sleep? Are there too many distractions going on? The answers to these questions might help you recognize the adjustments that need to be made.

You may feel resentful of the accommodations you have to make for your child. It may feel inconvenient to maintain routines in your life. You may wish that your child could be more like other children and handle unpredictability better. This is especially true when other family members are more spontaneous and flexible. It is not your child's fault that he responds to change and disruption with difficulty. Remember that he is "doing the best he can" (Linehan 1993a) and that you are also doing the best you can to provide an environment within which he can thrive.

DEVELOP CONSISTENT RULES AND EXPECTATIONS

Rules and expectations in a home need to be consistent and explicit. Your child needs the guidance and discipline created by rules that he knows and understands. Consistency is important. If your rule is that there is no TV in the morning before school, maintain this rule regardless of your child's demands or emotionality. If your child isn't allowed out on weekends until his room is cleaned up, do not make an exception because he has someplace exciting to go. The more exceptions you make, the more your child will expect and demand them. Consistent expectations will help your child know what to expect, lessen his confusion, and enable him to have more control of his emotions.

LIMIT ACTIVITIES

If your child is easily overwhelmed by demands and activities, try limiting the number of activities he participates in. It's often tempting to allow your child to be busy and out of the house, although there are often consequences when your child doesn't have the time to calm himself. Your child may have an outburst at dinner or at bedtime. A child who is overwhelmed or exhausted usually has a harder time settling down for routine activities. Instead, have him choose one extracurricular activity or sport rather than several. Teach him the importance and positive consequences of wise choices.

Your child may not want to limit his activities; you may find yourself struggling with him when you set limits on favored activities. He may enjoy sports and want to take part in as many events as possible. Especially when you know how generally unhappy your child is, you may want to let him do whatever makes him happy. However, your child may not always make decisions that are in his best interest. This is when you need to make reasonable and wise decisions about your child's level of participation. Think about balancing—giving your child some of what he wants *and* setting appropriate limits on his activities. Make decisions in consultation with your child and don't let your child make the decisions on his own. When your child has intense emotionality, it's possible to have too much of a good thing. As much as you want your child to be happy, limiting his activities will pay positive dividends over and over again.

If your child participates in an activity, you may make changes in how much he takes part when the demands from activities that he enjoys begin to overwhelm him or when he feels unable to continue at the level expected of him. The child who loves noncompetitive sports may feel threatened when competition becomes important. The child who enjoys playing local sports may not be able to handle the expectations of traveling teams. What happens when an activity demands so much from your child that there isn't enough time for other, necessary activities (such as sleep, quiet time, or homework)? When your child is unable to admit his anxieties or see their consequences, you will be the one to recognize his vulnerabilities and make effective accommodations.

If you have more than one child, you may find yourself taking one child to the activities of the other as you try to be there for everyone. If one child is easily overwhelmed, you may have to (1) limit *your* participation in events or (2) find someone who can spend time with one child while you're with the other. This has the added benefit that both children get one-on-one time with an adult. Another solution might be to (3) try to schedule alternating days of activities and quiet times at home. Finding ways for your child to have some downtime may have the positive consequence of fewer emotional meltdowns.

HOME AS A SAFE HAVEN

You may wonder why your child is able to contain his emotional intensity with friends or relatives and why he is unable to control his outbursts at home. Home tends to be the place where we can most comfortably be ourselves. We all need the safety of our home to let go of the stress of a hard day, a place to kick back and let our inner child come out to play (Wolfe 2002). Your child is no different. He needs to know there is a place where he is safe to let some of his emotions out. Your child needs to know that your love is unconditional and he will be loved despite his behavior.

To help your child manage his emotions at home, encourage him to:

- Release his emotions in ways that are not disruptive to the whole family

- Find a place in the home where he is allowed to go and be undisturbed; don't let others in the family bother him when he is there

- Use a quiet and soothing place that is filled with favorite toys, stuffed animals, and other calming items and activities

- Find ways to quiet and calm himself

Although it may be difficult to accept that your child needs to release some of his emotions at home, do not judge him for this. Validation and acceptance (Linehan 1993a) are key here. Your child's emotional outbursts do not occur at home just to bother you; the love and safety in his home allow him to express his emotions so that he can manage the rest of his life. If you can help him learn effective ways to manage his emotions, your child will be less disruptive when he expresses them.

Provide Opportunities for Pleasure and Mastery

Your child will be less vulnerable to overwhelming negative emotions if he participates in activities that he enjoys, that help him feel good, and that he feels competent doing.

LET YOUR CHILD DO WHAT HE ENJOYS

If your child is vulnerable to emotional intensity, you may be tempted to use activities he enjoys as rewards for good behavior or take them away as punishments. You may want to take away his computer time or a DVD if he has an outburst. Or perhaps you think your child *should* only use the computer for a limited amount of time. Are these effective or wise decisions? Are they helping him? Taking away things that your child enjoys may not be effective in helping him to manage his emotions.

In order to minimize the possibility of emotional outbursts, let your child engage in activities that he enjoys and finds relaxing at reasonable times and in realistic ways. You can allow him to enjoy his favorite activities to calm or relax himself without giving him total control over the activities in your home. Find a balance that allows your child to distract himself with soothing activities while also meeting certain household expectations.

Here or in your notebook, write down activities that your child enjoys doing.

_____

_____

_____

FIND ACTIVITIES THAT YOUR CHILD DOES WELL

When your child is expected to participate in activities that he doesn't feel he does well, this increases his vulnerability to negative emotions. When he feels that he can't complete a task or an activity well or when an activity threatens his sense of well-being, the possibility of an emotional outburst increases. You may see this when your child is doing homework that he feels is too difficult for him.

On the other hand, when your child participates in activities that he does well, he will feel more capable, feel better about himself, and feel less vulnerable to negative emotions. Help your child find those activities in which he can excel. For some children this is sports; for others it may be music, arts, or other hobbies, while others may enjoy working on projects with a parent. You don't want these activities to burden or overwhelm your child or the rest of your family, so provide a reasonable number of opportunities for your child to participate in activities that feel good to him.

Sometimes it's difficult to find an activity at which your child feels competent. If you live in an area where sports are important and your child is not athletic, he may begin to feel inadequate. If his friends get trophies or awards and he doesn't, this may lead to lower self-esteem. This, too, can lead to an increase in outbursts. Sometimes your child's strengths may not be those that are rewarded with trophies. Your job will be to help your child see his strengths and find those activities that he is most capable of doing.

Here or in your notebook, list some activities that your child does well.

_____

_____

_____

DE-ESCALATING YOUR CHILD'S EMOTIONAL OUTBURSTS

Children's outbursts differ in their causes and intensity. Some parents describe children as "raging," "practically foaming at the mouth," and/or racing throughout the house in a totally unmanageable way. For other children, an outburst may be screaming at a parent or slamming a door. Some outbursts last minutes and some last for hours. If your child's outburst is disruptive or threatening to your family, then you will want to take steps to de-escalate it.

When your child's emotional responses are escalating, you may begin to feel tense and anxious and react emotionally to him. An emotional reaction from you or any other member of the family increases the emotional intensity of your child. Decreasing your own emotionality therefore is the first step in de-escalating your child's emotions and behaviors. When you can remain calm in the face of your child's outburst, you will be able to respond in a validating and nonjudgmental manner, which are both necessary to help de-escalate your child's emotional outburst.

Guidelines for remaining calm and in control when your child is escalating include these actions:

- Speak to your child in a soft tone, in a soothing manner, and in a low voice. Slow down your own body by speaking slowly and taking slow, deep breaths, which will calm down your emotions as well.

- Think reasonably and wisely by observing your situation and by staying present in that moment (Linehan 1993a), without fears and worries about what might happen.

- Step back from the immediacy of the situation for just a few seconds to find a more effective response to your child.

- Be aware of thoughts such as, "Here we go again," or "Oh no, not again," or "I can't manage this." These thoughts escalate your own emotions. Remind yourself that your child is doing the best he can.

- Remember the story of emotion from chapter 1 (Linehan 1993b) and make calming statements to yourself. Practice statements such as, "We will get through this" or "I can help my child to calm down if I stay calm."

Helping Your Child Calm Down

Use the skills we discussed in chapters 2 and 3 to help your child calm down during an outburst. Let your child know you are listening by remaining nonjudgmental and validating; provide calming activities and a calming space and minimize demands and expectations until he is calmer. When your child feels accepted and heard, he will de-escalate quicker. More details about helping your child calm down follow.

COACH YOUR CHILD TO USE CALMING ACTIVITIES

Distress tolerance skills are specifically designed to help people calm down in the face of stressful situations. These skills include engaging in activities that distract from painful emotions and that soothe and calm a person so that he can feel better immediately (Linehan 1993a).

You can get some ideas for distress-tolerance/calming activities from the list below and from a more in-depth discussion in chapter 5.

Examples of Calming Activities

- Listen to music

- Draw or paint

- Play on the computer; use a handheld game

- Take a warm bath

- Eat or drink something enjoyable

- Suck on a candy

- Pet your dog

- Exercise

Add some of your own ideas:

- _____

- _____

- _____

When your child is escalating emotionally, your role is to coach him through the crisis by first validating and then suggesting a calming activity, hopefully one that your child has chosen in advance. The way that you will say this to your child is, "I can see that you're very angry. What can we do to help you feel better right now?" This is not the time to discuss all the things that are bothering your child. It is the time to help your child *do something* calming. This will help him de-escalate his emotions and behaviors.

PROVIDE A SAFE AND SOOTHING SPACE

We have already discussed the importance of providing your child with a place in your home that is comforting to him. Going to that place may help him calm down. It's best if the place is quiet and has soft lighting. Including an aquarium can be additionally soothing. Bright lights and noise are often not soothing. This place will be prepared when your child is calm and waiting for him when he is escalating emotionally. This space will be safe for your child physically and emotionally. That is, he cannot get hurt or destroy anything, and he can feel free to express his feelings in ways that are not dangerous.

DON'T MAKE DEMANDS ON YOUR CHILD IN THE MIDST OF AN OUTBURST

When your child is beginning to escalate or is in the middle of an outburst, reminding him of chores, responsibilities, or expectations may cause him to further escalate. It is also not effective to threaten him with consequences. When your child is emotionally dysregulated, he will not be able to hear anything until he has calmed down, and he may become angrier if he feels threatened or ashamed. When your child is in the midst of an emotional outburst, help him calm down using the techniques that we have discussed above. There will be opportunities for everything else later.

Validating Your Child When the Anger Is Aimed at You

Parents often ask how they can validate their child when their child's anger is directed at them. They wonder how they can possibly validate a child who is yelling and saying things that are hurtful for them to hear. As we discussed in chapter 2 and review here, the essence of validation is to let someone know that you hear what he is saying and acknowledge his *feelings* without necessarily agreeing with what is being said (Linehan 1993a). If you can find the essence of the feelings behind his words, as we discussed in chapter 3, you will be able to genuinely validate your child—even if you don't like what he is doing or saying.

What you *can* acknowledge and validate is your child's anger by honestly saying, "I can see that you're angry at me," or "I'm sorry that you're so angry at me. What can we do to make this better?" These words can be very comforting to a child who is feeling out of control. It helps him to emotionally de-escalate and calm down.

What can you say to your child when he is angry at you? Write your ideas here or in your notebook.

_____

_____

_____

Remaining Nonjudgmental When Your Child's Emotions Are Escalated

A child who is emotionally and behaviorally intense often has many painful feelings about himself and his own behavior. While much of the emotion he feels may be directed at others as anger, he may, in fact, be feeling ashamed of himself or guilty about his behavior. Labeling or judging your child when you may be angry at him exacerbates his own negative feelings about himself. When you are accepting and nonjudgmental of your child, he will feel less guilty and will be able to reduce his negative feelings and de-escalate his outburst.

ACCEPTING VS. DENYING DIFFICULT REALITIES

Willingness and *willfulness* differentiate the behaviors of people who are able to accept reality as it is (people who are "willing") and those who believe that they can change reality if they try hard enough, act perfectly, or demand enough (people who are "willful") (May 1982). Your child may believe that he can change things by refusing to accept the way they are and by demanding that they be different. In evaluative terms, you might think this child is stubborn, oppositional, or defiant and be very frustrated by his *unwillingness to understand*.

When your child denies things as they are and seems unable to accept the reality of a situation, your judgments will make you more frustrated and will add to his own already negative emotions. This may lead to an emotional outburst. Your child denies the reality of a situation because the reality is too painful or difficult for him to manage, not because he wants to be stubborn or unreasonable. Help him by acknowledging his frustrations while also helping him to accept what he cannot change.

Some realities are easier to accept than others. That your child has intense emotions and may need special accommodations to remain stable may be a difficult reality for you to accept. However, it is only when these realities are accepted that you can move toward constructive ways of improving the situation. We will discuss ways for *you* to accept difficult realities in chapter 11.

It may be hard, as well, for your child to accept that he is different from other children. He may wish that his whole life were different, that he didn't feel sad or angry so much. It's as painful for you, as a parent, to watch your child suffer with these feelings as it is for him. Some realities can't be changed, despite your strong desire to change them. You can only learn to cope as best you can with things as they are. Accepting those things that cannot be changed helps minimize suffering while you work on adjusting.

Helping Your Child Accept a Difficult Reality

You can help your child become more willing to accept a situation that he cannot change by taking the following steps:

- Talk to him in a calm and soothing voice.

- Validate him by acknowledging that he is having difficulty with the situation, how he might be feeling, and how difficult it is when something doesn't turn out the way he was hoping.

- Help him understand that this situation cannot be changed, no matter how much both of you might want it to. Give him time. Depending on the situation, accept that this may be an ongoing process and may require continued discussions.

- Help him find ways to distract himself from the negative emotions that accepting might create.

- Reinforce his acceptance of a difficult reality.

WHEN EMOTIONS ARE AIMED TOWARD ONESELF

Some children respond to overwhelming negative emotions by having "silent outbursts" (becoming depressed or negative about themselves) or by turning their aggression toward themselves (through self-injury). Your child may respond to his emotional pain by shutting down and becoming uncommunicative. If your child turns his feelings inward, he may not leave his room, participate in activities, or even attend school. The anxiety that he feels makes it impossible for him to meet any expectations, increasing his own sense of despair. When you try to get your child to participate in any way, he may actually "explode" as a way to protect himself from doing something he's afraid of. This explosion tends to be unexpected by parents who are used to a child who is more brooding and quiet. If your child seems to be losing interest in activities or school, you may want to seek professional help.

Some of these children release some of their internal pain by hurting themselves rather than by lashing out toward others. Self-injury and suicidal behaviors are not limited to adults. A child is sending you a message of desperation when he talks about wanting to die or harm himself. When your child talks about wanting to hurt himself, he is telling you that something is hurting him. It may be time to validate his pain and seek professional help. We will discuss this more in chapter 8.

Listen to your child. Talk to him. Validate his pain.

SUMMARY

When you see your child behaving in an unpredictable way, it can be very scary. It's easy to understand how your child's outburst can lead to one of your own. You want your child to just stop what he is doing. It's not always that easy. We have seen that there are a number of factors that contribute to these outbursts (temperament, vulnerability, emotional intensity) and that maintain them (they relieve emotional distress, children find that they get attention, and so on). We have also seen the interaction between your emotional reactions to these outbursts and their outcome. This is not to say that outbursts are your fault. This is not a framework of blame and fault. While you may not be in control of your child's emotional responses, you can take the steps discussed in this chapter to respond in an effective manner to minimize and/or de-escalate your child's outbursts.

Some of the strategies discussed in this chapter include:

- Developing a home with routines, consistency, and a balance of limit setting and pleasurable activities

- Maintaining your own calm and using nonevaluative, validating responses

- Coaching your child to use calming activities

- Helping your child to accept reality as it is

In the next chapter, you will learn how to help your child understand his own emotionality and how he can change the outcome of his own story of emotion.

CHAPTER 5

Teaching Your Child to Manage Feelings

When your child is emotionally dysregulated, what you want to do immediately is calm her down as quickly as possible. This is a short-term, crisis-driven strategy. After the immediate situation is over, do you sometimes wonder if your child will ever be able to manage her own emotions or calm *herself* down? Do you worry that your child will not develop the self-awareness necessary to soothe herself or that she will always be dependent on you to help her manage emotional situations? Teaching your child to respond effectively to her own emotionality is a long-term goal and requires a long-term strategy. When you are accepting and validating of your child, she will be less defensive and more accepting of learning to make changes in her behavioral responses. It will also help her develop the self-awareness necessary to recognize her own vulnerabilities, triggers, and warning signs. As your child learns her own story of emotion (Linehan 1993b), she will need less coaching from you and will become more independent in using the skills that change the outcome of her story.

YOUR CHILD'S AWARENESS OF SELF

As we have discussed, DBT skills enable you to be more aware of yourself, your body sensations, and your feelings in the present and to *use* this heightened awareness to manage the emotions you're experiencing in the moment (Linehan 1993b). When you help your child become more aware of herself in the present moment, she, too, will become more effective at learning to modulate and manage her emotions. Your child can develop heightened awareness of herself and her experiences by learning to observe things outside of herself. Try practicing the exercise below with your child.

A Child's Awareness Exercise

1. Find a favored toy or object (a stuffed animal, a toy truck, a blanket) that your young child uses often. With older children, use a rock or shell that your child has found.

2. Let your child hold the toy/object for at least a minute (or longer, for an older child).

3. While your child is holding the toy/object, encourage her to touch it, smell it, squeeze it, look at it, and use as many senses as she can.

4. When your child has finished experiencing the toy/object, help her find words to describe it. You can ask her if she has discovered something she didn't notice before, whether it is smooth or rough, how it smells, and so on.

Repeat this as often as you and your child enjoy it.

Teaching Self-Awareness of Experience

When your child has learned how to observe and describe objects, help her use these skills to describe her own sensations. Help her to notice feelings and then describe them by asking her to:

- Make a fist, squeeze it, and then open it

- Tip her foot up toward the sky and then tilt it toward the ground

- Squint and then open her eyes wide

- Breathe in and breathe out

After each exercise, encourage your child to notice how each feels and describe her sensations with words. For example: after your child squeezes her fist, ask her how she feels inside. You can ask her if her hand feels tight or loose, relaxed or tense, and if she ever feels like that inside the rest of her body.

With these exercises, you're helping your child to differentiate between when her body is tense (the fist, the foot tilted upward, furrowed brow) and when it is relaxed (fist open, foot tilted down, and so on). By connecting these same sensations to feeling words like anxious or angry (hand tensed) and happy or calm (hand relaxed), you will be helping your child identify what she is feeling when she experiences emotion.

Another way you can help your child identify when she's becoming overwhelmed by emotions is to point out the signs that *you* see by saying in a calm, accepting way:

- "I see that your face is getting red. Is anything bothering you?"

- "When you begin to clench your fist, it usually tells me that you're angry. Is that how you're feeling?"

You can also make a more general statement, like, "When people start to breathe fast, it sometimes means that they're angry or scared. Are you feeling that way?"

The sooner your child can develop the self-awareness to recognize her own body sensations and the feelings that they represent, the sooner she will be able to independently find ways to soothe and calm herself.

Mindfulness/Calm for Your Child

Another way for a child to develop an awareness of herself is to become more mindful of her own body sensations through mindfulness or calming exercises. When your child is aware of her own body, you can help her let go of overwhelming emotions by encouraging her to relax or "untense" her body. Relaxing her fingers, relaxing her legs (by pointing her toes downward), or slowing down her breathing will help relax her body, which, in turn, helps her to feel calmer.

To help your child feel calm, you can:

- Use lotions on her hands, arms, or feet.

- Model for your child by doing yoga, mindfulness, or meditation. Listen to soothing music or sounds.

- Do relaxation/mindfulness CDs *with* her.

When you make these exercises feel like games, your child will want to do them without even realizing that she is learning to soothe herself.

You can teach your child the elements of relaxation/mindfulness exercises by following the steps below. Often, remembering a sense of calm helps to bring that calm into the moment.

EXERCISE: Learning to Calm

Have your child see, smell, touch, and hear as many sights and sounds as possible on a day you spent together.

1. In a calm and soothing voice, explain to your child that you are going to practice calming.

2. Have her sit in a comfortable chair with her hands on the arms of the chair and her feet down. Tell her she can close her eyes or keep them open if she chooses.

3. Have her take a deep breath in and count 1 aloud with her. Tell her this is called her inhale. Have her hold her breath for an additional second.

4. Then have her let the breath out slowly and count 2 aloud with her. Tell her this is called her exhale.

5. Have her inhale and count 1 to herself and then exhale and count 2 to herself. Have her repeat this a few more times until she seems comfortable and relaxed (Linehan 1993b).

6. Have her continue to breathe in and out as you tell her you're going to help her remember when she had a really good time.

7. *Calmly, slowly, and in a soft voice describe a trip, a party, or another event when you and she felt relaxed and comfortable.* Create the image for your child. Describe:

   - How it looked (where you were, what you saw, who was with you, and so on)

   - How your child felt ("Remember telling me how warm you were," "Remember how the sand felt hot when you walked on it")

   - Scents you remember ("Remember the smell of popcorn")

   - Things your child touched (such as seashells on the beach)

8. Have your child continue to breathe for another minute, reminding her how calm she felt that day.

9. Then have her look at you and remember the calm.

Following Up to Increase Self-Awareness

Revisiting an emotional outburst after your child has calmed down will help her develop self-awareness and insight into her own story of emotion.

In a calm and validating manner, use the following questions and topics to guide your follow-up:

What *risk factors* and *triggers* led to the emotional outburst?

- Explore the issues, concerns, and/or situation she was facing.

- Revisit what happened right before the outburst.

- Discuss what she was thinking about.

What *name* would you or she give to describe how she felt?

- Make general connections between experiences and feelings (emotion names) by saying, for example, "When someone yells at me, I feel angry," or "When children get a good grade, they usually feel proud."

- Link your child's trigger with an emotion name: "I saw what your brother did to you. How did you feel about it? Did it make you angry, sad, or frustrated?"

- Ask your child if she can name her feelings. She can use a chart if this helps her until she can name her emotion more spontaneously.

If your child gets angry at you for suggesting her feelings, validate her concerns and do not argue with her. Let your child be the one to define her feelings. She is entitled to name her feelings the way that she wants to, or she can refuse to talk about her feelings at all. Remember: you can plant the seeds of ideas and see if they germinate.

What are the *consequences* to her for responding in this way?

- Did her outburst waste a significant amount of time that she might have spent having fun?

- Does she feel ashamed about her behavior after she has calmed down?

- How did her behaviors make others around her feel? Are people afraid or angry at her?

What other way could she *express her emotions*?

- What will she do differently the next time to avoid similar negative consequences in the future?

- Make suggestions without telling her what to do.

- Help her see the benefits of more effective responses.

Ultimately, it will be up to her, with your support, to make the necessary changes to bring about a better outcome to her story.

CALMING ACTIVITIES

In chapter 4, we introduced the idea of coaching your child through difficult situations by using calming activities. These DBT distress tolerance skills (Linehan 1993b) help your child distract herself from her internal conflicts and turn her attention to activities that calm or soothe her (such as playing on the computer, drawing, taking a warm bath, or using body lotions). Emotional escalation makes independently accessing these activities more difficult for her. Do not hesitate to help your child remember how to calm herself or to ask her, "Do you think a calming activity would be helpful now?" Your child may learn to use these strategies independently, as we will discuss in this section. However, there may always be times when you need to coach or remind her to use her skills.

When teaching your child to use these skills independently, help her:

- Understand that a calming activity is not a punishment

- Learn that using a calming activity will help her feel better and lessen the possibility of negative consequences

- See the ultimate benefits of using calming activities

Working together, you and your child can learn to implement calming activities into her daily life or when they're most needed.

Getting Your Child's Input

Your child's input and involvement in choosing helpful, calming activities is crucial; she will only use them if she is invested in them. Discussions with your child about these activities will be more effective if they take place when she is calm. At those times, she will be better able to hear you and be more receptive to what you're saying. You and your child will then be able to generate enough activities to give her a variety of choices and minimize the possibility that she will get bored with any of them.

Brainstorm ideas with your child by asking her what she likes to do when she feels bad, what helps her calm down when she is mad, or what helps her feel better when she is sad. You can also let her know that she has your support by asking, "What can I do to help you the next time you're upset?" Listen carefully to her answers with acceptance and validation.

You can also offer your child the following types of observations and suggestions:

- "The last time you were upset, I noticed that you went to your room. Did that help you feel better?"

- "I know that you like to take a warm bath; sometimes baths help people calm down when they're upset. Do you think that would help you?"

- "You seem to have a better afternoon when you've had some quiet time in your room after lunch. Do you think you might like to do that more often?"

As you and your child come up with calming activities, develop a chart like the one on the next page. Use words, drawings done by your child, pictures from magazines, or stickers to represent the activities that she has suggested. Put the chart somewhere easily accessible so that your child can refer to it when she feels herself becoming emotional.

What Helps You Feel Better?

When I am sad, I feel better when I:

_____

_____

When I am mad, I feel better when I:

_____

_____

When I am upset, I feel better when I:

_____

_____

When somebody hurts my feelings, I feel better when I:

_____

_____

Talking About It Is Not Always Calming

There is a myth that talking about it will help a person feel better about a difficult situation. This is not always the case. There are times when talking about a troubling situation, especially before a person has calmed down, actually escalates the person's emotions.

Before you discuss what is bothering your child, help her calm herself down using any of the activities or skills discussed earlier. Do not make demands on her to talk. Tell her you will talk later. There are always opportunities to talk about a situation and find ways to resolve it when your child's emotionality is diminished and she is better able to engage effectively in the discussion.

The Consequences of Calming Activities
for Your Child

You will want your child to use a calming activity before she becomes so escalated that her behaviors are out of control. To accomplish this, you can help her recognize the benefits of these activities and how they work in response to triggers or tension in her body. Help your child see that these activities lead to more effective behavioral responses and positive consequences. Show your child that her choices can affect what happens. The two paths are illustrated in the figures that follow.

Figure 5.1: Not Using a Calming Activity

Trigger → Emotion → Continued escalating emotion → Escalated behavioral response → Negative consequence (family angry and upset; child feeling ashamed) → Possible punishment

---

Figure 5.2: Using a Calming Activity

Trigger → Emotion → Calming activity → Emotions subside → No behavioral outburst → Child feels okay → Family feels okay → Positive consequences (go on with the day without interruption)

Your child will feel so much better about her actions and herself after she uses a calming activity that she will be more likely to use one of the activities again in the future. Calming herself becomes a self-rewarding activity; the more she does it, the greater the possibility that she will do it in the future.

Help your younger child choose to calm herself by suggesting:

- "It looks like you're getting mad. Please go to your room and play with some of your quiet toys so that you can calm yourself."

- "I think that quiet time will help you settle down so you won't get any madder."

- "Can we watch a movie and calm down a little bit together?"

To an older child you may, calmly, suggest:

- "It seems like you're getting mad. Is there something from your chart that you can do that will help you calm down so we can avoid another outburst?"

- "It looks like you're really angry. I'm worried that you'll do something you may regret later. How can I help you calm down? Will something on your chart help you feel better?"

Let's look at the following examples of a child's reactions and notice how using a calming activity can change the outcome of the story.

> Amy, age seven, gets angry when her father, Tom, doesn't allow her to do something that she wants to do or when he asks her to do something she doesn't want to do. One Saturday morning, Tom asks her to get off the computer so the family can leave for an outing. Amy is enjoying the game she is playing on the computer and doesn't want to stop playing. Her father repeats his request calmly and Amy continues to ignore him. When Tom asks again, Amy shouts, "No!" Her face is getting redder, and her father is getting angry and frustrated. Amy continues to concentrate on the computer and yells at her father that he always interrupts her fun. Tom now raises his voice, tells her she is being disrespectful, and approaches the computer to turn it off. Amy begins to block Tom physically and is ready to hit him if he comes any closer. Her father is totally exasperated and continues to yell at her. Amy begins to pound on the computer keys. After a half hour, Amy finally calms down. At that point Tom puts her in her room and tells her that she has ruined the afternoon for the whole family. Her siblings are upset because they have witnessed another episode of Amy being out of control.

Now see what happens when a parent introduces a calming activity into the situation.

Amy's father, Tom, asks her to get off the computer in five minutes to prepare for a family outing. When he reminds her again after the five minutes have passed, she ignores him and he repeats himself calmly. She tells him loudly, "I want to play on the computer. Leave me alone!" She continues to get louder, and when her face gets red, he realizes that she has been triggered by his insistence that she get off the computer. Tom does not want her behavior to escalate. After the last incident, he and Amy discussed ways for her calm herself and wrote them on a paper in her room.

- Tom remains calm, validates her feelings about not wanting to be disturbed, and acknowledges her anger when he says, "I know that you're upset that you can't continue your computer game."

- He then reminds her about her calming activities by saying, "The last time you got upset about this, you ended up in your room and the day was ruined for everyone. Do you think that you can look on the chart and do something that will calm you for a few minutes so that we can all go out?"

- Amy chooses to draw in the kitchen while the family prepares to go out.

- Amy is calm when she joins the rest of the family for the outing. The family is pleased that an incident has been avoided and their afternoon has not been disrupted.

Considerations

Your child will be able to use activities that require more concentration (like reading) in the early stages of emotional escalation. The more upset she is, the more she will need something that relaxes her physically and that doesn't require much cognitive energy. Develop a list of different activities: some for mild upsets, some for when she is more upset, and others for when she is intensely emotional.

- Do not assume that an activity that was very effective one day will always be effective. You and your child will need to continue to reassess what is helpful and what is not.

- Sometimes she will need to be alone, and sometimes she may need to be close to people. Let her tell you what she needs and accept her suggestions.

- When you work on the chart, find activities that you and your child agree to. These activities should be easily accessible within your home, your child should be able to do them independently, and they should not depend on or interfere with anyone else.

- Don't get into a power struggle if your child refuses to use a calming activity. Remain calm. Continue to validate your child's feelings.

- If your child is involved in a calming activity, don't interrupt, make demands, or interfere until she has completely calmed herself down. An interruption may cause an escalation before she is able to tolerate any frustrations.

You and your child will find that when you work together with patience and acceptance, you will find the activities that work most effectively in different situations.

SUMMARY

As your child develops self-awareness, she will learn the skills necessary to recognize and manage her own emotions. You can help her make effective choices when emotions threaten to overwhelm her by encouraging her to independently use the lists of calming activities that you develop together. When your child is able to experience the positive consequences of managing her emotions effectively, she will work harder at developing healthy responses that she will need throughout her lifetime. Your child will always face difficult situations, and she will be better able to manage these situations effectively when you have taught her these skills early in her life.

The skills that were discussed in this chapter include:

- Mindfulness and relaxation exercises to help your child develop self-awareness

- Follow-up questions to help your child learn her story of emotion and use it to change the outcome of her story

- Developing calming activity charts and encouraging your child to use these activities before her negative emotions overwhelm her

In the next chapters, we will discuss how to help your child change her behavioral responses to intense emotions.

PART 3

Responding to Your Child's Behaviors

CHAPTER 6

Behavioral Principles and Intense Behaviors

When your child's emotions dominate your life, you might feel like it's impossible to meet the basic responsibilities of parenting. How do you teach your child the lessons that all children need to learn about how to behave, what is expected of him, and the values and morals of your community? Your responsibility as a parent is to prepare your child for all aspects of his life. The temperament of some children makes this easy; they are able to accept what they're told and follow through on expectations without question or incident. When your child has intense emotions, they get in the way of his learning certain behaviors, maintaining expected behaviors, and/or responding to your limits. Even when your child knows *how* he is supposed to behave, his emotions may interfere with his *ability* to behave in expected ways. The task of teaching your child how to behave is much harder.

As we've discussed throughout this book, parenting a child with intense emotions requires special skills from parents. Teaching effective behaviors and responding in a way that encourages your child to use those behaviors requires special skills as well. The strategies that parents use to increase their child's adaptive behaviors and decrease his ineffective behaviors follow behavioral principles that developed from years of empirical research. In this chapter, we will discuss these principles, and in the following two chapters, we will discuss how to apply these principles to certain problematic behaviors.

PRINCIPLES OF EFFECTIVE PARENTING REVISITED

When your child is not responding to you, it's easy to become emotional and ineffective yourself. Here we offer some reminders about effective parenting that will make it easier for you to use the behavioral principles described below:

- **Do not assume the worst.** There may be many reasons why your child is behaving the way he is. Respond to his behavior, not assumptions about his intentions.

- **Don't be judgmental.** If you are thinking negatively about your child, gently remind yourself that your child is doing the best he can.

- **Validate your child.** Respond to your child's truth and feelings, even if it's difficult.

- **Be responsive, not reactive.** Take a few seconds to keep your emotions in check before you respond to your child's behaviors.

- **You can lose the battle and still win the war.** It's not essential that you have absolute control of your child. Choose your battles so that you can have a more positive relationship with him. This will enable you to reinforce positive changes over time.

- **It takes two to engage in power struggles.** You can walk away without feeling like you're giving in. You can enforce limits without arguing about them. Your child doesn't have to agree that you're right, nor do you have to prove he's wrong.

- **Balance your responses.** Balanced parenting means being able to give your child some choices and control while still setting behavioral guidelines.

- **Choose the most effective response.** Are you achieving your long-term goals? If what you're doing isn't working, try something else.

UNDERSTANDING AND USING BEHAVIORAL PRINCIPLES

According to the behavioral model of psychology, behaviors are caused and/or maintained by something that either precedes or follows them. When a behavior is prompted by something that comes before it, that behavior is a *conditioned response* (Pavlov 1928). Such is the response when you smell dinner being cooked and feel hungry. Other behaviors are learned by the consequences that come after them—behaviors are strengthened when followed by something pleasurable and weakened when followed by something unpleasant or punishing (Skinner 1953). An example of this would be giving your child a treat when he has cleaned his room in the hope that he will clean his room the next time you ask. Conversely, if your child has hit his brother and you put him in his room without TV, he may not repeat this behavior the next time he's tempted to do so.

Behavioral principles provide a great deal of information about (1) how behaviors are learned, (2) how they can be unlearned, and (3) how new behaviors can be learned to take their place. In this chapter, we will use these principles to guide you in developing more effective responses to your child and teaching him effective behaviors to take the place of less effective or problematic behaviors. This focus on behaviors makes your child less defensive, less ashamed, and more open to change.

Describing Behaviors

All behaviors can be described in very specific, nonjudgmental terms. It helps to describe behaviors by the specific actions you see, without interpretation or judgment. If you say that your child "was out of control," what does that mean? Some people might interpret that to mean that he screamed at you; others might think that your child was verbally threatening, while others might think that he destroyed things in your home. Interpretations are based on individual experiences, while descriptions are recognized in the same way by everyone. You and your child need to have the same understanding of exactly what behavior you're trying to change.

Evaluate the following two statements and write down what each leads you to think:

- "My son got upset and was disrespectful"

vs.

- "When my child was not allowed to do what he wanted, he told me that I was mean and then did not talk to me."

_____

_____

In this exercise, notice that the words "upset" and "disrespectful" can be defined differently by different people, leaving the first statement open to interpretation. The second statement is a clearer description that everyone can understand and does not create as much confusion or emotion.

Behavioral Terms

As you can see in the charts on the next page, every behavior is preceded by something (the *antecedent*) and is followed by something (the *consequence*). Principles for changing behaviors usually derive from *operant conditioning*, which means increasing or decreasing the likelihood that a behavior will occur by choosing the consequence that follows it (Skinner 1953). To change a behavior, the consequence must be contingent upon the behavior; that is, the behavior must occur for the consequence to occur. The consistency of the consequence is very important and will contribute to its effectiveness.

Whether or not a consequence is positive or negative is idiosyncratic—a consequence that may be positive for one child may be negative for another. A child who likes ice cream may increase a behavior when ice cream is promised afterward; this consequence will have no impact on a child who doesn't like ice cream. Praise may increase behaviors for some children but may decrease behaviors in a child who is embarrassed by it. The effectiveness of a consequence can only be judged by whether or not there is a change in the behavior it follows.

The box that follows breaks down this dynamic and introduces some important terms for further discussion.

ANTECEDENT → BEHAVIOR

The antecedent/precipitating or prompting event describes what is going on right before a behavior occurs.

Look at all aspects of the environment to determine what might lead to a behavior.

Something is always happening.

ACTION → RESPONSE

BEHAVIOR → CONSEQUENCE

Any action or behavior will produce a response or consequence from the environment.

POSSIBLE CONSEQUENCES

- **REINFORCEMENT:** *Increases* the probability of occurrence of the behavior it follows

- **PUNISHMENT:** *Decreases* the probability of occurrence of the behavior it follows

Following are important terms you'll need to understand when using behavioral principles to modify or change your child's behavior.

REINFORCERS

Sometimes known as "rewards," *reinforcers* are consequences that increase the possibility that a behavior will occur again (Skinner 1953) and/or will increase how often the behavior occurs. A reinforcer is generally something that your child likes or enjoys. It may also be taking away something that is disliked. For example, if your child is whining that he wants a cookie, you may decide to give him the cookie so that he will stop whining. You have increased the probability that your child will whine when he wants something because you gave him what he wanted. In addition, you have been reinforced for giving him the cookie and will do it more often because giving it to him *stopped* the complaining, a positive outcome for your behavior. You and your child reinforce each other, sometimes in ways that you don't even realize.

If you're consistently using a reinforcer to increase a specific behavior and you're not seeing any change in the behavior, the reinforcer you have chosen for your child is not working. There may be several reasons for this:

- The reinforcer should be available to your child *only* after, or contingent upon, the targeted behavior. If your child is able to use the computer whenever he chooses, it will not reinforce a particular behavior.

- It may not be effectively reinforcing for your child. Allowance will be an effective reinforcer only if your child likes to buy things and realizes that earning allowance allows him to buy what he wants.

- The reinforcer may not work because your child has tired of it, even if he initially chose it.

For reinforcers to be effective, (1) choose them with your child, (2) be willing to choose another if one isn't working (even if your child chose it), (3) use it at a time when your child has not had access to it, and (4) provide several choices so that your child doesn't get bored.

Examples: Reinforcers

- Special time with a parent

- A later bedtime

- An event your child wants to attend

- Extra time on the computer, TV, video game console, and so on

- Money to save for a special toy

- Stickers or stars on a chart (that may or may not be turned into something concrete)

Reinforcers are not bribes. Some parents reject the idea of reinforcers because they don't believe they should be "bribing" or paying their child to do what is expected of him. These parents believe that their child *should* behave a certain way and should not be rewarded for doing what is "right." In actuality, life is filled with reinforcers. People go to work in order to get paid and don't consider their paycheck a bribe. We do things for others when they express their appreciation. Everyone likes to be reinforced in one way or another. Concrete reinforcers (those that a child can hold, eat, or use) may give way to more social reinforcers (praise, attention) as a child grows. If your child is emotionally intense, it's harder for him to learn and maintain behaviors that are easy for others. Expecting him to behave in a way that is difficult for him without providing external incentives may not work. He may need an added incentive and additional motivation. Effective parenting means doing what works for your particular child. Reinforcing effective behaviors in your child may be one way to parent him effectively.

A caution about reinforcers: *Give your child reinforcers as immediately as possible.* When you act promptly to reinforce behaviors you prefer, your child will link the reinforcement to the behavior that immediately precedes it. If you have told your child that you'll go to the playground when he has picked up his toys, try to take him as soon as his toys are picked up. If you delay the trip, you may face the following dilemma: Your child has a tantrum before the time you have chosen to go.

- Do you take him to the playground even if it will seem to him that you are reinforcing his tantrum?

- Do you deny him the trip even though he's earned it? Will he trust you the next time you promise him a reinforcer?

Your actions sometimes have unintended consequences. Reinforce behaviors immediately so that your child links the *desired behavior* to the reinforcer.

SHAPING

Shaping is the way you teach your child how to complete a series of tasks by reinforcing small, gradual steps that increasingly approach the goal (Skinner 1953). The steps of effective shaping are:

1. Break the overall behavioral goal into small, manageable behaviors that your child can accomplish.

2. Reinforce completion of the first behavior until he is able to follow through consistently on that behavior.

3. When the first behavior becomes consistent, add another expectation and reinforce when both behaviors occur.

4. Add another behavior to *all* previous behaviors and only reinforce when that new behavior joins all the others.

5. Repeat until all expectations can be met by your child and reinforcement occurs only when your child has met the overall goal.

By following the steps above, you'll be increasing the expectations for your child to earn a reinforcer. You are gradually shaping more positive and effective skills by requiring and reinforcing more effective behaviors. In this way, you will eventually have taught your child how to reach a more difficult goal.

Following is an example of how shaping might work with your child.

If your child is overwhelmed in social situations and grabs things from other children, you might want to teach him more effective social behaviors. Telling him to "be nice" is ineffective; it lacks specificity, and your child will not know what to do. Instead:

1. Tell your child that you are going to help him get along with other children more effectively (or "better," if your child is young).

2. Let him know that if he sits next to another child in the sandbox and doesn't grab anything that does not belong to him for fifteen minutes, you will give him a special snack. Reinforce him whenever he is able to do this.

3. When your child is able to sit without grabbing for fifteen minutes (even if this takes several trips to the playground), tell him that you're proud of him. Then tell him that he'll have to sit in the sandbox and not grab a toy for a half hour. Show him on a timer how long this is. Tell him if he can do this for a half hour, you will go to his favorite ice cream store for a treat.

4. When your child is able to consistently be with another child in the sandbox without grabbing and consistently goes for ice cream, continue to praise his efforts. Then tell him that if he can share one of his toys with another child (or offer to do so), then you will buy him a new toy.

THE PREMACK PRINCIPLE

The Premack principle reminds you to make a behavior that is likely to occur contingent upon a behavior that is less likely to happen (Premack 1959). For example, if your child wants to watch TV, allow him to do that *after* he has completed his chore. In this way, the less likely behavior (doing chores) is reinforced by the more likely behavior (watching TV). This is the principle you're using, often without realizing it, when you tell your child to eat his dinner before he can have dessert.

INTERMITTENT REINFORCEMENT

When you reinforce your child only *occasionally,* or once in a while, you're engaging in *intermittent reinforcement* (Skinner 1953). Your child never knows when his behavior will result in a reward and continues the behavior because of the likelihood that eventually he will get what he wants. This creates very persistent behavior, similar to that of an adult at a casino. Spontaneously rewarding your child for an effective behavior when he is not expecting or demanding it can have long lasting positive results. It is also why responding, even occasionally, to an ineffective behavior may result in repetition of this behavior for a long time, as you can see from the example below.

Your child is having a temper tantrum, and your strategy is to ignore tantrums. You walk away and don't respond to your child until he stops his tantrum. Then you pay attention to him so that he realizes that positive behaviors are positively reinforced. You do this several times.

Then your child has a tantrum in the grocery store. You're embarrassed by this behavior and realize that others are staring at you and your child. You begin to hear mumblings about what a "bad parent" you are because you're not "doing anything" about your child's behavior. You tell your child that just this one time he can have what he wants if he stops his tantrum. His tantrum has the desired impact on you: *he has gotten what he wants.*

In the days to come, you return to your strategy of ignoring tantrums. Then your child has a tantrum in front of your extended family. Again, you may feel embarrassed and judged and give your child what he wants "just this one time."

The result is that your child continues to throw a tantrum no matter how many times you ignore him. He will keep waiting for that "one time" when you decide to give in and respond to his tantrum. Your strategy, when applied inconsistently, is not effective.

Intermittent reinforcement of negative behaviors inadvertently teaches your child that he will eventually be able to wear you down and get what he wants, regardless of any statements you may make to the contrary. Consistency is very important when you're trying to change behaviors.

PUNISHMENT

Punishment is any action that decreases the probability that a behavior will occur (Skinner 1953). Punishment can be taking away something that your child likes or doing something that your child does not like. For example, if your child is calling his sibling names, you may tell him that he can't play with a friend as expected that afternoon because of his behavior (taking away something). Or, you may ask him to apologize for his behavior (doing something he doesn't like) and not allow him to rejoin the family activity until he has done so. Punishments should matter to your child and should happen immediately so the child understands what behavior is being punished.

Effective punishment. To be most effective, punishment needs to be specific and time limited. Punishments that go on for days or weeks lose their effectiveness. Both you and your child will be anxious for the punishment to be over and may forget what led to it in the first place. More effective punishments are short and reasonable in length.

Try to make the punishment fit the "crime." That is, the punishment should teach your child the true consequence of his behavior. Not allowing your child to watch TV when he has taken something that doesn't belong to him doesn't teach him why his behavior is problematic. If your child apologizes for his behavior and has to return what he has taken, he will have a better understanding of its impact.

Natural consequences. When you allow the natural outcome of the behavior to punish it, you're using *natural consequences*. If your child forgets to bring his homework to school, you may bring his homework to school once or twice. If the behavior occurs consistently, eventually he will have to experience the natural consequence of forgetting his homework (imposed by his teacher) when you don't bring his homework to school for him. *Saving* or *protecting* your child from natural consequences does not help him learn to be responsible for his own behaviors.

Natural consequences can be quite effective, and you don't have to add your own punishment on top of them. If your child yells out in class despite his teacher's reminders not to and is kept after class, he may not need additional punishment at home.

Reinforcement is more effective than punishment. Though punishment might work, reinforcement generally works more effectively (Kodak et al. 2007). Your goal is to teach your child *how to* behave. Punishment teaches your child how *not* to behave without giving him alternative strategies. Often punishment teaches children not to get caught and to avoid punishment without teaching them what behavior would have a *positive* outcome. Reinforcement actually encourages new behaviors. Because reinforcement is more effective as well as more pleasant, most of the examples in this chapter will focus on reinforcement as a technique.

To decrease an ineffective behavior, you might reinforce an opposite or incompatible behavior, thereby teaching your child what *to do*. You can see some examples of this strategy in the table and comments below.

Table 6.1: Reinforcing Incompatible Behaviors

Behavior to Decrease	Behavior to Increase/Reinforce
Yelling	Using a softer voice
Demanding	Using the word "please"
Cursing	Days with no abusive language
Destruction	Days or periods of time without aggression
Hitting others	Expressing anger in words

Reinforcing incompatible behaviors in response to aggressive outbursts. To reduce your child's explosive and destructive behaviors, reinforcing him when he *is* behaving is more effective than punishing him when he is *not*. As we've said, when you reinforce him for effective behaviors, he will learn how *to* behave, not merely how *not to*.

When your child's intense emotions often lead to strong behavioral responses, you may be surprised to find that there are many opportunities to reinforce him for behaving effectively. Try to recognize and acknowledge those times when your child is calm and doing what is expected of him. One benefit of using reinforcing strategies is that you become more aware of positive moments when they occur. Acknowledging positives helps your child—and you—feel better.

You can also shape your child's behaviors by reinforcing specific behaviors that show a modulated response on the part of your child or a closer approximation of the behavior you're looking for. For example, reinforce your child when he:

- Takes space or goes to his room when he shows signs of being angry

- Responds to a prompt (or reminder) and ends his verbal abuse

- Reduces his outbursts by remaining outburst-free for gradually longer periods of time

- Uses feeling words rather than being aggressive

In each of the examples above, you are encouraging your child to use more effective ways to manage his feelings. Validate your child and acknowledge that (1) he is doing the best he can, (2) he can do better, and (3) you will help him to do better.

Guidelines for using punishment when necessary. There are times when you will need to use a negative consequence. At these times, try to institute a time-out for your child. This takes him from a social situation, where he might be inadvertently reinforced for his behavior, and gives him time to calm down. Let your child know that he can come out of time-out *when he is calm, but not before.* If your child refuses to go to time-out, usually because he doesn't want to leave the situation, you may have to take away something that your child likes. Use this method cautiously; we have talked to parents who have taken away all of their child's favorite toys, leaving their child depressed, bored, and with no better behaviors.

Rather than taking away something, let your child have access to it *only* when he's behaving effectively. Reminding your child when he can *earn* something is much more pleasant (and effective) than threatening to take something away. For example, tell your child that he can play his video game only on the days when he has not had an outburst. In this way, he is earning the video game for behaving rather than losing it when he is not.

Although follow-through is often difficult for parents, a punishment might mean prohibiting your child from participating in an activity he enjoys. Your child will begin to accept responsibility for his behaviors, and you will feel less guilty when he is gently reminded that you're not taking away this activity—*he* is not *earning* the right to participate.

Modeling. Your child follows your example. If you yell at him as punishment, he will learn to yell as well. Aggressive behavior on the part of the parent teaches the child to act aggressively. Focus on reinforcing positive behaviors in your child and he will use more positive behaviors and have a more positive view of himself as well.

CONTRACTS

Contracts are agreements between you and your child developed to (1) decrease a behavior that is problematic (like throwing things) or (2) increase adaptive behaviors that do not occur often enough (such as going to bed on time). A contract explicitly states the conditions under which your child will receive a reinforcer and what that reinforcer will be.

You set up contracts by stating:

"*If you* (state the behavior the child must do) *then* (you will respond in a certain way)."

Contracts are helpful to parents and children because expectations and consequences are clear and explicit. These consequences are not determined by the emotional mood of either parent or child but, instead, are based on wise decisions that are made in advance. The child is in control of whether or not he receives the consequence and learns that he is responsible for his behavior and its consequences.

Contracts require follow-through and ongoing attention, which make them difficult for parents at times. Following through on a contract increases the trust between you and your child as well as your child's recognition that you mean what you say. Contracts are effective only when consistently followed.

Elements of Contracting

Remember the following guidelines when developing a contract:

- Be specific about the behavior you are modifying so that you and your child know what is expected. For example, if you want your child to *complete* his homework, reinforce him when his homework is complete (regardless of how much time he has spent on it); if you want your child to do homework for a *certain amount of time*, reinforce him when he has done it for that amount of time (regardless of how much he has completed).

- Be able to confirm that a behavior has occurred either by seeing it yourself or by depending on the report of someone you trust (like a teacher or a babysitter).

- Have the reinforcer in your control and be able to follow through. For example, you can promise your child that he can play with his sibling when he finishes his homework only if you know his sibling is willing and able to do this.

- Only use consequences that you can and will follow through on. If you tell your child that he can go out to dinner with the family only if his homework is complete, be prepared for the possibility that either the whole family will have to stay home (which is more of a negative consequence to you than it is to him) or you will have to get him a babysitter.

- To develop a longer-term contract, have your child earn an immediate reinforcer (such as a sticker or star) and collect them until he has earned a predetermined number. These can then be exchanged for a special treat, activity, or prize. Keep repeating this process over time until your child's behaviors become consistent. Use bonuses for consistent behavior in the long term.

Contracts have two goals: (1) to increase your child's use of effective behaviors and (2) to enable your child to feel good about his success. Develop contracts that will be possible for your child to accomplish. *Successful contracts do not require perfection, only improvement.*

Sam's example demonstrates how contracts can work.

Sam is a ten-year-old boy who has explosive and aggressive outbursts at least once a day. These outbursts often come after his parents have asked him to do something he doesn't want to do. For example, completing homework has become what his parents call a "nightmare." He demands that they sit next to him and help him, which they do to avoid the inevitable struggle with him. (*He reinforces their behavior by not having a tantrum.*) When they sit quietly, Sam works on his homework. (*He reinforces them for sitting silently.*) When they leave or when he is frustrated with his homework, his outbursts can be violent.

His parents try to ignore his outbursts but intervene when they fear he will get hurt. (*They intermittently reinforce the outburst with their attention.*) Sam's parents recognize that they are overwhelmed and do anything they can to avoid his outbursts. They don't realize that they are reinforcing his behavior by meeting all of his demands.

Shaping and Reinforcing Effective Behaviors

- Sam's parents would like to decrease his outbursts, reinforce the completion of his homework, and eventually reinforce him for completing his homework independently.

- In order to decrease Sam's outbursts, his parents will reinforce effective and calm behaviors (for example, completing his homework without an outburst).

- Eventually, they will shape him to do his homework more independently by reinforcing him when he works for incrementally longer periods of time without their presence.

- Sam loves to play his video games, use the computer, and spend money.

Sam's parents realize that they will need to find reinforcers that will work for Sam and put together a contract that will include shaping his behavior toward the bigger goal. They recognize that even though Sam loves his video games, at the present time he is only allowed to play them for a half hour per day. He would like to be able to play them more often, and his parents know they can incorporate this wish into his contract as an effective reinforcer. They then develop a contract for Sam that looks like this:

- When Sam completes his homework by 7 p.m. without an outburst (no cursing, yelling, or running around the house), he will earn fifteen additional minutes playing his video games. When he has an outburst, he must calm down before he is able to have his half hour with the games.

- Sam receives fifty cents for each half hour that he works on his homework independently.

- Sam can be given one prompt to calm down and will receive his reinforcer if he is able to calm down within two minutes after receiving the prompt.

- Each day that Sam is outburst-free, he will be given a sticker at the end of the day and an extra fifteen minutes on his computer. When he has five stickers, his parents will give him two dollars.

Here are specifics about Sam's contract that you can consider:

- Sam is reinforced for *completion* of his homework (not just doing some of it) and remaining outburst-free.

- Sam is not required to be perfect, only better; prompts and reminders help shape his behavior.

- Children give up if reinforcers are based on consecutive days of effective behaviors. Think about how frustrating it is for a child when he has to be free of outbursts for five consecutive days. If, after the fourth day, he has an outburst, he has to start all over again and may become discouraged. However, when you give him the reinforcer *whenever* he has earned the fifth sticker, he could have an outburst on the fourth day and still get the reinforcer after one more outburst-free day. He never has to start all over again. And, when he does have an outburst, he can be encouraged to earn his sticker the next day and add it to those he's already earned.

Contracts encourage parents to find ways to reinforce positive behaviors rather than punish negative behaviors, just as Sam's parents have done. They do require time and patience on the part of the parents as well as the child in order to be effective. They can be used to change many different behaviors.

Applying Consequences in Special Situations

If your child is having an outburst in an area with other people, he may want to stay with everyone else and may refuse to go to time-out. If possible, you may want to have the others leave the area instead. Although this may not seem fair, it may be effective. Children may be reinforced by the reactions of others and can calm down easier when others aren't there. It is also safer to remove others in case your child becomes violent.

If your child is often triggered into intense or explosive responses, address only those behaviors that are most disruptive. You may have to let go of some expectations (like chores or a clean room). Your goal is to help your child control his behaviors without overwhelming him beyond his ability to manage his emotions.

Choosing Target Behaviors

How do you choose the behavior that you want to change or modify? Ask yourself the following questions:

- **Does my child have unsafe or dangerous behaviors?** If your child is dangerous to himself or others, these behaviors must be addressed and are the first targets for change.

- **What non-dangerous behavior has the most detrimental consequences for my child?** If your child is having frequent temper tantrums that interfere with daily activities, they may be your target behavior.

- **What behavior is most problematic and/or interferes most in the family?** When your child has difficulty interacting with others, teaching him social skills will have a positive impact inside and outside the family.

- **What are my child's goals and what behaviors get in the way?** Your child may be most motivated to work on behaviors that matter to him. Help him see the short- and long-term consequences of his behaviors as incentive for him to make changes in them.

Now that you have a basic understanding of behavioral principles that can help you and your child work on behavioral change, it's time to practice what you have learned. The exercise that follows will help guide your efforts. Use the blank spaces or your notebook to answer the questions. Choose your reinforcers based on the principles discussed above. As an example, we have completed the exercise above for Sam.

EXAMPLE: Behavioral Practice Exercise

WHAT BEHAVIOR DO YOU WANT TO CHANGE?

Sam has outbursts while doing his homework. They last for about an hour. They happen almost daily.

WHAT CONSEQUENCES USUALLY FOLLOW THE BEHAVIOR?

After the outburst, Sam ignores his parents when they talk to him and doesn't complete his homework. His parents are frustrated and angry.

DO YOU WANT TO INCREASE OR DECREASE THE BEHAVIOR?

Sam's parents want to increase the behavior of completing his homework calmly and independently. They will shape him and reinforce him for increasing these behaviors.

WHAT SPECIFIC REINFORCER or PUNISHMENT DID YOU CHOOSE?

His parents will let him use his video game longer when his homework is completed on time and without an outburst. He gets stickers (and money) for outburst-free days.

WHAT WAS THE IMMEDIATE AND LONG-TERM IMPACT OF YOUR CONSEQUENCE?

Sam begins to respond to prompts and reminders to calm down and has fewer outbursts. Eventually he needs fewer prompts, has fewer outbursts, and is able to do his homework independently for longer periods of time.

Behavioral Practice Exercise

The response that follows any behavior can increase, decrease, or maintain the frequency of that behavior.

Use your responses strategically.

WHAT BEHAVIOR DO YOU WANT TO CHANGE?

Describe the behavior specifically. How often does it occur?

_____

WHAT CONSEQUENCES USUALLY FOLLOW THE BEHAVIOR?

_____

DO YOU WANT TO INCREASE OR DECREASE THE BEHAVIOR?

What technique will you use? Reinforcement? Punishment? Shaping? A combination of them?

_____

WHAT SPECIFIC REINFORCER OR PUNISHMENT DID YOU CHOOSE?

Why did you choose that particular consequence?

Are you able to be consistent in applying this contingency?

_____

WHAT WAS THE IMMEDIATE AND LONG-TERM IMPACT OF YOUR CONSEQUENCE?

What was your child's reaction to the consequence? Did the behavior increase or decrease over time?

_____

SUMMARY

Teaching a child with intense emotional and behavioral dysregulation how to behave effectively requires parents to be patient and consistent. Your responses to your child may inadvertently or deliberately maintain, increase, or decrease your child's behaviors. In this chapter, we've discussed behavioral principles and skills to increase your effectiveness in modifying your child's behaviors. These include:

- Applying consequences (reinforcers or punishers) in a planful way to increase or decrease certain targeted behaviors

- Using contracts to consistently reinforce behaviors so that your child's effective behaviors will be more consistent

- Deciding which behaviors will be targeted and prioritized for change

In the following chapter, we'll examine how to establish and maintain limits, routines, and expectations for your child.

CHAPTER 7

Maintaining Expectations, Limits, and Routines

Parents are often frustrated when their child "doesn't listen"—either not doing what is asked (not responding to requests) or continuing to do something when asked not to (not responding to limits). How do you apply the principles you learned in chapter 6 to the multitude of problems you encounter, many on a daily basis? How do you get your child up and ready for school without an ordeal or get her to bed by a reasonable hour without a fight? Do you find yourself ignoring behaviors because other behaviors seem so much more important or because requesting something seems not worth the effort? When your child has intense emotions, a request to do something or an attempt to set a limit can lead to a full-blown tantrum or aggressive behaviors that may last for hours.

In previous chapters (2 and 6), we provided guidance for choosing *what* behaviors are most important for your child to learn. In this chapter and the next one, you will learn how to apply the behavioral principles we discussed in chapter 6 to teach your child *how to consistently use* effective behaviors (such as asking for something she wants) rather than more problematic behaviors (screaming or having a tantrum).

EXPECTATIONS, ROUTINES, AND LIMITS

Every child needs rules and limits to know what's expected and what's not permitted. A child who is allowed to behave in any way she chooses will not learn how to live successfully in a world that has rules, laws, expectations, and consequences. When you respond to your child's behaviors thoughtfully, wisely, and consistently, she will learn how she is expected to behave in different situations.

As your child gets older, your expectations of her will change and she will demand privileges that will require more independent judgment and responsibility on her part. Your expectations and rules will shift with the changing needs and capabilities of your child. When your child's demands and her behaviors are based on emotions, you will face difficult ongoing decisions that balance what your child wants, what she needs, and what you think she is capable of managing safely and effectively. In this section, we will address how to determine, explain, and maintain your expectations, routines, and limits for your child.

Be Explicit

As we discussed earlier, using behavioral principles means that both you and your child are clear about expectations, rules, and limits. Don't assume that your child knows what you think she should know; she might have difficulty reading social cues and making appropriate judgments. She may, for example, believe you're angry at her when you're actually frustrated about something else. When your child has intense emotions that interfere with her ability to think reasonably, be prepared to teach her skills that other children acquire independently. This is not her fault or yours. Being clear and consistent about acceptable and unacceptable behaviors and their consequences will make it a little easier (although not always *easy*) for your child to meet expectations and accept limits.

Family rules and expectations develop and change over time and are somewhat dependent on shifting societal developments (at what age you give your child a cell phone is a fairly recent dilemma, for example). Every family is unique, and the following lists are far from exhaustive; however, you can use these questions and examples to guide the development of clear expectations, rules, and limits for your family.

ROUTINES

What *routines* do you have in your home? What can your child do independently and what does she need help with? Do you need to negotiate so that your expectations and hers are the same? Two examples of routines include:

- **Bedtime**: Your child's bedtime routine may include activities like bathing, brushing her teeth, getting into bed by a certain time, reading stories, and/or turning lights out by a certain time.

- **Getting up in the morning**: Her morning routine probably consists of waking up by a certain time (be clear about who is responsible for waking your child—you or an alarm clock), getting out of bed by a certain time, washing up, brushing her teeth, combing her hair, and getting dressed in clean clothes appropriate to the weather.

List your child's home routines here or in your notebook:

_____

_____

_____

EXPECTATIONS

What *expectations* do you have of your child? How do you want her to behave in certain situations? Some examples include making agreements about:

- **Privacy:** Knocking before entering someone else's room, not opening another person's mail, and so on

- **Socializing:** Getting permission to have friends over, no friends' visits without supervision, and so on

- **Electronics:** The amount of television and/or computer time allowed on school days and weekends

- **Religious observance:** Attending religious school or services

- **Time management:** Prioritizing academic and extracurricular activities

List your expectations here or in your notebook:

_____

_____

_____

LIMITS

What are the limits or rules in your house? What's allowed and what is not allowed? For example:

- **Language:** No swearing and no abusive or threatening language

- **Computer use:** Using the Internet only for homework

- **Strangers:** No talking to strangers

- **Safety for younger children:** No crossing the street without an adult

- **Safety for older children:** No accepting rides from people you don't know

List your limits and rules here or in your notebook:

_____

_____

_____

SOCIAL RULES

What *social rules* do you expect your child to follow? Some examples might include:

- **Addressing adults :** Referring to adults as Mr. or Mrs., Aunt or Uncle, instead of by first names

- **Sharing:** Sharing toys (or keeping a special toy in a private space)

- **Avoiding aggression:** Not hitting or threatening friends or siblings

List your limits and rules:

_____

_____

_____

CHORES

What chores (daily and weekly) are expected? Does your child get an allowance based on completing chores or do you consider doing chores a responsibility of everyone in the family? Do chores change as your child gets older so that older siblings have different chores? Some examples of chores are making the bed, emptying the dishwasher, setting the table, and taking out the trash.

List the chores you expect from your child:

_____

_____

_____

Bedtime routines. Bedtime routines are often difficult for parents and children. You may wonder why bedtime is such a struggle. The answer is that you and your child don't have the same goals. Your goal at bedtime is to get your child to bed (especially if she has to get up early the next morning), while your child's goal is to stay awake and involved in family activities or things she enjoys. If either or both of you are tired, which is often the case, this vulnerability inevitably leads to a lack of cooperation and behavioral incidents on the part of your child and less patience on your part. If you approach bedtime as a nightly struggle that you dread, your apprehension and anxiety will fuel that of your child. You may find yourself engaged in a nightly struggle that leaves everyone exhausted and frustrated.

As with all routines, you can follow some basic guidelines. These include:

- Maintaining your calm

- Developing a consistent start time and allowing sufficient time to complete all parts of the routine before you expect your child to be in bed

- Making the steps of the routine explicit and consistent and maintaining the order of the routine so it's easier to follow

- Changing any aspect of the routine only under special circumstances

- Building in some calming and relaxing activities before your child goes to bed, especially if you have or she has had a comparatively difficult day; for instance, letting her play a little longer in a bath, reading a calming bedtime story, and not trying to rush the routine, which will cause more anxiety for both of you

- Developing a contract that reinforces your child for each step of her routine and for being in bed on time, particularly if she typically refuses to go through the routine or finds ways to avoid it

- Accepting that there will still be nights when the bedtime routine is a struggle despite your efforts

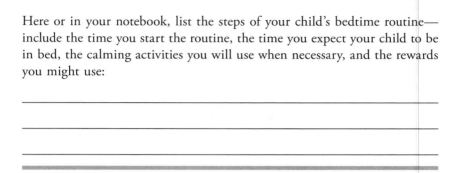

Here or in your notebook, list the steps of your child's bedtime routine—include the time you start the routine, the time you expect your child to be in bed, the calming activities you will use when necessary, and the rewards you might use:

_____

_____

_____

Discuss the routine with your child and get her input on calming activities and rewards. Use the routine you have developed consistently and make changes if and only as necessary.

Maintaining Expectations, Rules, and Limits

Once you and your child know the rules and expectations, apply behavioral principles to increase the likelihood that your child will follow them. (1) Remember to be consistent and expect your child to meet expectations and follow rules despite excuses and attempts by her to avoid them. (2) All parenting adults should have the same expectations and use the same consequences when necessary. (3) Choose reinforcers (rewards) over punishment and be sure to use rewards that work for your child. (4) Calmly and without defensiveness, provide prompts and reminders for your child while validating her feelings about rules, expectations, and limits. (5) Remind your child about consequences, but do not threaten her with them.

There are other important things to remember that will help your child follow routines and expectations without escalating emotionally. Your child may have a different sense of time than you do. You should give her time to respond to you and try not to rush her. Demanding that chores be done immediately may result in a negative response from her. It's often more helpful to give her a time when the chore has to be completed, which empowers her to choose when to do it. Remind her that she cannot do other activities that she enjoys until she has met her obligations. As we mentioned earlier, if the expectation is too great, shape your child's behavior in incremental steps or develop a contract. Remember to praise your child or otherwise reinforce her when she has met your expectations.

WHEN TO USE REWARDS

No child is going to be perfect. Accept that your child will forget sometimes or will choose not to hear you at other times. Be patient and remind yourself that your child is doing the best she can. Some children need more help than others. When you are nonjudgmental and calm, you can provide support for your child *and* remind her of her responsibilities.

Reward your child when she does meet expectations or follows rules. Sometimes an added incentive can help. You can arrange this with your child in advance by saying something like, "When you let me talk on the phone without interrupting, I will put a quarter in a jar (or a sticker on a chart)." Acknowledge when she follows through.

If following a routine is a struggle for your child, let her know she will be rewarded on those days when she does the routine without causing difficulties. For example, you can tell her, "If you brush your teeth and get into bed on time, you can have fifteen extra minutes to read before lights-out." Don't hesitate to give your child these extra few minutes. She will probably go to bed the same time she usually does, but she will spend the extra time quietly in bed rather than struggling with you.

Don't give reinforcers or favored activities *before* your child has successfully completed the task you requested. Children often tell parents that they will do what is asked *after* a parent does or gives the child what the child wants. Your child may plead, promise, and beg. However, once your child has gotten what she wants, she will have no incentive to do what you've asked. You may find yourself angry and resentful when your child doesn't follow through. When you expect her to meet your expectations *first*, you will be more effective and less frustrated.

Consistently reinforce your child until the behavior occurs more often and more spontaneously. She may need prompts occasionally. When your child is overwhelmed by emotions, it will be very difficult for her to meet expectations. Gently and calmly remind her of the rewards she can receive. If she doesn't earn them, don't worry. Help your child understand that *she* earns or doesn't earn her rewards; *you* do not choose whether to give them to her. This helps your child accept responsibility for her behaviors rather than blaming you or others.

Be cautious about giving your child too many prompts when she is highly emotional; she may feel overwhelmed by reminders or feel ashamed that she cannot follow through. Give her time to calm down, and gently remind her of the rewards she might earn if she does. You can make your requests or discuss options when she is calm. There will be times when your child does not successfully meet expectations, even though she will continue to need the structure they provide.

Creating a Contract

Using the principles discussed in chapter 6, develop a contract for (1) getting your child to bed or (2) completing the morning routine. Think about the specific behaviors you want to increase, choose rewards that will work for your child, and think about how often she can earn the rewards. Remember that your child will not be perfect. You can use the worksheet on changing behaviors in chapter 6 as a guide.

WHEN TO USE PUNISHMENT

There may be times when you feel that punishment is necessary. Follow the guidelines presented in chapter 6, and remember to use negative consequences sparingly and minimally so that your child doesn't feel hopeless or defeated. Use time-outs as punishment as often as possible so that your child is in a quiet space without access to fun activities.

AVOID POWER STRUGGLES

When your child doesn't respond to you, you can easily get into a power struggle with her, demanding that she listen while she refuses to do so. You may become angry and start to yell; she may escalate and become more resistant. A full-blown outburst may occur. To avoid power struggles, calmly:

- Give your child warnings and prompts about upcoming expectations.

- Walk away and tell her to complete the expectation within the next few minutes.

- Nonjudgmentally remind her of the reward she may not earn.

- Let it go if she does not follow through. Remember, you may lose some battles and still win the war. However, if you continue to engage in a power struggle, you will almost inevitably end up in a war.

Remember your own story of emotion (Linehan 1993b). Know your triggers and be aware of what you are thinking and feeling when your child isn't listening to you. If you're frustrated with her, take a break or a time-out. Calm yourself down so that you can respond wisely and effectively.

SUMMARY

When your child has intense emotions, it may feel impossible to develop routines and rules in your home. Your child may respond so negatively to requests or limits that you would rather not ask anything of her. However, it's important for your child to learn how to behave. Therefore, maintaining consistency, routines, and expectations, despite the reactivity of your child, is your goal and your challenge.

Skills we discussed in this chapter include:

- Making expectations and limits explicit

- Developing and maintaining routines

- Using reward and punishment to change behaviors

Next we'll be discussing aggression and other problem behavior you may be dealing with.

CHAPTER 8

Decreasing Tantrums, Aggression, and Other Problem Behaviors

Young children may have tantrums as a way of expressing anger or frustration (Goodenough 1931). Tantrums come in different shapes and sizes, with a range of emotional intensity. Your child may scream and get red for a few minutes, or he may throw himself on the ground (even in public), screaming, kicking, and banging his fists. As a child gets older, tantrums may take more aggressive forms. He might throw books and toys at others and/or tip furniture as he runs through the house without regard to his safety or the safety of others. If you have experienced behaviors similar to this, you have probably felt frustration, embarrassment, and fear that someone would get hurt. You may have vacillated between wanting to ignore this behavior (so that you aren't reinforcing it with attention) and wanting to give your child what he wants (so that the tantrum ends).

Over time, your child learns what to expect from you. If you've begun to make different and more effective choices about how you respond to him, your child may initially react negatively to these changes. He will want you to change back and will "punish" you by escalating his behavior. This will create a dilemma for you as you balance your emotions and your desire for effective results. Some of these dilemmas include:

- Being consistent while your child is letting you know, verbally and physically, how angry he is

- Making effective choices versus maintaining immediate safety

- Promoting positive long-term change versus dealing with immediate, short-term negative behaviors

DBT is focused on long-term change (Linehan 1993a) and helps parents to manage the difficulties along the way (see chapter 11). It takes great strength and courage to help your child make changes in his behaviors by changing your own.

RESPONDING TO TANTRUMS

Most children have tantrums. Younger children will have them more often; in older children, they may be a sign of more serious difficulties (Belden, Thomson, and Luby 2008). When your child has intense emotions, his tantrums will be more intense as well. Parents don't cause tantrums but, as we have mentioned, your responses can affect whether they increase or decrease over time. If you respond to your child's tantrums with an increase in attention or by meeting his demands, your child will see tantrums as an effective way of getting his needs met. If you ignore a tantrum, your child will learn more effective ways to communicate with you.

When your young child is having a tantrum, do not panic and try to ignore it—even if it occurs in public. Reward your child if he is able to use his words or take space. Making effective choices may mean that you give your child a few minutes of your attention even if you're busy; a few positive minutes may prevent a tantrum altogether. Remember to validate your child's frustration or disappointment when he doesn't get something he wants. This will help to defuse his emotionality and minimize the possibility of a tantrum.

Reassessing Your Responses to Tantrums

If you have been responding ineffectively to your child's tantrums and now they are (1) occurring more often, (2) becoming longer, (3) increasing in intensity, or (4) continuing in an older child who is not learning age-appropriate ways to get his needs met, you can teach him alternative behaviors and respond more effectively by:

- Not giving in to your child's demands

- Calmly and consistently ignoring the tantrums, even if they initially increase (Skinner 1938)

- Rewarding positive behaviors (such as asking appropriately) at other times and/or developing a contract for tantrum-free days

- Distracting or calming him before the tantrum escalates

If your attempts to decrease tantrums have not been effective, consider seeking professional help for you and/or your child. Eventually your child will learn more effective ways to express his needs and feelings.

Changing Responses to Your Child's Tantrum

Think about a specific time when your child had a tantrum. Without judging yourself, answer the following questions in your notebook to develop new responses:

- What led to this tantrum? What did your child want?

- How did you respond? Did you get angry or frustrated? Did you give in to what he wanted? Were you embarrassed or worried about judgments from others?

- If you had remained calm, would the tantrum have ended sooner?

- Did you miss an opportunity to respond when he asked for something effectively?

If you feel that you are inadvertently reinforcing your child, don't judge yourself. Learn to remain calm by soothing yourself or practicing mindfulness. Changing your behaviors and your child's takes time; be patient with yourself and with him.

RESPONDING TO AGGRESSIVE BEHAVIORS

What do you do when your child's tantrums become aggressive and dangerous? How do you respond when your child's reaction to a limit is to destroy his favorite toy, an action that may lead to guilt, remorse, and sadness when he has finally calmed down? What do you do when your child's response to any expectation is to throw household items at you or his siblings? How can you act effectively when you are afraid of your child's behaviors?

These are very difficult and painful questions. When your child's intense emotions have spiraled into dangerous behaviors, you may find yourself facing situations like those mentioned above. Your reactions to these behaviors may include anger, frustration, disappointment, anxiety, fear, and grief. Aggressive behavior causes an emotional reaction in everyone who witnesses it, including siblings.

Parents describe walking on eggshells, always feeling on edge, trying desperately to do everything they can to avoid upsetting their child. You may avoid setting any limits or making any demands only to see another aggressive outburst happen anyway. You may be anxious, always waiting for the next outburst, because you know how little it takes to trigger one. You may fear for your child and the rest of your family. You can influence your child's behavior and still be unable to control it (Mason and Kreger 1998). The pain that your child is reacting to is inside him and ultimately it will be up to him to find ways to manage it.

Remember that your child is not his behaviors. Help him to see that *he can* express his feelings in ways that don't hurt others and that people will listen to him more if he does. Remind him that you accept and love him, even while you are helping him find better ways to express his intense feelings.

Seek Supportive Professional Help

If your child's behaviors are so out of control that you fear his reactions and worry about the safety of your family, you and your child might benefit from the help of a mental health professional, especially one experienced in working with children and families. Even if these problems are not of your making, learning new responses can still be helpful to your whole family. If you feel that the professional who is working with you and/or your child is blaming you for your child's problems, find a more supportive, less judgmental professional who understands and validates *your* feelings as well as your child's.

Therapeutic Holds

If you have to restrain your child because he is dangerous to himself or others, try to get training on how to hold your child in a safe and effective way (a *therapeutic hold*). Use therapeutic holds only to avoid imminent harm to your child or others. Restraining a child is inevitably traumatic for the child (who may feel smothered) and the parent (who senses how out of control the situation feels), and you want to make sure that it is done in the least traumatic way possible.

When you are facing an aggressive, dangerous outburst, remember to use the skills you have learned:

- Validate your child as often as possible to avoid escalating the outburst

- Teach your child to take a time-out (in a safe, quiet space) or to soothe himself

- Give your child safe toys (such as stress balls or stuffed animals) that he can use when he is escalating

- Maintain safety, including keeping your other children away when your child is aggressive. You may also need to stop driving or doing any other potentially dangerous activities until your child is able to be calm

Though it may occur rarely, some children become so dangerous that parents need to seek immediate help from specially trained police officers who can take the child to a hospital to be evaluated. The decision to hospitalize a child is a difficult and painful one; parents will need to think wisely about the immediate and long-term needs of their child.

Effective Responses Before and After an Aggressive Outburst

You can't parent a child effectively when you're afraid of him or feel guilty. Reacting emotionally makes it harder to make long-term decisions in a planful, thoughtful manner. If you continue to walk on eggshells, your child won't learn how to control his behaviors and your family will live in fear. Instead, respond wisely to your child in the moment. Because you may be overwhelmed during a crisis, develop a safety plan in advance for you and other family members. This plan can include restraining him, getting other children to safety, or calling 911. When the incident is over, talk to your other children and validate their feelings. When your child is calm, help him take responsibility for his behaviors without judging him or increasing his shame. Remind him that you love him.

Jason's experience can shed further light on this issue.

Jason is an eight-year-old boy with an older brother and a younger sister. He began having tantrums when he was two years old, just as his brother had. However, unlike his brother, his tantrums continued and became more violent as he got older. If Jason didn't get attention from his mother when he wanted it or was told he could not do something he wanted to do, he would break things. He hit, pushed, and spit at his siblings so that they became afraid of him. When he would begin to yell, his brother and sister would hide in their rooms. Jason and his siblings were not able to have friends over because fights always erupted, especially when Jason didn't win the game they were playing. At first, Jason only had these difficulties at home, but they began to interfere in school as well.

Jason's parents sought out professional help, and a child therapist began teaching Jason to recognize and manage his feelings more effectively. He was also put in a social-skills group at school and was allowed to meet with the guidance counselor if he became upset in school.

In addition, his parents instituted the following practices:

- Jason's parents spent individual, uninterrupted time (fifteen minutes) with each child at least five times a week.

- His parents validated the feelings of their other children, even when the children were angry at them or at each other.

- Jason was given a contract to earn daily rewards and something he really wanted. He received (1) a sticker on a chart (and lots of praise) for every hour he was outburst-free, even if he received one prompt, (2) two bonus stickers at the end of an outburst-free day, and (3) his treat immediately after earning the predetermined number of stickers.

- If Jason had an outburst, he didn't earn stickers during that time period.

- If Jason was unsafe, his parents would restrain him safely as they had been taught to do. Then, Jason had a calming-down period in his room after his parents let him go.

- When Jason was calm, his parents reassured him that they loved him even while they did not like his behaviors.

- After an incident ended, his parents would talk to his brother and sister about their feelings.

Having a plan in place allowed Jason's parents to feel more in control. Because Jason understood what was expected of him and what his consequences would be, he felt a little more in control as well. Jason's siblings were given the attention they needed to address their feelings about their brother's behaviors. Jason's parents learned to validate their own feelings as well. This plan addressed the emotional needs of every family member and specifically addressed Jason's behavioral problems as well.

OTHER BEHAVIORAL CONCERNS

Tantrums and aggressive behaviors are not the only problems you may face. In an effort to manage his anger, sadness, or pain, your child may turn to a variety of behaviors, each causing its own difficulties. Some of these behaviors include risk taking, overeating or refusing to eat, or setting fires.

Dangerous Behaviors

What do you do when your child runs into the street, plays with matches, or engages in other behaviors that may lead to him or someone else getting hurt? There may be no time to discuss rewards or remind him of consequences. In situations in which someone may get hurt:

- Get your child to safety immediately, even if that means picking him up in the street and/or risking an outburst.

- After your child is safe, discuss the dangerousness of his behavior. Do not hesitate to make the consequences scary to him (getting hit by a car, burning down the house, and so on).

- Tell him in a firm tone that this behavior is not allowed and that you will punish him if it happens again.

If a consequence does not stop your child from engaging in dangerous behaviors, you may need to limit his freedom and independence. Remind him that he can't be left alone if he does things that are unsafe. Continue to use time-outs and other punishment if necessary, and continue to discuss behaviors and consequences with him until he can behave in a safer manner.

When Your Child's Behaviors Interfere with Others

You may face situations in which your child's behaviors significantly interfere with others. How do you respond during those situations? Let's evaluate how to respond to the following scenario.

You and your child have been at the playground for several hours. Now you have to leave to pick up your other child from a friend's house. You don't want to be late because that would cause your other child to worry. You've given your child several prompts, and he has ignored them all. Now it's time to go, and he refuses to come out of the structure he's playing in. You're starting to get anxious about being late, and he's still not responding. Remain as calm as possible so you can wisely choose the most effective way to respond. Remember, if you remain calm, your child may as well.

Some effective responses may include:

- Promising him a treat if he comes with you when you ask

- Telling him that you will not be able to return to the playground unless he follows your directions

- Calling your other child (or the parent) to alert him or her that you may be late

A child who has intense emotions may not respond effectively to threats or demands in the moment. If you know that your child's behaviors may interfere with others, develop a plan *in advance* to minimize his anxiety. This can include:

- Giving yourself plenty of time to do things in a relaxed way

- Giving him plenty of time to respond to you

- Talking to your child about the positive consequences if he leaves the playground when you ask (he will return again) and the negative consequences if he does not (he may not return for a longer time)

If your child doesn't follow your expectations, you can turn down his next request to go to the playground. Validate his feelings of disappointment even while you maintain this limit. When he asks again the next time, remind him of the consequences for not listening and try taking him to the playground again. If he doesn't listen to you again, wait even longer before you take him back to the playground. Take opportunities to remind him, calmly and patiently, that you cannot take him places when he doesn't listen to you. Whenever your child *does* do what he is asked, reward and praise him and return to the playground as soon as possible.

Impulsive Behaviors

Impulsivity presents a major challenge if your child has intense emotional and behavioral reactions. Your child may get seriously hurt or hurt someone else, even if this was not his intention. For example, your child may not be thinking in a logical way when he runs out of the house and into the street without any awareness of an oncoming car. A child who realizes that his cough medicine makes him sleepy may accidentally take an overdose because he is so frustrated that he wants to escape into sleep. Or, a child who is angry because he feels that his younger sibling is getting too much attention may push his sibling's stroller down a hill without realizing how dangerous this might be.

Parents and professionals often question whether or not a child *meant* to hurt himself or others. The question of intent is important in treating your child. It is less important in making decisions about maintaining safety in your home. If your child is impulsive, whether due to intense emotions, attention disorders, or an inability to think about long-term consequences of behaviors, your attention to his safety and to the safety of those around him can't be minimized. You will not necessarily be able to give your child the responsibilities given to other children his age. You may ask yourself questions such as:

- Can I leave him alone in a room? In the house?

- How often do I have to check on him?

- Can he be left alone with a sibling for a few minutes? Longer?

- Can he have unsupervised time with playmates?

- Do I need to keep all potentially dangerous items out of reach?

- Should I keep the door locked so my child cannot run out of the house?

Questions such as these may anger or disappoint you. You want your child to be as "normal" as possible and want to let him have normal activities, especially when he *seems* calm. Like many parents, you would like to see your child become increasingly independent and you may feel uncomfortable continuing to monitor a child whom you (and he) consider "too old to be treated like a baby."

Keeping a child safe while encouraging age-appropriate development is a difficult balancing act (see chapter 2). Err on the side of safety while also allowing your child to experience non-dangerous natural consequences. Assess potential risks as you make wise decisions. Recognize that every child needs opportunities to learn. Help your child understand that he'll have more freedom and independence when he is able to show better judgment and effective management of his behaviors.

Emotional Withdrawal

Some children are so afraid of their emotions that they inhibit any emotional reaction and withdraw into themselves. While a quiet child does not generally cause the kind of anxiety that an aggressive child can, parents may become concerned if their child spends more and more time in his room alone, listens to depressing or angry music, and shows less and less interest in home or school. Some withdrawn children can become so overwhelmed by their emotions that they may suddenly explode, much to the surprise and dismay of their parents.

As we discussed in chapter 4, parents should be aware that some children secretly hurt themselves (for example, by cutting themselves or pulling at scabs until they bleed) as a way to alleviate emotional pain.

TAKE YOUR CHILD SERIOUSLY AND MAINTAIN SAFETY

Listening, validating, and attending to a quiet and withdrawn child is as important as using those skills with a more aggressive child. Children don't threaten to hurt themselves "to get attention." The desire to get away from the pain is real, and, because children do not think in terms of the future (Piaget 1928), an impulsive attempt to rid himself of the pain may be devastating.

While children who act on suicidal thoughts are still rare, more and more children are hurting themselves. If you are concerned about your child's desire to hurt himself in any way, create an environment that is safe for him. This might mean that you make sure that drugs are safely locked away and that knives are not easily accessible. If your child is talking about wanting to die or is hurting himself deliberately, seek professional advice to help your child maintain safety. If you are fearful that your child may immediately act on his threats, you can take him to the nearest hospital for an emergency evaluation.

Public Behavioral Difficulties

You are watching your child play in the sandbox with other children when your child bites another child. Or you've told your child that he has to hold your hand, and he runs through the parking lot, causing a car to stop short. Your overall sense of anxiety, frustration, and disappointment will be exacerbated by your embarrassment and guilt when these behaviors occur in public. You may feel inadequate and ineffective and wonder what others are thinking of you. If you feel an urgency to *do something*, try to respond wisely despite the judgments of others. You may have to tolerate some feelings of distress in the moment in order to parent effectively for the long run.

Use the skills we have already discussed to remind your child about safe and effective behaviors. Prepare your child in advance of outings by telling him your expectations and limits, and follow through with any rewards or consequences that you have discussed. If your child hurts another child, remove him from the situation and have him take a time-out by sitting next to you for a few minutes. Or you may decide to take him home. Remind your child that you will go home if he can't behave safely and follow your rules. Praise and reward safe and effective behaviors when they occur.

SUMMARY

In this chapter we discussed some specific behaviors that you might encounter when your child has intense emotions and an inability to modulate his behavioral responses. Different children will have different responses to their emotions, and your child may have a variety of responses to his own emotional turmoil. Your child may be cooperative at times and still become aggressive when emotionally challenged. He may be calm until he wants something and then may throw a tantrum until he gets it. Your role is to keep your child safe while being consistent in teaching him effective ways to manage his emotions.

The skills we discussed in this chapter include ways to:

- Maintain safety for your child and others

- Use contracts to reward safe behaviors

- Decrease tantrums and aggression by using positive and negative consequences

- Assess the need for professional help and support

In the next chapter we will look at problematic behaviors that are specifically related to school and help parents learn to advocate for their child and work together with school personnel.

CHAPTER 9

School-Related Difficulties

Is it a nightmare trying to get your child ready for school? Do you dread her return at the end of the day? Do you anticipate behavioral difficulties around homework completion? Do you send your child to school and await the call that she has had another difficult day or, worse, is being suspended? Do you go to school conferences and wonder how the child who is so difficult at home can be described as "wonderful" by her teacher? Or do you wonder who the teacher is talking about when she describes difficulties your usually cooperative, though very active, child has at school?

If your child struggles with intense emotions, school can be challenging for her and for you. Your child's school day experience and its impact on her return home may be a continuing source of anxiety and frustration for you. A child who works to manage her behaviors in the familiar surroundings of her home may find it even harder to manage in a classroom with other children, multiple distractions, different rules, and new learning to master. If the child has learning disabilities as well as emotion dysregulation, the struggle becomes even more difficult. Your child may have behavioral problems in school that interfere with her learning. Or she may manage the school day only to fall apart when she returns home.

School is a major part of your child's life and will be for many years. Understanding her problems at school, validating her feelings, helping her use skills to be more effective, and advocating for her needs will be a major part of your life. Here we will provide some tips to help you be effective in this role.

RECOGNIZING THE PROBLEM

If your child is struggling academically or emotionally at school, she may not tell you directly but may give you clues that there is a problem. She may frequently:

- Be difficult to get out of bed in the morning or delay getting ready for school

- Complain of physical ailments before school or have a tantrum and refuse to go to school

- Return home from school showing signs of vulnerability by whining, crying, or being very quiet

- Struggle with her homework or battle with you about getting it done

If you haven't recognized these signals as indications of a problem at school, a call from your child's teacher may be your first indication. When the teacher begins discussing your "difficult" child, you may become defensive and believe that the problem is caused by the teacher or the classroom, not by your child. Try to remain nonjudgmental and do not make assumptions. Remember that a child can behave differently in different situations. Even if you or your child try to deny what the teacher is saying, you will still have to listen to the teacher with an open mind and learn to work collaboratively together.

Conversely, you may have seen your child's school problems acted out at home (in the ways mentioned above), and the teacher may not have noticed any problems at school. When you go to a conference, the teacher may be surprised to hear that your child is having difficulties with homework. The teacher may blame you for these problems. While you may feel angry and defensive, try to respond wisely. Your goal in communication with the teacher is to (1) help the teacher understand that your child has difficulty regulating her emotions and (2) minimize any school difficulties that are affecting her behaviors at home.

As you recognize the possibility of school-related problems, you will need to work in collaboration with your child's teacher to find the most effective ways to help your child manage her difficulties.

Pros and Cons of Labeling

You may be worried that when you begin to discuss behavioral and school difficulties with your child's teacher, your child will be labeled in a way that will stigmatize her and cause others to see her as "the angry child," "the difficult child," or a "behavior problem." These worries are understandable; parents may fear that any labels applied to their child will follow her through her academic career and possibly further. You may be concerned that others will negatively judge your child and/or you.

If your child is diagnosed with a learning disability, identifying and naming the disability enables all of her teachers to be aware of the academic supports she needs in order to learn more effectively and with less frustration. Acknowledging your child's emotional disorder may benefit your child in the same way that labeling a learning disability does. Despite this reality, some parents find it so painful to hear that their child has been diagnosed with an emotional disturbance that they put off testing, learning more about their child's difficulties, or taking her to a mental health professional so that they don't have to face these labels. However, a better understanding of the problem will help professionals have a better understanding of her needs. The sooner your child is able to get the help she needs and the sooner accommodations are made in school and at home, the better the future will be for your child.

The Impact of Learning Disabilities

While the child who struggles with her emotionality may become easily frustrated during the school day, so does the child who struggles with a learning disability. What about the child who struggles with both? If your child has both an identified learning disability and intense emotionality, managing her intense emotions and the behaviors that result from them will be more of a challenge for her. If she is not receiving adequate educational support for her learning issues, her frustration in the classroom will be yet another trigger for an emotional and/or behavioral outburst.

Your advocacy can help her school experience become a more positive one. The key is effective communication between you, your child's teacher, and the support staff working with your child. If they are aware of your child's emotional needs as well as her academic needs, a learning plan can be put into place that will address and make accommodations for both. When all her needs are adequately met, her frustrations will be lessened, her outbursts will decrease, and her self-esteem may increase.

As your child's advocate, you can address some of the following issues:

- Whether she needs to be in a special or regular classroom

- The size of the classroom she is in and how much individual attention she receives

- Whether she can spend any time out of the classroom or otherwise take breaks from her work

- Whether she can be given more time to get her work done

- How to validate her feelings of frustration, disappointment, and anger without allowing her to make excuses

It might feel overwhelming to think about balancing your efforts at managing your child's school problems *and* her emotional problems. You already feel like there isn't enough time for what you need to do. A working collaboration with your child's teacher will benefit you as well as your child. You and her teacher can support one another, develop strategies together that assist you both, and become partners in helping your child manage her emotions and behaviors at school and the related issues that affect her behaviors at home.

BEING AN ADVOCATE FOR YOUR CHILD

When reading the preceding section or those below, you may feel some resistance, thinking (1) "I'm not comfortable speaking to my child's teacher this way" or (2) "I don't want to share so much personal information about my child or myself." Sharing information about your child's problems at home may make you feel uncomfortable and vulnerable because:

- You want others to think you're capable and competent

- You don't want the teacher to judge your child

- The sharing of such personal information may feel like an invasion of your (and your child's) privacy

These feelings are common and understandable. However, the outcome of sharing this information will be a more effective collaboration that benefits your child by making expectations and responses more consistent. Communication between you and your child's teacher will use a familiar frame of reference, enabling consistent comparisons of her functioning at home and in school. In addition, you will be able to help her teacher learn the importance of validation and nonjudgmental language in helping your child to remain calm.

Even if you are very involved in your child's school as a classroom volunteer, as a library aide, or in the parent-teacher organization and have a very good rapport with teachers and other school staff, advocating for your child may put you into unfamiliar and uncomfortable positions. As you open the discussion about your child's struggles with intense emotions, you may find yourself disagreeing with the teacher and challenging classroom protocols that don't meet your child's needs. This new role may feel outside your comfort zone; you may be someone who worries about rocking the boat, or you may be easily intimidated. You will have to balance your discomfort with your primary role as your child's chief advocate. Seeking help from the school social worker or guidance counselor may prove beneficial.

A number of skills we've discussed in previous chapters will help you become an effective advocate for your child. To ensure that your child is getting the emotional and academic support she needs, some helpful skills include:

- **Doing what is effective:** Know when to listen and when to talk; work in a cooperative manner so that you are heard.

- **Thinking wisely and remembering your story of emotion** (Linehan 1993b): Manage your feelings and don't let emotions guide your decisions or actions.

- **Remembering that there is no absolute truth**: Do not try to prove that you are right and they are wrong (see below). Work together to find compromises (Miller 2001).

Absolute Truth Revisited

When meeting with your child's teacher (and other support staff working with your child), remember that there is no absolute truth. Other people may have different, legitimate perspectives and insights about your child. You and her teacher may not agree about her behaviors at home and at school or about the specifics of how to resolve the problems she faces. This doesn't mean that one of you is right while the other one is wrong. Listen to and respect each other. Try to figure out the most effective strategy based on everyone's input. If one proposed strategy doesn't work for your child, there is another one to try. If you and your child's teacher agree that your primary goal is to help your child do the best she can, you will find it easier to work together to develop the most effective way to help her. Using effective advocacy skills can help you make a difference in your child's education and her life.

PROBLEMS WITH GOING TO SCHOOL

For some children, anxieties about school manifest during their morning routines. Your child may:

- Struggle to get out of bed despite going to bed on time the night before, requesting "five more minutes" several times before getting up

- Continue to move slowly as she washes, dresses, and picks at her breakfast

- Miss the bus often, necessitating that you drive her to school

These situations create stress and increased emotionality for you and your child.

In addition, some children complain of physical ailments in the morning. The most common complaints are headaches, stomachaches, and nausea. You may think that your child, who doesn't look sick, is faking it. Many children, however, actually do experience headaches, stomach pain, and nausea caused by the intensity of their feelings about going to school. It is difficult to decide what to do when your child complains about feeling sick before going to school.

If any of these behaviors become a pattern or occur frequently, you may need to address the problem. The following strategies may help.

Validate. Remember to validate your child's feelings while still expecting her to go to school.

Use behavioral principles. Use the principles discussed in chapter 6. In particular, you can:

- Develop a contract that reinforces her for the steps of her morning routine and making the school bus on time

- Use natural consequences and, if your child complains of being sick, have her stay in bed for the day

Communicate. When your child is calm after school or during less stressful times, talk to her about what might be bothering her and what would help her by asking the following questions:

- "Is there anyone or anything at school bothering or upsetting you?"

- "Is there anything happening at school that you would like to talk to me about?"

- "What can we do to make going to school easier for you?"

Refusal to Go to School

Some children, despite a parent's attempt to get them to school, may refuse outright. Use the calming skills we discussed earlier (mindfulness, calming activities) and validate her feelings. If your child continues to say that she's not going to school and escalates by having a tantrum or becoming more aggressive, make sure everyone is safe before trying a different, hopefully more effective strategy.

You may find it helpful to:

- Determine whether your child has experienced an undisclosed threat at school (such as from peers).

- Develop a contract and reinforce your child on those days when she goes to school without incident.

- Work with the school to find strategies to relieve your child's anxiety in school. Talk to them about the use of nonjudgmental language and validation.

- Work with a mental health professional, who will help your child learn to relax when facing her fears about school.

Eventually, your child will need to receive an education, and you and the school personnel can discuss the most effective way for this to happen.

Insist or Give In?

As the parent of a child who has intense emotions about school, you may face the following dilemma. You may wonder whether it is best to insist that your child attend school (with the resulting outbursts) or to allow her to stay at home (which may accommodate her anxiety and also feels like "giving in"). If you allow her to stay at home to lessen her stress level or to avoid power struggles at home, the risk is that she will miss learning opportunities and lessons and fall behind academically (Burland 2003). You may also wonder if you are reinforcing ineffective behaviors. However, if your child is forced to go to school despite her behaviors and feelings, she may have more outbursts at school, creating additional problems for your child, you, and the school. You may worry that the school can't effectively keep your child safe. You may question how to resolve this dilemma and make the most effective decision.

You don't need to make these decisions on your own. There may be many factors involved in this complex situation, and others may be able to help you sort them out. Consult with your child's pediatrician, the professional who has known and cared for her over a period of time. Along with the doctor's guidance, any medical reasons for your child's current difficulties can be eliminated as contributing factors. You may also consult with your child's teacher, who works closely with her and can provide valuable information about her school performance, relationships with peers, and overall comfort level in the classroom. School counseling staff (the social worker, guidance counselor, or psychologist) may be able to provide valuable insights after observing your child in the classroom. You may also consult with an independent mental health professional, who will objectively provide support and new strategies for you and your child.

These professionals may help you make the most effective decisions to resolve immediate situations and the longer-term problems. There may be times when you allow your child to stay home and others when you push her to go to school. You and your child should be clear about the expectations and consequences for each situation.

HOMEWORK ISSUES

Most children would prefer to come home from school and not think about it for the rest of the day. Homework is a daily reminder of school and any difficulties your child is having there. When your child struggles with intense emotions, the overwhelming feelings she has about these struggles make her vulnerable, and homework can easily trigger an intense emotional or behavioral response.

Your child may use a great deal of energy managing her various struggles at school and may need some downtime when she returns home. She may need time to play outside to release some of her energy or some time for a soothing activity that you and she have chosen. If she is expected to do her homework immediately, her frustrations about school will not diminish and she will be emotionally dysregulated as she attempts her homework. Remember her story of emotion (Linehan 1993b), validate her feelings, and make accommodations that allow your child to be more successful.

Your child may also struggle with homework because she is unable to successfully complete the assignment or do the work. She may indeed have been in the classroom when the teacher presented the information she needs to complete the work; however, it may have been difficult for her to pay attention because her emotionality interferes with her learning. Or she may have missed the lesson because she was asked to leave the classroom when her behaviors were disruptive to the other children. Your child may also miss class time because she is in the bathroom, in the nurse's office, or with a counselor in an effort to avoid going back to class or otherwise managing her emotions.

To help your child with homework issues:

- Give her time after school to do things that she enjoys, that she does well, and that relax her

- Develop a consistent routine (see below)

- Allow her to take short breaks to relax while she does her homework

- Provide a comfortable space for homework

- Allow her to leave homework incomplete if she is too overwhelmed to finish it, and tell her that you'll write a note to the teacher explaining this decision

- Discuss ways to make homework time easier for her

Homework Routines

The strategies we discussed in chapter 7 for developing routines can be applied to your child's homework routine. You can use any or all of the following skills:

- Develop a reasonable and consistent start time.

- Make expectations explicit and consistent. Discuss *when* and *where* homework is done (before or after dinner? In the kitchen with parent supervision/independently in the child's room?), how much help you will give her, and how your child can let you know that she is too tired to do any more.

- Provide reinforcers for effective work and/or homework completion.

- Validate your child's struggles and frustration and continue to encourage her work.

- Provide prompts and reminders when necessary.

- Gently remind your child of any natural consequences for not completing homework.

Creating an Effective Homework Routine

In your notebook, write a plan for your child's homework routine. Get input from your child. Think about what her needs are in order to decide:

- When homework is done

- How long your child can tolerate the work before taking a break or being done for the night

- Where your child can do homework so that she can remain focused and where you can also supervise her activities and be available for support

- What kind of a contract would work best to reward successful homework completion

Remember the benefits of consistency. You may be inclined to give in to your child when she requests putting off her homework "just this one time" or wants to watch TV before getting her work done. Try to resist this temptation; the change in routine may disrupt the rest of your child's day, and she may not complete her homework as promised. As we noted earlier, once you allow this, your child will continue to ask for exceptions and may not readily accept your limits because you've changed your mind in the past. Children who struggle to maintain their emotions need the consistency that you provide.

Sharon's experience illustrates how one family collaborated to establish a homework routine.

Sharon, a third grader, was assigned a book to read outside of class and a book report to write answering specific questions. Sharon enjoyed the book and read each evening until she finished it. When it came time to write the report, Sharon stared at the questions and complained that she couldn't remember details of the story. Her mother, Andrea, tried to help her by showing her how to find the answers in the book and made other attempts to help and give her strategies. Sharon remained overwhelmed and unable to work, and her mother became impatient. Sharon escalated, screaming threateningly at her mother. When Sharon calmed down, Andrea helped her complete the report.

Homework struggles like this have become an almost daily event for Sharon, and Andrea is no longer sure that helping Sharon complete her assignments is effective. Should she stop helping her and allow her to turn in incomplete or incorrect assignments? How would this affect Sharon's already poor self-image? Should Andrea let Sharon's teacher know about the homework battles?

PARENT/TEACHER COLLABORATION

Andrea recognizes her need for help and arranges to meet with Sharon's teacher. They discuss the frequent homework difficulties occurring at home and concerns about Sharon's emotionality and academic work in school. Andrea also takes the opportunity to share some of the intense emotional reactions Sharon has at home and the strategies Andrea uses to minimize them. This leads to a discussion about possible strategies that may be effective in school to help Sharon remain calm, such as:

- Allowing her to take space or talk to a counselor when she's upset

- Recognizing when Sharon's feeling highly emotional and not calling on her or making demands when she's stressed

- Having soothing activities available to her at school

- Validating her feelings when necessary

Andrea shares some of the behavioral techniques she uses at home, including:

- Using stickers or stars on a behavioral chart

- Breaking up assignments into smaller, more manageable steps for Sharon

Sharon's teacher and Andrea discuss similar techniques that could help Sharon manage more effectively at school.

They begin to talk about ways to communicate with each other that will provide Andrea with insight about Sharon's day at school and provide Sharon's teacher with information about Sharon's behaviors at home. These ways include:

- Communicating daily by e-mail or in a notebook that Sharon carries between school and home

- Scheduling regular phone calls for more detailed communication

- Alerting each other immediately through e-mail or phone calls when there has been any unusual situation or problem

In addition, Andrea and the teacher develop the following strategies to minimize stress during homework time:

- Andrea will determine how much time Sharon will spend on her homework at a given time and let her know when the predetermined time has elapsed. At that point, Sharon can move on to do other things. Sharon's attempts at her homework can be communicated to her teacher through Sharon's notebook or by e-mail. If Sharon did not make any attempt at her homework, this can be noted as well.

- The teacher will let Andrea know if school has been particularly difficult so that Andrea can prepare for Sharon's vulnerability when she returns home.

- Andrea will let the teacher know if Sharon came home from school too dysregulated to complete or even attempt her homework.

When both parent and teacher are aware of a child's story of emotion, they can work together to help the child manage her vulnerabilities and triggers more effectively.

COOPERATIVE AT SCHOOL, DISRUPTIVE AT HOME

What happens when you speak with your child's teacher and learn that your child doesn't have the same emotional intensity or behavioral problems at school that you see at home? Remind yourself that this does *not* mean that you can't handle your child, even if others believe this to be the case, and it does not mean that your child is doing this to you "on purpose." It means that your child is able to regulate her emotions and behaviors for limited amounts of time and in certain situations. The problem for you is that your child needs an outlet for all of the emotions that she has worked so hard to keep in control at school. In this situation, home is the place where your child feels comfortable being herself and where she can allow her emotions their full expression. Appreciate the fact that she can be successful at school even while you try to manage her behaviors at home.

When your child comes home, allow her time to soothe herself, relax, or engage in calming activities. Make fewer demands on her until she is more in control of herself. Do not be judgmental, and remember that your child is not choosing to misbehave with you. She is doing the best she can, given her emotional intensity.

Working with your child's teacher will be beneficial in this circumstance as well. If the teacher is aware of your child's vulnerabilities and potential stressors during the school day, she can make modifications in your child's school routines or workload that may decrease her stress. This may positively affect the behaviors of the child who arrives back home to you at the end of the school day.

SUMMARY

The preceding chapters have focused on how *you* can help your child manage her emotional intensity and resulting behaviors. However, your child spends time away from you, most of it at school. In this chapter, we discussed behaviors you may see that are indicative of problems at school and we have provided suggestions on how to manage them. We've also discussed the importance of collaborating with your child's teacher and school support staff, as well as advocating for the necessary strategies to help your child succeed at school and in her schoolwork at home.

Strategies we discussed in this chapter include ways to:

- Share information about your child with school personnel

- Advocate for your child

- Help your child if she has both learning disabilities and intense emotionality

- Respond when your child refuses to go to school

- Develop effective homework routines

In the next chapter, we'll be looking at the effect of your child's emotionality on the rest of the family.

PART 4

Helping Your Whole Family: Minimizing Collateral Damage

CHAPTER 10

The Impact of Intense Emotions on the Entire Family

How do you respond when your parents or in-laws wonder why you can't control your child and have lots of advice about how you should do so? What do you do when your cousin tells you that she won't let her children play with your child? How do you respond when your child has become unmanageable during a family celebration? How can you attend to other children's "normal" questions and concerns when the child who has emotional intensity dominates your time and energy? How much do you share with your other children and how do you help them to feel special as well?

THE STONE IN THE POND

When one member of a family has intense emotions, the impact can be felt by relatives near and far. It is as if a pebble has been thrown into a pond, creating a ripple effect. The closer the relationship, the more profound the effect. All family members are affected when a child has emotion dysregulation—members of the nuclear family most of all.

When a child begins to show signs of intense emotionality, you may be so bewildered and confused that your anxiety might overwhelm you. As you seek answers to unending questions, your other children may be bewildered not only by the behavior of their sibling, but by your confusion as well. You may not realize that your other children need to understand what's happening, and you may not have the words or understanding to explain it to them. As you learn, recognize that they can too.

Helping your other children manage their lives as normally as possible in a home that may be chaotic at times is a difficult but necessary responsibility. Private and group discussions with parents and with adult and college-age siblings have made clear the long-term impact of having a sibling with intense emotions or a disorder related to emotion regulation. Although this emotionality is a consequence of life circumstances and is nobody's fault, siblings grow up with issues of their own that often go unrecognized by others whose attention is necessarily focused elsewhere. It might feel very difficult to respond to other children's needs when one child takes up so much of your emotional and physical energy; in this chapter we'll discuss ways for you to do just that.

It's also up to you to educate other family members about your child's problems so that they will be able to accept your child and you. You may not consider it your responsibility to help everyone understand, and you may feel angry that they don't. However, your child's behaviors may seem inexplicable unless you live with him. Stigma continues to exist. You will be the only one able to help others understand. Educate yourself; the more understanding and knowledge you have, the easier it will be for you to explain your child's problems to others.

Your explanations may never be enough to satisfy some members of your family. This is sad but true. You may find that you drift away from those family members because their judgments are too painful. You may not be able to change others, but you can protect your child and yourself from their harsh and invalidating judgments. In the next chapter, we will discuss ways that you will take care of yourself. In this chapter, we'll discuss how you can find teachable moments to educate those family members who are trying to understand.

SIBLINGS

Siblings of children with intense emotions have shared with us the ways they try to adjust to their life circumstance. They describe trying to be "perfect" because they don't want to create any more difficulties for their parents; feeling bad about the demands they see their sibling making on their parents and trying to keep theirs at a minimum; and pretending they don't have a sibling, especially when that sibling attends a special school. Siblings describe feeling "invisible" and talk about searching for ways to be acknowledged for their accomplishments or escalate their own behaviors in order to be noticed. Finally, some siblings say they wish they understood more about their sibling's difficulties.

One of the more difficult and painful consequences of having a child with intense emotionality and difficulty regulating his behaviors is the effect he has on the household and especially on your other child or children. There is little you can do to change the fact that difficulties in one family member will inevitably affect the others. You can, however, minimize the damage and trauma to siblings and find ways to help siblings grow in healthy ways. The way you respond to situations will be a model for your other children. Your calm validation and acceptance of them will be very beneficial. If you can live a satisfying life, they will be able to as well.

In the rest of this section, we'll focus on how to meet the demands of each of your children when one child seems to dominate your thoughts, time, and energy.

A Parental Balancing Act

You are chasing after your child while he's running through the house in the midst of a behavioral outburst. A few minutes before, you were sitting at the kitchen table helping your other children do their homework. Suddenly, you don't have time to help them, nor do you even have time to think about where they are. This scene may be familiar to the members of your family but no less traumatic to any of them. You want your home to be a place of safety for all your children, and yet it seems so difficult to achieve this goal.

How do you help one child understand the other without minimizing the feelings of either? How do you explain why your expectations are different without making it look like a child who cannot maintain control has a better deal? How do you ensure your other children don't interpret your attention to the child with behavioral outbursts as a reward for acting that way? How do you minimize the trauma in the family when the ordeal is ongoing and causing stress for you as well?

You may feel constant tension about the seemingly impossible task of trying to meet the needs of all your children. You may feel guilty when you're unable to accomplish this. You may find yourself asking any or all of the following questions:

- How can I explain emotion dysregulation to other children? How much do I tell my other children about the problem without invading the privacy of the child with intense emotions?

- How can I help my "healthier" children validate and be nonjudgmental of their sibling while also validating their feelings?

- What language do I give my other children so they can talk to others about their sibling without judging, minimizing, or exaggerating the reality of the situation?

- How do I help my children feel safe when their sibling is behaving aggressively?

- Do I encourage my other children to include their sibling when they're playing with friends?

- How do I take one child to a party when another child is in the midst of a tantrum?

- How much time do I spend helping one child with homework when she seems more capable of doing it independently and her sibling needs the help so much more?

- How can I listen patiently to one child's issues and feelings when I know this causes my other child to spin out of control?

- How do I praise my healthier child without making my other child feel bad about what he cannot accomplish?

In addition to your sensitivity and awareness, "healthier" siblings will also need consistency, rules, and expectations, even if those necessarily differ from the ones you have for their sibling(s). Healthier siblings will be raised to understand that fairness is relative, and that everything is not always equal. What they need from you is:

- Understanding and acceptance of their feelings

- Validation that their issues are important

- Recognition that even though their sibling has special needs, their needs are special too (Safer 2002)

- Recognition of their uniqueness

- Reinforcement for overcoming their own challenges

- Acknowledgement of their accomplishments

The Impact of Birth Order

Birth order plays a role in the experiences of parents and other children. If your older child is the one with intense emotions, you may:

- Not have the time to address or enjoy the normal developmental steps of a younger child

- Be overly sensitive to the behaviors of other children and worry that they will have similar problems

- Feel sadness when a younger sibling passes milestones that his older sibling has not been able to accomplish

- Be grateful when a younger child becomes more responsible and demands less of your attention, even if they're not quite ready for this responsibility

If your younger child is the one who has difficulty regulating emotions, you may:

- Expect your older child to be more independent and responsible sooner than you otherwise might

- React with bittersweet feelings to their accomplishments as you recognize what your other child may not be able to accomplish

- Demand that the older child refrain from doing anything that might trigger his sibling

- Blame the older child when the younger one is escalated

To counteract these difficulties, try to see that each of your children is a unique individual and needs to be treated as such. Recognize that all of your children have their own strengths, weaknesses, and accomplishments. Try to be present in the moment so that you can appreciate the unique abilities of each child without worries, comparisons, or disappointments.

Explaining Sibling Differences

Consider that your children all have chores to do after dinner except the child who has intense emotions, who is allowed to go to his room and relax. You have found that when you give your child this time, the rest of the evening is much easier for everyone. Your other children, however, resent the special treatment they think he is receiving. While the child with intense emotions is calm, your other children are fighting with you. You want to go away and take a break. In fact, a time-out for you might be helpful right now.

You may be wondering how to:

- Explain special circumstances to siblings who may be naturally competing for your time and attention

- Encourage acceptance to replace their resentment

- Teach that what may *be effective* may not *feel fair*

The truth is that each of your children is different and has different needs. No child's needs are any more special than another's. However, what is effective for one child may not be effective for the others. One child may need strict limits and guidelines because he tends to be impulsive; another child may be so disciplined that you encourage a more laid-back style. One child may be distracted by a computer in his room, and another may need the computer in his room so that he can do homework without distractions. Make individual decisions based on the individual needs of each of your children and explain to all of them that you understand their feelings even as you make effective decisions.

Your other children will be very aware of the difficulties of their sibling, and trying to keep the situation a secret or being unwilling or unable to discuss it will have long-term negative consequences. Secrets are almost always destructive in families (Imber-Black 1993). Children will create explanations for an unanswered question, and these may not be helpful or healthy. Your other children may blame themselves and feel ashamed, embarrassed, or isolated. Acceptance and understanding of the emotion dysregulation problems of a family member makes it easier to discuss, share, and manage. To promote this understanding, you can (1) talk to siblings about emotions and behaviors and how some people's brains work differently; (2) give them a way to talk to their friends, if they choose to do so; and (3) let them talk to school counselors or other parents. The more your healthier children are able to share, the better their adjustment to life will be.

The explanations that you give your other children will need to be developmentally appropriate and will change accordingly. You can:

- Tell a young child that his sibling "has some difficulties with his anger, and he doesn't mean to be so destructive in the house, even if it seems like he does. He really doesn't know how to control himself, but we're trying to help him learn." Let your child know that you recognize the problem and are trying to take corrective action.

- Tell an older child, "Your sibling has some difficulties that he was born with. While you can be mad and manage those feelings, he can't. That doesn't mean it's okay when he's destructive, and we're trying to get him the help he needs to change his behavior." If you have a diagnosis for your child, you may share it with his sibling and explain what it means.

- Discuss that each person has something they have to overcome and challenges they live with. Explain that everyone is doing the best they can under difficult and sometimes frightening circumstances.

- Provide enough information without overwhelming your child or creating pity for a sibling.

In these interactions with your other children, remember to:

- Validate each child's feelings by listening with attentiveness and not dismissing any feelings, even if they seem trivial or negative to you

- Reassure them that their sibling's problems are not anyone's fault

- Resist comparing your children and *find time to spend one-on-one time with each child as often as possible*

- Try to pay attention to the accomplishments, activities, and interests of each of your children

- Listen to the fears of your other children (especially after an aggressive outburst)

- Provide reassurance that you will work to keep them safe

- Develop a safety plan—a place for each child to go in the house when a sibling is getting out of control

In addition, develop calming activities for your other children to use when they are afraid or worried. You can share ideas about what helps you. It may also help to involve your "healthier" child in activities outside the home if he wants to do them. However, be careful not to push him out of the house as a way to protect him; this may lead to resentment later in life. Finally, accept when your healthier child is resentful, angry, judgmental, and unwilling to do what you're asking, despite your efforts. Provide active reassurance that you love him.

If you think that the difficulties in the home are having a significant impact on your other children and beginning to affect their friendships, their schoolwork, or other areas of their life, don't hesitate to ask them if they would like to talk to someone professional. Be aware of the fact that your healthier children may be very anxious that they too will have the problems of their sibling and your suggestion that they see a counselor may enhance their fears. Reassure them that it's helpful to talk to someone, and that it doesn't mean that they will be like their sibling. Offer them help, but don't force the issue.

As we said at the outset, this is a balancing act for parents. You may feel stuck mediating the needs of different family members, and you may be so overwhelmed by one that you can't address the needs of the other. Short-term solutions may lead to long-term problems; when you have the time and energy, talk to the healthier siblings, make their needs important, and remind each of your children that he is special in different ways.

EXTENDED FAMILY

Every extended family is different, and each has its own expectations and rules, both implicit and explicit. How are elder family members treated? Is this a family that maintains secrets or whose communication style precludes open conversation? How does the family negotiate and understand the feelings of its members? Does the family accept the idea that intense emotions may be disorders of the brain and not a function of faulty parenting?

The answers to these questions will affect how you handle the fact that your child doesn't follow the norm expected in the family. Think wisely about your answers to the following questions. What will be the consequence of forcing your child to meet the family expectation that he attend a family gathering despite the intensity of his emotions? If your family is unable to talk about difficult feelings, how can you explain that even *you* don't always understand the behavior of your child? How do you teach others to validate your child when they would rather ignore that a problem exists or, worse, blame the child for his behaviors? How do you help your child when family expectations exceed his skills? Is every family event a cause for anxiety in you and in your child? What do you do if you're aware that every visit causes your child to feel worse about himself because he realizes that he doesn't behave like the others and that he isn't accepted as he is?

Grandparents

What happens when the rule in your extended family is that grandchildren welcome grandparents with open arms? How do you react if your child is anxious when his routine is changed and a visit from a grandparent is a trigger for him? If you're practicing effective parenting, you may give him permission to stay in his room until he feels comfortable and calm enough to come out and join the rest of the family. However, you may feel stuck between supporting your child and trying to please a parent who doesn't have the understanding that you do.

At times such as these, remember your own triggers and find ways to manage your own anxiety. You may be tempted to give in to your own parent and expect your child to behave like the others. Or you may feel that you have to protect your child from people who don't understand. If you feel yourself becoming angry and frustrated, find a way to take a break. Recognize that it's usually not possible to please everyone, and think through the most effective path to handling this situation. Consider the following:

- Your child's needs are very important, and he needs to know that you support his efforts at managing his emotions.

- You can calmly explain why your child is in his room and encourage your parent to be patient until your child is ready for the visit.

- Your parent may be taking this situation as a personal rejection of the love she wants to give her grandchild. As hard as it is, *try to validate her feelings of rejection and confusion.*

- Pushing a child with intense emotions into an emotionally laden situation will probably end in a way that is unfavorable to everyone.

- You can help your parent understand that this is not your child's—or your—fault.

- Encouraging grandparents to accept the individuality and strengths of *each* grandchild can help.

If your parent is judgmental of you or your child, try not to become defensive. Just as you can't control the behavior of your child, so you cannot control the attitudes of your relatives. You can validate their feelings even if you don't like or agree with them.

Grandparents may want to discipline your child if they feel that his behavior is not appropriate. Or they may demand that you discipline your child for behaviors that you respond to differently or have learned to ignore. Grandparents may not understand why you're validating a child that they judge as "spoiled" or "getting away with murder." You can explain, without defensiveness, that (1) your child has some difficulties that you're responding to in a planful, effective way; (2) their "discipline" may not be as helpful as they think in the long run, and (3) validation will help your child feel better about himself and improve his behaviors. Ultimately, this is your child, and you may need to remind yourself that you are parenting effectively. Don't let the judgments of others (even if you love them) affect your decisions or choices. As hard as it is, continue on the path you have wisely decided to follow.

Educating Relatives

If your relatives are receptive to new ideas, you can teach them some of what you've learned about intense emotions. Share books, magazines, and newspaper articles; find teachable moments to educate them that:

- Your child's emotional intensity is something that he was born with and is not his fault. Nor can it be blamed on your parenting.

- Your child is doing the best he can—and so are you.

- His behaviors are ways that he has found to manage his emotions, and you're trying to help him learn more effective behaviors.

- It will be easier for him to spend time with family members if he feels accepted and validated.

- Insisting that he conform or behave in a certain way will actually backfire by increasing his emotionality and the probability of problematic behaviors.

- Your child is learning skills that may mean he leaves the group for a while or spends time by himself. Encourage family members not to take this behavior personally or judge him harshly.

- Your child's life is painful, even if he seems calm at times, and he will always have to work harder to maintain appropriate behaviors.

If you find it difficult to share this information with your relatives, if your family usually maintains secrets, or if your relatives are unable to accept your child, you may need to protect your child and yourself by accepting that some relatives may have a diminished role in your life. Surround yourself with people who are supportive of you and accepting of your child. When you do spend time with your family, don't expect them to be different than they are. If you can accept them, even though you disagree with them, you will be less angry, less hurt, and less frustrated. You will, in fact, be helping your child by modeling effective interpersonal skills.

When Your Child Behaves Better with Relatives

Some children are able to behave better with other family members than with you for a variety of reasons. Your child may feel that a visit with an aunt or a grandparent is a special occasion and does not create any stress for him or make any uncomfortable demands on him. Your child may flourish from one-to-one time with a relative. He may even be treated to special activities that he finds pleasant and empowering, and therefore he may not become emotionally intense or behaviorally dysregulated. This may lead other family members to believe that any difficulty you have with your child is your fault and that if you knew how to parent better, he wouldn't have these difficulties. This can be an enormous trigger for you, or for any parent who is working very hard to effectively parent a child who has emotional and behavioral outbursts.

It may be painful when you're judged by others who don't share your experiences, who do not live with your child, and who don't have the responsibility to raise your child. As much as you may try to help others understand the nature of your child's difficulties and the attempts you're making to do the best you can, you won't be able to control their thinking. You will feel better if you can accept that they don't understand. Calmly remind yourself to think wisely as you consider the following:

- If your child benefits from visits with this relative, you may want the visits to continue. If he feels conflicted during these visits or confused by statements made by the relatives about you, you may want to discontinue the visits.

- It benefits your child if he has a relative he enjoys; it also gives you a break from his behaviors.

- If you become defensive or angry in response to relatives' reactions, it will only reinforce their negative judgments of you.

- You don't have to accept the judgments of others or respond to them.

- It will be helpful to find a support network of other parents who understand what you're going through.

When family expectations are making your life more difficult, try to remember the old adage that you cannot choose your relatives. You can, however, choose how much time you spend with them and how much you listen to what they're saying. You can't control your relatives, but you *can* control your responses to them. As tempted as you may be, try not to respond emotionally; continue to evaluate your parenting by whether or not it's effective for your child—not whether or not it pleases your relatives.

If your family is understanding and accepting of your child, or if some members of your family are, appreciate this. Accept their help and support without embarrassment or guilt. Receiving support and validation will make it easier for you to parent your child effectively and will therefore benefit you both.

SUMMARY

When you're immersed in parenting a child with intense emotions, you may not realize the stress experienced by your other children or how the reactions from relatives may either increase your stress or provide much-needed support. Siblings and relatives need to be given information so they can become more accepting and understanding. Their needs and feelings also need to be validated. Try to make wise decisions that are effective for your child, your other children, and you.

In this chapter we discussed ways to:

- Address the needs, feelings, and questions of your healthier children in developmentally appropriate ways

- Educate extended family members and help them accept your child and your parenting

- Make wise choices and decisions in response to the expectations of the extended family

In our final chapter, we'll be exploring ways for you to take care of yourself and maintain your own health and well-being while effectively raising your child.

CHAPTER 11

Caring for Yourself and Living Your Life

Do you ask yourself how you can remain calm when there is so much emotionality spinning around you? Do you wonder how you can be mindful of addressing everyone else's needs when you feel as though you're drowning? Do you feel overwhelmed by the chaos in your home? Do you ever feel like running away?

Raising a child with intense emotions can create an overwhelming mix of feelings in a parent. You may not know how you can do one more thing, much less do it effectively. Now we're going to add something else important for you to do: take care of yourself by treating yourself well, doing things that you enjoy, and attending to your own needs. You deserve some pleasure, and you *are allowed* the time to take care of yourself.

SELF-CARE IS ESSENTIAL

You may question how you can take care of daily demands, advocate for your child while keeping her safe and parenting her effectively, be sensitive to the needs of your other children, *and* take care of yourself. Actually, doing everything else depends on it. You cannot take care of others or remain calm in the face of chaos if you don't take care of yourself. Think of the flight attendant who reminds you that if the oxygen mask descends, you should put it on yourself *first*. Without your own oxygen, you will not be able to take care of others. The same principle applies here—you can't do what you need to do for your family if you are depleted yourself. If you take care of yourself, taking care of others will be easier. Parents in our groups who have learned the importance of caring for themselves have confirmed this to be true.

Through our discussions with parents, we have heard many of the concerns that you may have as the parent of a child with intense emotions. Some of them include:

- A sense of overriding dread, worry, and anxiety

- Self-doubt about your abilities to parent (or love) your child

- Fears that your child will not get better and the feelings of grief and loss that result

- Fear of being judged as an incompetent parent by others (including teachers and social service workers)

- An inability to enjoy things or relax because you always feel on call

- A constant struggle to find the best help for your child combined with anger, frustration, and disappointment when following the advice you receive makes no difference in your child's behavior

- Guilt about what your other children are experiencing in the home and/or your inability to attend to them as often as you'd like

- Isolation based on a lack of patience with what *you* might consider trivialities and the feeling that no one really understands what you're going through (Karp 2001)

- Disagreement with and stress between you and your child's other parent or your partner

- Financial concerns as special needs use up valuable financial resources

You may experience some, none, or all of the concerns we've listed above. You may simply feel as though every day is a marathon, and you don't look forward to running it. You may feel that your family life is a storm that you can't navigate.

The same skills that help your child calm down will form the foundation of ways to help yourself as well. Acceptance that you *deserve* and *need* to take care of yourself will enable you to have a more satisfying life. You will then be able to effectively parent your child. In this chapter, we will present some guidelines for doing what is effective in your own life.

ACCEPTANCE

When your child has intense emotions, your life is difficult and challenging. You may be angry or resentful, and you may believe that your child's emotional vulnerability isn't fair to your child, to you, or to your family. It may be true that you and your family have been dealt a difficult hand. However, your life is what it is, and denying your reality only leads to more suffering (Linehan 1993b) and to a diminished ability to move forward. You have to play the cards you have been dealt. There are certain realities that won't change, no matter how hard you try. Accepting what you can't change makes it easier to recognize opportunities to change what you can.

Getting to this point of acceptance isn't easy, and it's not a passive process. It takes:

- Recognizing what can be changed and what can't be

- Reminding yourself that denying reality doesn't make it go away

- Actively relaxing so that you can see things in new and different ways (Linehan 1993b)

- Validating yourself and being patient as you move toward change

- Remembering the assumptions (chapter 2) and believing that you're doing the best you can even while you try to do it better

Do Not Judge Yourself

We have found that even as parents become less judgmental of their child, they continue to be judgmental of themselves. You may continue to be annoyed with yourself when you yell at your child or forget to use the skills you're learning. You may be frustrated when you get overwhelmed, cannot control situations, or are *less effective* than you think you "should" be. You may feel that you can't meet your own expectations for yourself.

Remember the guidelines for being nonjudgmental:

- Do not compare yourself to others; everyone else's life looks better on the outside.

- Avoid thinking in terms of right and wrong or good and bad. Think about whether or not you've been effective.

- Don't label yourself.

- Remind yourself that change is possible.

- Think of yourself in accepting terms.

Just as you don't expect perfection from your child, don't expect it of yourself. Expecting that you will always get it right is a prescription for being disappointed in yourself. Be realistic about what you can do and what you can't. Be patient. Forgive yourself. You're doing the best you can; on other days, you'll do it better.

Just as your child's intense emotions interfere with listening and effectiveness, so will your emotions affect your ability to be accepting of yourself and effective with others. The more you take care of yourself, the better you feel physically and emotionally, the more accepting—and effective—you'll be.

You can't deny the difficulties of your life. The first step toward making your life better is accepting your life as it is. When you recognize and accept what can and cannot be changed, you will feel less frustrated and disappointed. Though it may be quite difficult at times, the skills in this book can help you create a meaningful and fulfilling life for yourself and every member of your family.

CALMING AND SOOTHING ACTIVITIES FOR YOU

As we have already discussed in chapters 4 and 5, distress tolerance skills (Linehan 1993a) help you manage times of crisis or stress and help you manage the long-term difficulties of your life.

These skills are as important for you as they are for your child. Remember that doing pleasant activities and taking care of your own health makes you less vulnerable to negative emotions. You will handle situations or difficulties that arise more effectively when you take time to:

- Get enough sleep and take care of your physical health

- Soothe yourself

- Take a walk or engage in other calming activities

- Exercise or practice mindfulness

Your story of emotion (chapter 1) will teach you to recognize when you are stressed. Try not to ignore the signals. When you take care of your emotions early, your story will probably have a better outcome. Calm yourself by taking a few deep breaths, doing a short mindfulness exercise, or taking a mental vacation. Even in the middle of a storm, these few seconds can be quite helpful.

A Short Mindfulness Exercise

When you need to take a moment to catch your breath and feel calmer, try this brief exercise in mindfulness.

1. Take a deep breath.

2. Remember a place you have visited that was peaceful and calming (this can be on a beach, in the mountains, walking along a stream, and so on). See with your mind's eye what you saw then, in as much detail as you can recall.

3. Recall what you heard (the sound of the waves, birds singing), how it smelled (the scent of the ocean), what you felt (the wind blowing, the sun on your face, the sand under your feet).

4. Stay with the vision for a few seconds or a few minutes.

5. Feel the calm you felt that day.

6. Take another deep breath.

Sometimes calm comes when you can simply take a small break from what is going on in the moment.

Take a Mental Vacation

Choose one or more of these short exercises to take a vacation in your mind.

- Sit at your desk with your eyes closed and your feet up and take a few deep breaths.

- Close your eyes for a second and mentally visit a place you enjoy.

- Go into the bathroom, splash a little water on your face, and take a few breaths.

- Walk slowly and mindfully around your home or office.

Calming Activities

Take care of yourself on a regular basis so that you have the strength to handle situations when they arise. Parents tell us that they become so focused on the needs of their child that they forget to do those things that have always relaxed them. Now you need those skills more than ever. Doing things that help you feel good about yourself provides the foundation for making more effective decisions and responding wisely.

In the midst of the storm, you may forget about distress tolerance skills. If you're constantly putting out fires, it's hard to remember what helps you think clearly, plan effectively, and remain calm. Just as you did with your child, create a list of activities that you enjoy and that soothe you. Keep the list handy and refer to it when you're stressed or otherwise emotional. Share your list with a significant other or a good friend who can coach you to use the skill when you forget. Remember that different levels of stress respond better to different activities; a high level of anxiety might respond to a hot bath or soothing lotion but might make it difficult to read.

Some calming and soothing activities that parents have told us help them include:

- Running or other exercise

- Spending uninterrupted time reading an entertaining book

- Having a massage

- Gardening

- Hobbies such as knitting, needlepoint, and/or painting

- Watching a favorite TV show or sports event

- Listening to or playing music

- Calling or meeting a friend

- Helping other parents or doing volunteer work

Your Soothing Activities

Write your own list of calming activities by answering these questions in your notebook or here, on the lines provided:

What soothes you?

_____

_____

What activities relax you?

_____

_____

What activities do you feel good doing?

_____

_____

List other calming activities.

_____

_____

Remember to validate yourself and to cheerlead your efforts (Linehan 1993a). Your child isn't the only person who feels better when her efforts or accomplishments are acknowledged. Without letting negative emotions take over, accept any mistakes you make as lessons for the future. Focus on the present and enjoy what's positive. Surround yourself with people who understand what your life is like and who are able to provide validation on those days when you're not able to do it yourself. All the skills that you've learned for your child apply to you as well.

Couple Time as a Calming Activity

Finding time to go out with friends or as a couple is not easy. You may have difficulty finding a babysitter, or your child's anxiety over your leaving may cause an outburst just as you're about to leave. However, finding time to be together under pleasant circumstances helps parents work more effectively as a team. It gives you opportunities to enjoy yourself, appreciate the positives, and renew and strengthen your relationship, and it reminds you that you don't have to face situations alone. Carve out this time and make it a priority. It will pay dividends the next time your family is involved in a chaotic situation. Working together gives you the strength to handle the situation more effectively.

Asking for Help

Parents sometimes believe (erroneously) that they should be able to handle their child and meet the needs of their family by themselves. You may feel that your family is *your* responsibility and that taking care of them should be something you can do. You may be afraid that asking for help shows that you're weak or incompetent.

In reality, accepting the difficulties you face and admitting that you need help shows courage and strength. When your child has intense emotions that affect the entire family, asking for help from others is an effective and wise choice. If friends or family can't help you, find support groups or other parents whose lives are challenging as well.

There may be many ways that others might be able to help you. They might:

- Provide validation and listen when you need to talk

- Coach you to use calming skills when you're stressed

- Watch your children so that you can have a break or share enjoyable time with your partner or spouse

- Cheerlead your efforts at helping your child and yourself

- Help your other children when your child with intense emotions is in crisis

MOTHERS AND FATHERS, WIVES AND HUSBANDS

When your child has intense emotions and behaviors, when experts disagree on the best course of action, when it seems like nothing is working and frustration is rampant, parents tend to blame each other. Each parent may tend to believe that only he or she has the right answers and the other parent must be wrong. In these situations, remind yourself that there is no absolute truth (Miller 2001), that agreeing to disagree may be useful, and that accepting that other opinions are also valid helps you to feel better and, paradoxically, more in control. Think about being effective by listening to each other, respecting each other, and trying to come up with a compromise (or a totally new solution) that satisfies both of you.

You may feel sometimes that your child is "manipulating" you. When your child doesn't get the answer she wants from you, she may go to her other parent. Parents can stop this behavior by being consistent and supportive of each other's decisions. If you disagree with your partner, discuss this later in private and come to agreements for the future. If one of you feels your child is right and the other parent is wrong, support your partner and privately share your feelings later. Remember that your child needs consistency and that parents need to be partners in this effort.

To parent most effectively together and to maintain your relationship:

- Don't make assumptions about your partner or his or her intentions

- Validate your partner's point of view

- Work to develop consistency in your responses to your child, even if you don't always agree, despite how difficult this might be

- Talk to each other, share your concerns, and learn how to support each other

- Remember that your child's welfare is the goal for both of you and the most effective response is the one that works best

SUPPORT AND PSYCHOEDUCATIONAL GROUPS

There may be a point in your life, which you may or may not have already reached, when you realize you need help and support for you and/or your child. You may look for professionals to help your child and search for information for yourself. If you are reading this, you may be in the early stages of your search to understand or you may have already walked far along this road.

Parents seek out information by attending educational or support groups, some facilitated by parents and others by professionals. You may get referred to these groups by school personnel, mental health professionals, friends, or other parents. At first, you may feel scared or sad seeing parents whose children may be more ill than yours or who have been wrestling with problems longer. If you attend a group that has parents whose children are already adults, you may begin to feel hopeless and defeated. Don't give up on all groups because of one negative experience. Ultimately, the parents we work with report that it was a group of parents who shared their worries and fears that helped them move forward and find peace with their lives. Look for a group:

- That you feel comfortable in

- With parents you can talk to whose children are close in age to yours

- That provides you with support and helpful information

- That helps you feel better

- That you look forward to returning to

Some groups provide information, some provide support, and some provide both. In the more formal and time-limited psychoeducational groups, you'll learn about emotion dysregulation and other disorders, as well as effective strategies and treatments. You will also receive information about helpful resources. Sometimes participants continue to meet informally after the group officially ends.

In the more informal support groups, you'll have time to talk about your specific concerns as well as hear the stories of other parents. You will get to know what strategies have worked for other parents and use the group when you most need or want to attend.

Some parents find the structure of psychoeducational groups to be more helpful, and others find the support and informality of the support groups to be beneficial. Some parents attend both. You can experiment with different groups until you find what's most helpful to you.

In the appendix, you will find information about groups and resources for parents. The benefit of any group is talking to and sharing with parents who have similar experiences and "have been there." Knowing that you're not alone can be quite healing. You'll also find that giving and receiving support and sharing with other parents can be invaluable.

LIVING IN THE MOMENT

DBT teaches you to regulate emotions by encouraging you to appreciate the moment and be "unmindful of worries" (Linehan 1993b, 155). For parents who are constantly worrying about what their child will do next, this is especially relevant advice. When your child is doing well or when you're enjoying time with her, be mindful of it, acknowledge it, and savor the moment. Try not to think about what happened before or worry about what might happen next. Learn to live for that moment and appreciate it.

Worrying about something *does not* prevent it from happening. Worrying *does* take away any pleasure that you have in the moment. We encourage parents whose children have emotion dysregulation to take an imaginary snapshot of moments that feel good so they can be remembered later. When you're fully present and aware of moments of pleasure and peace, you will enjoy them more and you'll be able to revisit those moments (and those pleasurable feelings) in the future.

Learning to focus on positive moments without worrying about what will happen next can be life-altering. Attend to those ordinary family moments; they are special in your family. You will start to find more of these moments when you begin to focus on them. They might be:

- The one day of the week when your child gets up and gets ready for school easily

- A week without a call from the school

- A few minutes when your children are talking to or playing with each other

- The spontaneous hug your child gives you for no reason at all

- Your child's pleasure over her own accomplishment or success

- A quiet hour when everyone is doing what they're supposed to be doing

- A special activity that you can share with your child when her siblings are busy elsewhere

Take a snapshot; savor the moment; remember it when you want or need to.

LIVING YOUR LIFE

You deserve to have your own satisfying life despite the difficulties your child's intense emotions create. You *can* have your own life. In order to do this, you may need to mourn the child that you dreamed of in order to accept the child that you have. You may also have to make some compromises and accept that your life might not be what you expected.

Use the skills we have discussed to accept that you:

- Might not be able to do everything that you want to do

- Can ask for help from others so that you can have opportunities to enjoy your life

- Can trust family or friends to take care of your child in effective ways so that you're comfortable going away and leaving her

- Can let go of blame (that you caused the problems) and guilt (that you cannot make your child well)

Making the most of the life you have may mean letting go of any guilt you feel when you enjoy yourself or take care of yourself. Your child will not suffer less if you suffer more. You *and* your child will benefit when you are able to (1) take time for yourself for pleasant activities without feeling guilty and without fearing that everything will fall apart, (2) respect your own limits and encourage others to respect them as well, (3) accept that you can't please everyone all the time, and (4) believe that you—and your child—are doing the best you can even while you're working quite hard to do things better.

When you create a life that is meaningful and fulfilling, you will be able to:

- Think and respond wisely (chapter 1)

- Parent your child with a more balanced focus (chapter 2)

- Respond more effectively to your child when she's overwhelmed by her emotions (chapter 4)

- Help your child learn effective skills for managing her emotions and behaviors (chapters 5 and 8)

- Help the rest of your family effectively manage and minimize the collateral damage from the emotional and behavioral chaos created by a child who has emotional intensity (chapter 10)

It is possible to live your life and enjoy it. We have met many parents over the years who have learned the beneficial impact of taking care of themselves and using the skills we have discussed. They describe lives that feel more fulfilling and satisfying. We hope these skills will help you live your life fully and peacefully as well.

SUMMARY

In this chapter we addressed your needs as the parent of a child with intense emotions. We have encouraged you to (1) find ways to take care of yourself so that you will be less vulnerable to negative emotions, (2) live in the present, and (3) live your life in ways that feel good to you and that bring you calm and pleasure. We hope you have come to see that taking care of yourself enables you to do everything else more effectively.

Some of the skills discussed in this chapter include:

- Calming skills for parents

- Learning to appreciate the moment

- Remembering that there is no absolute truth

- Accepting life as it is

- Learning that you can have a satisfying and fulfilling life even while parenting a child who has intense emotions

We've seen these skills increase the calm in other parents' lives as well as bring them closer to their children. Our hope is that with knowledge, calm, and patience, along with acceptance of your child and yourself, you will experience a similar outcome. We hope you're feeling validated and empowered by the skills and information you've learned here and that you are experiencing a renewed sense of hope. Recognize the courage you showed in reading this book and acknowledge the strength in your willingness to change and we are confident that you will move forward to parenting in a more effective way.

APPENDIX

Resources for Parents

INFORMATIONAL WEB RESOURCES

Behavioral Tech, LLC

This is the official DBT website, created by Marsha Linehan, Ph.D. Here you will find general information about DBT, a directory to help you find a therapist who uses DBT, listings and registrations for conferences, and resources such as books and videos.

www.behavioraltech.com

BPChildren

This website provides information about bipolar disorder, a newsletter, and resources for parents that include mood charts, posters, books, and magnets. It has information for children, teens, and parents and also includes interactive games designed especially for children.

www.bpchildren.org

National Alliance on Mental Illness

NAMI is often the first stop for parents who think their child has an emotional problem. They provide parent-led information and support groups (including a new program for parents of children, called NAMI Basics), usually free of charge. The organization provides a program to help parents and schools work together more effectively and has a Child and Adolescent Action Center with resources specifically for parents and children. The website provides resources and information about serious emotional disturbance, mental illness, and mental health public policy and legislation. You will also find information about ways to reach your state or local NAMI affiliate.

www.nami.org

National Education Alliance for Borderline Personality Disorder (NEA-BPD)

This organization and website provide information about borderline personality disorder and audio and video lectures from experts in the field of emotion dysregulation. You will also find out how to participate in one of the Family Connections Programs for parents and family members.

www.borderlinepersonalitydisorder.com

Treatment and Research Advancements
National Association for Personality Disorder (TARA)

This organization and its website provide information and resources about disorders of emotion dysregulation and DBT. It also offers information about DBT Family Workshops.

www.tara4bpd.org

ADDITIONAL WEB RESOURCES

Annenberg Foundation Trust at Sunnylands

This site provides information on the Adolescent Mental Health Institute, which is a resource for adolescents with mental health issues. You can also access books written by and about teens with various mental health problems.

www.sunnylands.org

Creative Therapy Associates

You can find numerous feelings posters, magnets, and other items that can help you and your child understand and address emotions.

www.ctherapy.com

Iris the Dragon

On this website you will find illustrated children's books specifically for children with emotional and behavioral challenges. These books will help your child gain self-awareness and know that he or she is not alone in his or her difficulties.

www.iristhedragon.com

Pat Harvey, LCSW-C

Pat Harvey's website contains information about DBT and more information about DBT skills training for parents and siblings, as well as links to additional resources.

www.patharveymsw.com

BOOKS

Brach, T. 2003. *Radical Acceptance*. New York: Bantam Books.
Radical Acceptance provides guidance in bringing a sense of calm and acceptance into your life.

Brantley, J. 2007. *Calming Your Anxious Mind*. Oakland, CA: New Harbinger Publications, Inc.
Brantley's book provides exercises and examples that will help you find calm even if your life is filled with emotional intensity.

DeGangi, G., and A. Kendall. 2008. *Effective Parenting for the Hard-to-Manage Child: A Skills-Based Book*. New York: Taylor and Francis Group.
This book provides additional parenting techniques and mindfulness exercises to help you parent your child who has intense emotions.

Griffith, G. 2005. *Will's Choice*. New York: HarperCollins.
This is a firsthand account of a mother's attempts to find the most effective treatment for her teenage son following a suicide attempt. It explores the dilemmas parents face when a child's emotion dysregulation causes him to behave in an unsafe way.

Nhat Hanh, T. 1991. *Peace Is Every Step*. New York: Bantam Books.
Peace Is Every Step will help you find ways to use mindfulness in your life.

Karp, D. A. 2001. *The Burden of Sympathy: How Families Cope with Mental Illness*. New York: Oxford University Press, Inc.
Karp's sensitive sociological perspective validates the feelings of family members who are questioning how to respond to the needs of a loved one who has a mental illness.

Kreger, R. 2008. The *Essential Family Guide to Borderline Personality Disorder*. Center City, Minnesota: Hazelden.
Kreger's newest book provides useful advice for any family in which one member has any emotion dysregulation (it need not be diagnosed as borderline personality disorder).

Kundtz, D. 2000. *Quiet Mind: One-Minute Retreats from a Busy World*. Berkeley, CA: Conari Press.
Quiet Mind is filled with quick and easy exercises for using mindfulness and awareness in your life.

Mason, M. S., and R. Kreger. 1998. *Stop Walking on Eggshells: Taking Your Life Back When Someone You Care About Has Borderline Personality Disorder*. Oakland, CA: New Harbinger Publications, Inc.
This book provides helpful guidance for family members who are trying to respond effectively to someone with emotion dysregulation.

McKay, M., J. C. Wood, and J. Brantley. 2007. *The Dialectical Behavior Therapy Workbook: Exercises for Learning Mindfulness, Interpersonal Effectiveness, Emotion Regulation, and Distress Tolerance*. Oakland, CA: New Harbinger Publications, Inc.
This workbook provides more specific details about the DBT skills that are discussed throughout this book. It provides easy-to-follow exercises in how to apply the skills to your life.

Moorman, M. 1992. *My Sister's Keeper*. New York: Norton and Company.
My Sister's Keeper by Margaret Moorman is a very poignant account of how the mental illness of one sibling affects the lives of her mother and sister, as seen through the eyes of the sister.

Raeburn, P. 2004. *Acquainted with the Night*. New York: Broadway Books.
This first-person account of the struggles of one father when his children begin to show signs of emotion dysregulation validates the feelings of parents as they search for answers to very difficult questions and situations.

Spradlin, S. 2003. *Don't Let Your Emotions Run Your Life*. Oakland, CA: New Harbinger Publications, Inc.
This workbook walks you through the DBT module of emotion regulation using exercises, examples, and easy-to-follow explanations.

ARTICLE

Penzo, J. A. and P. Harvey. 2008. Understanding parental grief as a response to mental illness: Implications for practice. *Journal of Family Social Work* 11:323-328.

References

Beck, A. T. 1972. *Depression: Causes and Treatment*. Philadelphia: University of Pennsylvania Press.

Belden, A. C., N. R. Thomson, and J. L. Luby. 2008. Temper tantrums in healthy versus depressed and disruptive preschoolers: Defining tantrum behaviors associated with clinical problems. *The Journal of Pediatrics* 152:117-122.

Burland, J. 2003. *Parents and Teachers as Allies*. Arlington, VA: National Alliance for the Mentally Ill (NAMI).

Chess, S., A. Thomas, and H. Birch. 1959. Characteristics of the individual child's behavioral responses to the environment. *American Journal of Orthopsychiatry* 29: 791–802.

Ciottone, R. 2008. Conversation with authors on May 20, 2008, in Worcester, MA.

Fox, N. A., and S. D. Calkins. 2003. The development of self-control of emotions: Intrinsic and extrinsic influences. *Motivation and Emotion* 27: 7–26.

Fruzetti, A. E. 2005. Validating and invalidating responses in families. Paper presented at Borderline Personality Disorder: Historical and Future Perspectives sponsored by National Education Alliance for Borderline Personality Disorder (NEA-BPD) and McLean Hospital. Burlington, MA.

Goodenough, F. L. 1931. *Anger in Young Children*. Minneapolis, MN: University of Minnesota Press.

Imber-Black, E., ed. 1993. *Secrets in Families and Family Therapy*. New York: Norton.

Karp, D. A. 2001. *The Burden of Sympathy: How Families Cope with Mental Illness*. New York: Oxford University Press, Inc.

Kodak, T., D. C. Lerman, V. Volkert, and N. Trosclair. 2007. Further examination of factors that influence preference for positive versus negative reinforcement. *Journal of Applied Behavior Analysis* 40: 25–44.

Lazarus, R. S., and S. Folkman. 1984. *Stress, Appraisal, and Coping*. New York: Springer Publishing Company.

Linehan, M. M. 1993a. *Cognitive Behavioral Treatment of Borderline Personality Disorder*. New York: Guilford Press.

Linehan, M. M. 1993b. *Skills Training Manual for Treating Borderline Personality Disorder*. New York: Guilford Press.

Mason, M. S., and R. Kreger. 1998. *Stop Walking on Eggshells: Taking Your Life Back When Someone You Care About Has Borderline Personality Disorder*. Oakland, CA: New Harbinger Publications, Inc.

May, G. 1982. *Will and Spirit*. San Francisco: Harper & Row.

Miller, A. L., and C. Swenson. 2001. Notes taken at Advanced Topics in Dialectical Behavior Therapy Conference, October 18–19, Holyoke, MA.

Miller, A. L., J. H. Rathus, M. M. Linehan, and C. Swenson. 2007. *Dialectical Behavioral Therapy with Suicidal Adolescents*. New York: Guilford Press.

Pavlov, I. P. 1928. *Lectures on Conditioned Reflexes*. Trans. W.H. Gantt. New York: Liveright Publishing Company.

Peterson, L. E., and P. D. Gerson. 1975. Changing thoughts, feelings, and behaviors: A common-sense approach. Paper presented at the Massachusetts Psychological Association Fall Meeting.

Piaget, J. 1926. *The Language and Thought of the Child*. New York: Harcourt Brace.

Piaget, J. 1928. *Judgment and Reasoning in the Child*. New York: Harcourt Brace.

Premack, D. 1959. Toward empirical behavior laws. *The Psychological Review* 66: 219–233.

Safer, J. 2002. *The Normal One: Life with a Difficult or Damaged Sibling.* New York: Bantam Dell.

Skinner, B. F. 1938. *The Behavior of Organisms.* Acton, MA: Copley Publishing Group.

Skinner, B. F. 1953. *The Science of Human Behavior.* New York: The Free Press.

Werner, H. 1948. *Comparative Psychology of Mental Development.* New York: International Universities Press, Inc.

Wolfe, A. E. 2002. *Get Out of My Life, but First Can You Drive Me & Cheryl to the Mall?: A Parent's Guide to the New Teenager, Revised and Updated.* New York: Farrar, Straus, & Giroux.

Pat Harvey, LCSW-C, has practiced clinical social work for more than thirty years, working with families and individuals with serious emotion dysregulation. She was instrumental in the development of an award-winning dialectical behavior therapy (DBT) adherent adolescent group home. Pat now specializes in facilitating DBT skills groups for parents and family members, coaching and supporting parents of individuals with intense emotions or mental illness, consulting, and training others to use DBT skills with many populations.

Jeanine A. Penzo, LICSW, is a licensed clinical social worker with the VA Boston Healthcare System, where she utilizes dialectical behavior therapy (DBT) skills in her work with spinal-cord-injured patients and their caregivers. She is also a trained teacher who has worked with elementary and middle school students. Jeanine is the mother of three children, one of whom suffers from emotion dysregulation.

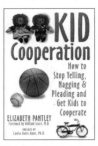
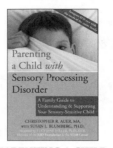

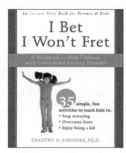

Sweet Seduction

CHOCOLATE TRUFFLES

D0951283

ADRIENNE WELCH

HARPER COLOPHON BOOKS
Harper & Row, Publishers
New York, Cambridge, Philadelphia, San Francisco
London, Mexico City, São Paulo, Sydney

TO DAVID

Sweet Seduction © 1984 by Smallwood and Stewart & Adrienne Welch

FIRST EDITION

Designed and Produced by Smallwood & Stewart, 6 Alconbury Road, London E.5.

Photographs by Bruce Wolf

Library of Congress Cataloging in Publication Data
Welch, Adrienne.
    Sweet seduction.
    Includes index.
    1. Candy.   2. Cookery (Chocolate)   I. Title.
TX791.W384   1984   641.6′374   84-47608
ISBN 0-06-091187-5 (pbk.)   84 85 86 87 88 10 9 8 7 6 5 4 3 2 1

Contents

INTRODUCTION

⋯•━━◆━━•⋯

L ike the elusive fungus of the same name, chocolate truffles are rich, supremely sophisticated delicacies. Also like truffles, once tasted they are never forgotten, and the finest are ardently sought-after. For although chocolate truffles are flavored with liqueurs, vanilla, coffee, nuts, caramel, fruit, and so on, these flavorings work primarily to enhance and enrich the pure pleasure of chocolate.

Heavenly pleasure they can be indeed. The ideal chocolate truffle, if it ever existed, would have an exquisite balance between its creamy chocolate heart, called a 'ganache', and thin, crisp coating of highly-refined chocolate known as 'couverture'. To achieve this delicate harmony, truffles must defy the laws of science, and the truffle-maker must work carefully with the best ingredients under favorable conditions. Chocolate is highly temperamental, easily influenced by any change in temperature or humidity. My directions describe the best working conditions and temperature but, of course, even a professional truffletier must cope with variations from this ideal. For the best results, try to come as close as possible to my recommended times, temperatures, ingredients, and quantities.

Fortunately, the rewards of truffle-making more than repay the time and care they require, although most of the recipes take only about 2 hours' work, aside from freezing times. Truffles are best enjoyed fresh, within a few days of making. My recipes use much more fresh cream than nearly all commercial varieties as well as liqueurs and liquor, which are illegal in store-bought candies, to heighten the flavor. All this produces chocolate truffles as they should be—richly flavored, refined delicacies.

Tempering, described in Chapter 2, is probably the most exacting technique you will have to master to make truffles. The truffle neophyte should begin with the Classic truffle, which does not use a tempered chocolate coating. However, I suggest you read through the techniques in Chapter 2 if you haven't worked with chocolate before.

In Chapter 4 I have included several other chocolate recipes, most of which can be made to use up chocolate leftover from making truffles. Bark and tuiles are very straightforward to make and can be varied in dozens of ways. For the more ambitious, I have included a spectacular truffle cake, a woven chocolate basket, and some unusual ganache-filled madeleines, as well as directions for molding chocolate.

The central interest of this book, however, remains the pure delight of truffles. While the original humor behind these irresistible gastronomic puns may have been lost, their sublime pleasures remain. Now I hope that you can experience the satisfaction and pure enjoyment of making and enjoying your own truffles.

1

Ingredients & Equipment

･････━━◆━━━･････

Chocolate lovers do not need to be told that chocolate is a very serious subject. People have devoted their whole lifetimes to understanding its complexities and perfecting its manufacture. Fortunately, you need know very little about chocolate to enjoy it. But to work with it successfully, and especially to make something as exquisite as truffles, you must get to know some of its idiosyncrasies.

All chocolate begins with the bean of the cocoa tree (*Theobroma cacao*, "the food of the gods"), native to South and Central America and also cultivated in Africa. From the tree's many aroma-less flowers only a few will bear the thick, woody pods that contain the cocoa bean. Anywhere from 20 to 40 beans, each about 1½-inches long, are contained in a single pod. At this point the fresh beans are extremely bitter. Before shipping to a manufacturer they are fermented and dried, mellowing their flavor considerably.

After cleaning and sorting, the beans are roasted, making it easier to remove the shells around the 'nibs,' or seeds. This develops the characteristic chocolate flavor and at the same time eliminates the vinegary, rather astringent aroma. The roasted nibs are then crushed and blended according to the manufacturer's own specifications, and crushed again, to form a thick, viscous mixture known as chocolate liquor. Once molded, cooled, and set, this is the unsweetened chocolate that is so ideal for cakes and pastries.

For anyone working with chocolate, either professionally or simply making one or two of the recipes in this book, the most important element to know about is cocoa butter. Cocoa beans naturally contain a high level of this fat, and all chocolate contains it in varying percentages.

Two properties of cocoa butter make important contributions to chocolate. As it cools, cocoa butter contracts, making molding of chocolate easier. Second, its melting point is very close to that of human body temperature (98.6°), which creates the pleasant 'mouth feel' of chocolate.

DARK CHOCOLATE (Sweet, Semi-sweet, and Bittersweet)

To produce a chocolate that can be eaten raw, sugar, cocoa butter, lecithin (an emulsifier), and vanilla are added to the liquor. Normally these are added during further refining and mixing to produce the correct consistency before molding and packaging.

Better, and generally more expensive, chocolate also receives further processing known as 'conching', during which the chocolate paste is kneaded for an extended period of time, sometimes as long as three days. During this very important refinement the moisture and the less aromatic, volatile acids evaporate, and a fine texture and chocolate flavor develop.

MILK CHOCOLATE

The manufacture of milk chocolate is similar to that of unsweetened dark chocolate but with the addition of dried milk powder and extra cocoa butter. The milk powder increases the content of, and modifies any fat which is present in the chocolate. At the same time it produces a softer chocolate because of the lower setting point of the butterfat in the milk powder. (The influence of butterfat also results in a lower temperature for dipping or molding.)

To further achieve the characteristic qualities of milk chocolate, the blend and variety of cocoa beans chosen for milk chocolate must be mildly flavored and lightly roasted. Extra cocoa butter is added to milk chocolate for smoothness.

WHITE CHOCOLATE

The manufacturing of white chocolate is similar to that of milk chocolate, except it contains cocoa butter instead of chocolate liquor. Like milk chocolate, the cocoa butter in white chocolate is made from mild, lightly roasted cocoa beans to produce the characteristic creamy milk flavor.

Because of the absence of chocolate liquor the U.S. Standard of Identity will not allow manufacturers to label white chocolate as 'chocolate', and it is generally referred to as white or ivory coating. Do not confuse it with white confectionary coating which contains vegetable fat as a substitute for cocoa butter. Read the ingredients label carefully before purchasing.

White chocolate is extremely susceptible to oxidative rancidity due to the butterfat content of powdered milk and the absence of chocolate liquor. Well wrapped, in a cool, dry, dark place, white chocolate will keep about eight months.

COUVERTURE

Couverture, the professional term for European coating chocolate, contains a much higher percentage of cocoa butter than any other chocolate. The finest quality brands will contain at least 32 percent cocoa butter and will have been conched for an extended time to produce a chocolate with a fine texture, well-balanced taste, and good flow properties, ideal for molding, machine enrobing, and hand dipping.

In order to achieve a high gloss and fine, homogenous texture when working with a couverture, it must first be tempered, which is explained in Chapter 2. Because different brands of couverture are processed differently, they require different tempering temperatures, which will fall within the ranges given for each type of chocolate.

CONFECTIONARY COATINGS

Confectionary coatings, or compound coatings as they are sometimes called, are sweetened combinations of cocoa powder and/or milk powder which contain vegetable fat as a complete or partial substitute for cocoa butter. Frequently these coatings come in a variety of flavors and pastel colors. As with white chocolate, they are not considered real chocolate by the U.S. Standard of Identity because of the absence of chocolate liquor.

Unlike cocoa butter, the vegetable fats contained in these coatings possess high melting points (above body temperature). The coating does not completely melt in the mouth before it is swallowed, causing an unpleasant waxy sensation, masking the flavor release of the coating.

Compound coatings are not recommended for use in these recipes.

UNSWEETENED COCOA POWDER

The dark, rich color of unsweetened cocoa powder, used as a coating on some of the truffles, gives them a seductive earthy look. I prefer Dutch cocoa for the recipes in this book. Dutch process treats the beans with an alkali-solution before or during roasting, resulting in a slightly less astringent flavor and a darker color. Droste, Poulain, Guittard, and Hershey are some of the popular brands of Dutch cocoa.

STORING CHOCOLATE

All chocolate should be wrapped in foil, then plastic wrap, and stored in a cool, dry place with good air circulation, out of sunlight. The ideal temperature for storage is 65° with 50 percent humidity. If chocolate is kept too cool or refrigerated and then exposed to room temperatures of 70° and above, it will sweat.

Storage in damp conditions will cause 'sugar bloom', as moisture collects on the surface of the chocolate. As it dries the bloom appears as tiny sugar crystals that have been leached out of the chocolate by the moisture and the chocolate becomes rough to the touch.

Chocolate that is stored in overly warm conditions will show 'fat bloom'. In this case, the stable cocoa butter crystals have melted reforming the unstable variety, eventually transforming back to the larger (but stable) crystals which appear as greasy blotches and streaks on the surface of the chocolate. Both types of bloom are often visible on truffles and chocolates sold in stores, especially in hot or humid weather.

Because cocoa butter, unlike most fats, contains natural oxidants that keep it from going rancid for a long period of time, dark chocolate that is wrapped well and stored in the proper conditions can be kept for as long as ten years. In fact, many people believe that its flavor actually improves with time. This is not true of milk or white chocolate. The butterfat contained in the milk solids eventually breaks down and becomes rancid, giving milk chocolate a life of about a year and white approximately eight months.

Of the other ingredients in the truffles, I use fresh, unsalted butter, ultra-pasteurized heavy cream (for longer storage life) and large eggs. Liqueurs and liquors are used to heighten the flavor of the fillings. If you cannot get the more unusual liqueurs, substitute an equal quantity of Cognac or rum. The liquor can be left out of the truffles completely if you substitute an equal amount of heavy cream.

VANILLA

In most of the truffle recipes that follow I suggest using vanilla beans rather than extract because I prefer the subtle, more rounded flavor of the real vanilla bean. Large beans should be used in the fillings; if you have smaller beans, increase the quantity indicated in the recipe.

Vanilla beans can be reused two or three times before their flavor is exhausted. Simply rinse them thoroughly in hot water and allow to dry before reusing or storing in sugar in an airtight container. (This also gives you vanilla flavored sugar for baking.) Where the beans are used in halves, cut crosswise.

If you prefer to use extract, substitute approximately ¾ teaspoon for 1 vanilla bean, and reduce the liquid proportionately, adding it to the truffle filling after the melted chocolate has been whisked in.

CRÈME FRAÎCHE

2 cups heavy cream
2 tablespoons buttermilk

Combine the heavy cream and buttermilk in a heavy saucepan. Gently heat to 90°. Immediately pour into a warm thermos. Cover and allow to sit in a warm place until the cream thickens, about 2½ days. Pour into a container, cover, and refrigerate. This recipe will make about 2 cups.

HAZELNUT OR WALNUT PRALINE

Made with hazelnuts or walnuts, praline adds texture and flavor to some of the truffles. The quantities can be doubled.

¼ teaspoon butter
½ cup coarsely chopped hazelnuts or walnuts
¼ cup sugar
⅓ cup water
¼ teaspoon lemon juice

To toast the hazelnuts, preheat the oven to 350°. Bake the nuts in a cake pan until the skins become loose and the nuts turn golden brown, about 10 minutes. Shake the pan from time to time to ensure even browning. As soon as the nuts are done, pour them on a clean tea towel. Cover the nuts with the towel and rub between your hands to loosen and remove the skins. Coarsely chop the nuts.

To prepare the praline, lightly butter a 4-inch square area on a baking sheet and set aside. In a small saucepan over low heat, stir the sugar, water, and lemon juice until the sugar has dissolved, about 2 minutes. Stop stirring and increase the heat so that the syrup boils. Dissolve any sugar crystals on the side of the pan with a pastry brush dipped in cold water. Swirling often, cook the syrup until it becomes a dark, golden brown, about 6 minutes. Watch the caramel very carefully; once it begins to color it should be swirled constantly. Remove the caramel from the heat. Add the chopped nuts and stir until they are evenly coated. Pour the praline onto the buttered baking sheet and quickly spread it to fill the 4-inch area. Cool about 20 minutes.

To make praline powder, chop the praline with a knife, then pulverize it into a coarse powder in a food processor with the metal blade or in a blender.(If you are using a blender, work in 4 batches to prevent the praline from becoming oily.)

EQUIPMENT

The recipes in this book require very little equipment beyond that normally found in a well equipped kitchen. The most important exception to this is the chocolate thermometer, which is used in tempering.

A cool kitchen with good air circulation is important to the chocolate maker, so I recommend using a fan, or better still, an air conditioner, to keep the working temperature about 68°. Water and humidity are two of the greatest enemies of the chocolate maker, and your equipment—pans and bowls, whisks and spatulas—and work surfaces should be clean and dry.

Chocolate thermometer.   Different from a candy thermometer, a chocolate thermometer must cover a range of 40-130°F in one degree increments to control the tempering process accurately. (Candy thermometers normally start above the minimum temperature needed in tempering.) Chocolate thermometers are available through mail order sources, but any good laboratory thermometer can be used for tempering.

Hot tray or flame tamer.   To melt chocolate, I use a hot tray with an adjustable control because it gives better temperature control than a double boiler and does not carry the risk of water or steam reaching the melting chocolate. As an alternative, you can use a flame tamer, which is a cheaper but less controllable method of keeping the pan away from direct heat.

Heating pad.   To maintain the constant low heat necessary for dipping chocolate, I have found a standard heating pad, the kind used for backaches, to be ideal. After melting chocolate, I set the pan on a heating pad covered with plastic wrap, with the temperature set to low (90°).

Small and medium-size bowls
Heavy 1 and 2-quart saucepans
Marble or formica work surface
Food processor or blender
Electric mixer
One-piece rubber spatulas
Finely meshed sieve
Wire whisks, preferably 9-inches
Melon baller, for shaping centers

Pie tins
Baking sheets and a heavy
   12 × 18-inch jelly roll pan
Baker's scraper and palette knife
Rolling pin (1¼-inch wooden)
Hair dryer, for warming molds
Pastry brush
Pastry bag with tubes
Parchment paper

HOW TO MAKE A PARCHMENT PAPER CONE

Because they're disposable and clean (free from any residue that would contaminate the chocolate), parchment cones are far better than cloth or plastic ones. Pre-cut triangles are available or you can cut one from a sheet of parchment—15-inch sides with a 21-inch base. To form the cone, place base-side down on a work surface. (To make shaping your first cone easier, number the base angles 1 and 2, and the apex 3.) With your right hand, curl point 1 over and bring forward to position it on point 3, to begin forming the cone. Hold points 1 and 3 with one hand, and bring point 2 over and round the back of the cone so that all points meet. Fold the three points down inside the top of the cone to secure.

To decorate coated truffles, hold the cone with the seam away from you. Spoon in about ¼ cup of tempered chocolate, gently pushing it towards the tip. Fold in the top sides and open end and roll to create a ball by which you can hold the cone. With scissors, cut a ¹⁄₁₆-inch opening in the tip of the cone. Pipe a little of the chocolate back into the pot to be sure the opening is large enough.

2

WORKING
WITH
CHOCOLATE

····——◆◈▶——····

For anyone working with chocolate, excessive heat or humidity and improper cooling conditions cause the most difficulties. Ideally the temperature in your kitchen should be about 68° and the humidity about 50 percent with good air circulation, for making truffles. When the temperature or humidity level rises much above this, you may find that after dipping your centers expand and crack their delicate chocolate coating or that some form of 'bloom' appears on the couverture.

MELTING CHOCOLATE

Many people use a double boiler for melting chocolate, but steam or even drops of water will cause the chocolate to sieze up or become lumpy. I find using a hot tray cleaner and much simpler.

Place pieces of chocolate about 1-inch in size in a heavy 2-quart saucepan. Adjust the dial on the hot tray to medium, no hotter than about 120°. Above 120° the chocolate will burn, become grainy, and lose some of its flavor. Stir frequently with a clean, dry spatula, scraping down the sides of the pot to get an even crystal melt, until the chocolate is completely melted. Remove from the heat.

It normally takes about 8 minutes to melt the quantities of chocolate I use in my truffle fillings. Milk chocolate, because of its milk solids, needs to be stirred more frequently than dark; white chocolate should be stirred constantly. If melting quantities much larger than 8 ounces, do not melt it all at once. Start with about 8 ounces and add the remainder gradually to melt the chocolate as evenly as possible.

TEMPERING

Tempered chocolate has a beautiful glossy finish, crisp texture, and it will keep longer. Tempering is actually raising, lowering, and raising again the temperature of the melted chocolate. Chocolate in 'poor temper' will look dull or grey, or streaked, or have a coarse, granular texture when broken up.

Because of the complexity of cocoa butter, the chemical and physical explanation behind the tempering process quickly becomes very difficult to follow. Basically, the process of heating to 120° then cooling to 80-82°, before raising the temperature slightly for dipping, aims to melt out the cocoa butter crystals, then reform them in their most stable (*beta*) state. When evenly distributed, the chocolate is then described as having been 'seeded' properly with the stable crystal.

Since unstable crystals begin to form at temperatures of about 82° and below, and above 93° the stable crystals begin to melt out, particular care should be taken in controlling the temperature of melted chocolate to preserve its temper. Check the temperature of the chocolate regularly, stirring it first to make sure your reading is accurate, and hold the thermometer in the chocolate, not resting on the bottom of the pan which will be hotter.

Because different brands and different types of chocolate contain different amounts of cocoa butter, the precise temperature for tempering will vary according to the chocolate you are using. Broadly, dark chocolate is tempered at 86-91° and white and milk at 84-86° (because of butterfat content in milk powder).

There are several methods for tempering, but I find the two described below work very well.

TABLE METHOD

The most professional and widely used technique for tempering small quantities of chocolate, the table method is also the most accurate and fail-safe. But it can be quite messy and requires a marble or formica work surface.

1. Melt about one third (no more than 8 ounces) of the broken chocolate couverture in a heavy 2-quart saucepan on a hot tray adjusted to medium setting. Gradually add the remainder until it is all melted and the temperature is 120°. Stir frequently with a clean, dry spatula.

2. Immediately remove from the heat and pour into a smaller 1-quart pan on a heating pad set to medium (about 100°). Pour three quarters of the melted chocolate onto a clean, dry surface such as marble or formica. With a palette knife, smear the chocolate evenly across the work surface, going back and forth over the chocolate. Bring the chocolate together with a scraper, and use the palette knife to clean the scraper. Repeat the spreading and scraping process, working quickly to prevent lumps from forming, and mixing the chocolate evenly.

Check the temperature of the chocolate; when it reaches 80-82° and takes on a dull, matte look, it is sufficiently seeded. Depending on the temperature of the kitchen, this will take anywhere from 5 to 20 minutes of continuous work.

3. Return the seeded paste to the rest of the chocolate in the pan. Stir gently and constantly with a rubber spatula, trying not to create air

bubbles, until the chocolate is smooth. Take the temperature of the chocolate; it should read 84-91°, depending on the type of chocolate you are tempering. If the chocolate is above 93° the stable crystals will melt out and you will have to begin tempering again from scratch. If it falls below this range, return the pan to the hot tray for 30 to 60 seconds to further heat the chocolate.

POT METHOD

This technique is a lot cleaner than the table method but takes longer and it is a little harder to get an even temper. Start with a couverture in good temper—showing a smooth grain and even color without grey streaks or blotches.

1. Break up all but 4 ounces of the chocolate couverture in 1-inch pieces. Melt in a heavy 2-quart pan on a hot tray adjusted to medium setting, stirring frequently. Bring the temperature to 120°.

2. Immediately remove from the heat and transfer the chocolate to a 1-quart saucepan. Place on a cake rack and add the 4-ounce lump of chocolate. If using 3-ounce bars, break into thirds and add one ounce at a time, allowing each to melt first.

Stir frequently until the chocolate reaches 82°. Add more chocolate a little at a time (about 2-ounce lumps) if it has all melted before this stage. Any lumps still present at 82° should be removed.

3. Return the pan to the hot tray and bring the temperature back to 84-91° (depending on the type of chocolate), stirring constantly and gently until smooth. Again, if the chocolate goes above 93° the stable crystals will melt out and you will have to begin tempering again.

CHOCOLATE TEMPERING RANGES

These are tempering ranges for the three types of chocolate couverture. Try to keep the temperature around the middle of these ranges so that as the viscosity of the chocolate increases with working, you can increase the temperature and still remain within the upper limit.

Dark Chocolate	86-91°
Milk and White Chocolate	84-86°

When you are working with tempered chocolate for more than about half an hour (for example, making a double batch of truffles, the filled madeleines, or molding), the viscosity of the chocolate will increase even if its temperature is kept constant. This is due to the agitation of the cocoa butter crystals, and it means that the tempered chocolate will become harder to work with. When this happens you can maintain the correct viscosity by adding small amounts of warm untempered chocolate at about 95-100°. Care must be taken, of course, not to add too much, or the stable crystals will melt out and the tempering process will have to be repeated.

Truffles deserve, and even depend on, being made with good chocolate. I've tested the recipes with a number of different chocolates. For the truffle and cake fillings, I recommend that you use any of the following: Dark—Lindt Excellence, Lindt Surfin, Tobler Tradition, and Suchard Bittra; Milk—Lindt Swiss Milk, Tobler Milk, and Suchard Milk; White—Lindt Swiss White and Tobler Narcisse. Add one extra ounce of chocolate if you use the Surfin, and two extra ounces of the Bittra to the quantity in the recipe.

If you prefer to use other chocolate, you may find that your results vary. Specifically, the chocolate flavor may be less intense or the fillings less easy to shape. To come as close as possible to my results, look for dark chocolate with 51 percent minimum cocoa solids, and milk and white chocolate 33 percent minimum. Some manufacturers include this information on the label.

All the coatings have been tested with Lindt dark, milk, and white couvertures. Other well-known brands of couverture include Valrhôna, Carma, Callebaut, Peter's by Nestlé, Guittard, and Wilbur. These and other couvertures are generally available through mail order sources. You can temper one of the chocolates suggested for the filling as a coating, but the shell will not be as thin and delicate.

DIPPING

To maintain the correct temperature of the chocolate during dipping, I have found that placing the pan on a heating pad adjusted to the lowest setting provides the ideal amount of heat. To protect the heating pad from stains, cover it in plastic wrap. Line a baking sheet with foil to receive the dipped truffles.

I use my fingers to dip truffles because it gives greater control than dipping forks. With practice you can learn to feel the temperature and viscosity changes in the couverture. The process is simple: lift the truffle center with your forefinger and second finger and dip into the melted chocolate. Toss the truffle between your fingers on the surface of the tempered chocolate to get an even coating. Lift out the truffle. Move your fingers in a scissor-type motion to release any drips, and scrape excess chocolate from your fingers on the edge of the pan. Place the truffle on a baking sheet removing your last finger with a slight twisting motion so that any drips form a finished, professional-looking twist on the top of the coated truffle.

3

THE TRUFFLES

····•————◄◆►————•····

I n the twenty recipes that follow I have selected some of the great variety of truffles you can make at home. Chocolate—dark, milk, or white—remains of course the soul of each truffle; but fruits, nuts, pralines, and liqueurs give it new dimensions.

The ideal truffle has a very delicate balance of flavors and textures that interplay around the chocolate ganache which is the essence of a truffle. Because of this, a slight change in the measures of the flavorings or variation in the types of flavorings will produce very different results. You will see that the quantities in my ingredients are very precise and should be followed as closely as possible.

Nearly all the recipes follow the same sequence of steps that with experience you will come to know intimately:

1. Infusing the cream with flavorings. Bring the cream to a gentle boil with flavorings such as vanilla beans and freshly ground coffee beans, then allow to cool for a few minutes to let the flavors permeate the cream fully.

2. Melting chocolate for the filling. As soon as the cream has been put on to heat, melt the chocolate following the method described in the previous chapter.

3. Mixing the filling. After sitting for the 5 or 10 minutes indicated in the recipe, strain the hot cream through a fine sieve to remove the vanilla, coffee, and other solid flavorings. Whisk the melted chocolate and other ingredients into the cream to complete the ganache. The mixture is allowed to cool to room temperature, covered in plastic wrap, and frozen overnight to allow the flavors to mellow.

4. Shaping the ganache. Using a melon baller, scoop a center. Roll it quickly and gently between the palms of your hands to form a smooth or irregularly-shaped ball, depending on the recipe. Dust your hands and the melon baller with confectioners' sugar if the filling becomes sticky. Cover and freeze until firm, about 2 hours.

5. Tempering the couverture. Follow one of the methods described in the previous chapter for tempering the chocolate.

6. Dipping and rolling. Dip the centers one at a time using the technique described in the previous chapter. Those truffles that have a coating such as cocoa or crushed cookie crumbs should be rolled immediately, before the couverture hardens.

7. Refrigerating and storing. Chill the coated truffles for 5 minutes to set the chocolate. Pack the truffles between layers of wax paper and store in an airtight container in the refrigerator. Take truffles from the refrigerator about 15 to 20 minutes before serving.

Truffles made with unpasteurized heavy cream can be refrigerated for one week; those made with ultra pasteurized cream, for ten days. Cover the airtight container with plastic wrap, then foil. Truffles can be frozen for up to two months. Thaw the unopened container overnight in the refrigerator.

Each of the recipes yields about 36 truffles. The recipes can be doubled, but you need add only 8 ounces of couverture to the amount indicated. Because it is difficult to temper the small quantity of chocolate couverture needed for a single recipe, you will find that you have plenty left over when all the centers have been dipped. Of course this chocolate need not go to waste, and I've given recipes for making bark, tuiles, and madeleines with the surplus.

If you're making your first truffles, I suggest that you begin with the Classic, since it does not require a tempered coating. On hot or humid days, it's probably safest to make one of the many rolled truffles so that any deterioration in the couverture is disguised. The Belgian, Bittermint, Bittersweet, Classic, Orangine, Raspberry, Saronno, and Walnut are all rolled truffles.

Classic Truffles

Start with this recipe if you've never made truffles before. These classic truffles are made with a lightly whipped ganache that is delicately flavored with dark rum or a liqueur of your choice. Unlike the other truffle recipes in this book, the filling is not frozen, but piped from a pastry bag fitted with a plain round tube. The centers are not dipped in tempered chocolate. They are simply rolled in cocoa, thus making the total preparation time very short—approximately 40 minutes. Have a bowl of ice water on hand for cooling the ganache.

Filling:

½ cup heavy cream
1 vanilla bean, cut in half
A few grains of salt
8 ounces bittersweet chocolate, in 1-inch pieces
1 ounce milk chocolate, in 1-inch pieces
2 egg yolks
1½ tablespoons dark rum or liqueur

Coating:

1½ cups unsweetened cocoa

Combine the heavy cream, vanilla bean, and salt in a small saucepan over medium heat. Bring to a gentle boil. Remove from the heat and allow to cool 5 minutes. While the cream is heating, melt the chocolate in a heavy 2-quart saucepan, stirring frequently with a rubber spatula. Set aside.

Strain the hot cream through a fine sieve into a small mixing bowl.

Whisk in the egg yolks and melted chocolate. Add the dark rum or liqueur and blend until smooth. Place the bowl of ganache in ice water, making sure that the water cannot slosh into the mixture. Stir constantly with a rubber spatula until the ganache is very thick and completely cool—approximately 5 minutes.

Immediately whip the ganache in an electric mixer, using a paddle attachment if you have one, until it lightens in color and forms soft peaks, about 15 to 30 seconds. Do not overbeat or the mixture will harden too quickly and the texture of the truffle will be grainy. Line a baking sheet with foil. Fit a pastry bag with a #8 round tube.

To shape the truffles, spoon half the ganache into the pastry bag. Pipe 6-inch long cylinders onto the baking sheet. Refill the pastry bag and continue to pipe. Refrigerate for 10 minutes to harden the truffles.

Slice the cylinders into 1½-inch pieces. Lightly dust the truffles with 1½ tablespoons unsweetened cocoa. With your fingertips, form each piece into an irregularly shaped 1-inch ball. Roll the truffles in cocoa and store.

BITTERSWEET TRUFFLES

My most popular truffle, the Bittersweet is the truffle for purists. Only vanilla adds its flavor to the dark chocolate ganache while unsweetened cocoa gives the finished truffle its characteristic earthy look. In a sense, all the truffles that follow are the children of this classic.

Filling:

¾ cup heavy cream
2 vanilla beans, cut in half
A few grains of salt
8 ounces bittersweet chocolate, in 1-inch pieces
½ tablespoon butter, cut in half, at
  room temperature
Confectioners' sugar, for shaping centers

Coating:

1½ pounds bittersweet chocolate couverture
4 cups unsweetened cocoa

To make the filling, combine the heavy cream, vanilla beans, and salt in a small saucepan over medium heat. Bring to a gentle boil. Remove from the heat and allow to cool for 5 minutes. While the cream is heating, melt the bittersweet chocolate in a heavy 2-quart saucepan, stirring frequently with a rubber spatula. Set aside.

Strain the hot cream through a fine sieve into a small mixing bowl. Whisk in the melted chocolate, then stir in the butter and blend until smooth. Allow to cool to room temperature, cover with plastic wrap, and freeze overnight.

To shape the centers, use a melon baller to scoop the filling and roll into irregularly-shaped 1-inch balls. Dust the melon baller and your hands with confectioners' sugar if necessary. Place the centers in pie tins, cover with plastic wrap, and freeze until firm, about 2 hours.

To coat the truffles, temper the chocolate couverture. Put the cocoa in an 8-inch square dish. Make troughs 8-inches long by 1-inch wide in the cocoa. Set the saucepan of tempered chocolate on a heating pad. Dip the frozen centers, one at a time, into the chocolate. As soon as each is coated, set it in a trough and cover with cocoa. When the truffles have set, transfer to a pie tin and refrigerate for 5 minutes to set the chocolate.

MOCHA TRUFFLES

This truffle attempts to capture the irresistable aroma of freshly ground coffee beans by pairing the beans with Tia Maria. A pinch of cocoa tops the glossy bittersweet couverture.

Filling:

⅔ cup heavy cream
1 vanilla bean, cut in half
1 tablespoon coarsely ground coffee beans,
    preferably Mocha
A few grains of salt
7 ounces bittersweet chocolate, in 1-inch pieces
2 ounces milk chocolate, in 1-inch pieces
1 tablespoon Tia Maria
2 teaspoons Cognac
½ tablespoon butter, cut in half, at
    room temperature
Confectioners' sugar, for shaping centers

Coating:

1½ pounds bittersweet chocolate couverture
¼ cup unsweetened cocoa

To make the filling, combine the heavy cream, vanilla bean, coffee, and salt in a small saucepan over medium heat. Bring to a gentle boil. Remove from the heat and allow to cool for 5 minutes. While the cream is heating, melt the chocolate in a heavy 2-quart saucepan, stirring frequently with a rubber spatula. Set aside.

Strain the hot cream through a fine sieve into a small mixing bowl. Whisk in the chocolate. Add the Tia Maria and Cognac. Stir in the butter and blend until smooth. Allow to cool to room temperature, cover with plastic wrap, and freeze overnight.

To shape the centers, use a melon baller to scoop the filling and roll into 1-inch balls. Dust the melon baller and your hands with confectioners' sugar if necessary. Place the centers in pie tins, cover with plastic wrap, and freeze until firm, about 2 hours.

To coat the truffles, temper the bittersweet couverture. Place the cocoa in a small bowl. Set the pan of tempered couverture on a heating pad. Dip the frozen centers one at a time into the chocolate and place on a baking sheet lined with foil. Sprinkle the top of each truffle with a pinch of cocoa powder immediately after placing it on the sheet. Refrigerate for 5 minutes to set the chocolate.

DUBLIN TRUFFLES

The macerated raisins spike this dark ganache, and I've added a little orange zest to fill out the flavor. The bittersweet coating is capped with a single golden raisin.

Drunken Raisins:

⅓ cup raisins, gold and dark
1½ tablespoons Irish whiskey
1½ teaspoons dark rum

Filling:

⅔ cup heavy cream
1 vanilla bean, cut in half
1 tablespoon coarsely ground coffee beans,
    preferably Mocha
1 teaspoon grated orange zest
A few grains of salt
8 ounces bittersweet chocolate, in 1-inch pieces
½ tablespoon butter, cut in half, at
    room temperature
Confectioners' sugar, for shaping centers

Coating:

1½ pounds bittersweet chocolate couverture
36 golden raisins

For the drunken raisins, combine the raisins, Irish whiskey, and dark rum in a small bowl. Cover and allow to sit overnight. Drain and reserve the soaking liquid. Finely chop the raisins and add them to the liquid. Set aside.

To make the filling, combine the heavy cream, vanilla bean, coffee, orange zest, and salt in a small saucepan over medium heat. Bring to a gentle boil. Remove from the heat and allow to cool for 5 minutes. While the cream is heating, melt the chocolate in a heavy 2-quart saucepan, stirring frequently with a rubber spatula. Set aside.

Strain the hot cream mixture through a fine sieve into a small mixing bowl. Whisk in the melted chocolate and drunken raisins. Add the butter and blend until smooth. Allow to cool to room temperature, cover with plastic wrap, and freeze overnight.

To shape the centers, use a melon baller to scoop the filling and roll into 1-inch balls. Dust the melon baller and your hands with confectioners' sugar if necessary. Place the centers in pie tins, cover with plastic wrap, and freeze until firm, about 2 hours.

To coat the truffles, temper the bittersweet chocolate couverture. Place the pan of tempered chocolate on a heating pad. Dip the frozen centers, one at a time, into the chocolate and transfer to a baking sheet lined with foil. Place a raisin on top of each truffle immediately after setting it on the baking sheet. Refrigerate for 5 minutes to set the chocolate.

BELGIAN TRUFFLES

Crème fraîche adds a tartness and Cognac a depth to the flavor of the ganache. Dipping the truffle in cocoa after the coating has set gives the truffle a softer look.

Filling:

⅔ cup Crème Fraîche (Page 11)
1 vanilla bean, cut in half
A few grains of salt
6 ounces bittersweet chocolate, in 1-inch pieces
3 ounces milk chocolate, in 1-inch pieces
1 egg yolk
2 teaspoons Cognac
½ tablespoon butter, cut in half, at
    room temperature
Confectioners' sugar, for shaping centers

Coating:

1½ pounds milk chocolate couverture
1 cup unsweetened cocoa

Opposite: Cocoa dusted Bittersweet truffles.

Overleaf, left: A composition of milk and dark, from left: Walnut truffle (top), raisin topped Dublin, dark ridged Bittermint, dark nubbly Jamaican, cocoa dusted Belgian, crunchy coated Saronno, nubbly milk Yucatan, praline topped Hazelnut Praline, cocoa dusted ridged Raspberry, and dark cocoa topped Mocha.

To make the filling, combine the crème fraîche, vanilla bean, and salt in a small saucepan over medium heat. Bring to a gentle boil. Remove from the heat and allow to cool for 5 minutes. While the cream is heating, melt the chocolate in a heavy 2-quart saucepan, stirring frequently with a rubber spatula. Set aside.

Strain the hot cream through a fine sieve into a small mixing bowl. Whisk in the egg yolk, then the chocolate. Add the Cognac and butter and blend until smooth. Allow to cool to room temperature, cover with plastic wrap, and freeze overnight.

To shape the centers, use a melon baller to scoop the filling and roll into irregularly-shaped 1-inch balls. Dust the melon baller and your hands with confectioners' sugar if necessary. Place the centers in pie tins, cover with plastic wrap, and freeze until firm, about 2 hours.

To coat the truffles, temper the milk chocolate couverture. Set the pan of tempered chocolate on a heating pad. Place the cocoa in a small bowl. Dip the frozen centers one at a time and transfer to a baking sheet lined with foil. When the truffles have been dipped, roll each in cocoa. Refrigerate for 5 minutes to set the chocolate.

Previous page, right: White chocolate bark surrounds cocoa dusted Capuccino, nubbly Coconut Lime, sleek ridged Pistachio, and the white dusted Orangine.

Opposite: Truffle Cake.

RASPBERRY TRUFFLES

Crème fraîche and raspberry are a classic filling of Belgian chocolates—the tartness of the cream enhancing the sweetness of the fruit in the liqueur. A crisp bittersweet couverture completes the traditional combination of flavors.

Filling:

⅓ cup Crème Fraîche (Page 11)
½ cup heavy cream
1 vanilla bean, cut in half
A few grains of salt
9 ounces bittersweet chocolate, in 1-inch pieces
1 egg yolk
3½ tablespoons Framboise
1 teaspoon Cognac
½ tablespoon butter, cut in half, at
   room temperature
Confectioners' sugar for shaping centers

Coating:

1½ pounds bittersweet chocolate couverture
1 cup unsweetened cocoa

To make the filling, combine the crème fraîche, heavy cream, vanilla bean, and salt in a small saucepan over medium heat. Bring to a gentle boil. Remove from the heat and allow to cool for 5 minutes. While the cream is heating, melt the chocolate in a heavy, 2-quart saucepan, stirring frequently with a rubber spatula. Set aside.

Strain the hot crème fraîche through a fine sieve into a small mixing bowl. Whisk in the egg yolk and chocolate. Add the Framboise, Cognac, and butter; blend until smooth. Allow to cool to room temperature, cover with plastic wrap, and freeze overnight.

To shape the centers, use a melon baller to scoop the filling and roll into 1-inch balls. Dust the melon baller and your hands with confectioners' sugar if necessary. Place the centers in pie tins, cover with plastic wrap, and freeze until firm, about 2 hours.

To coat the truffles, temper the chocolate couverture. Make a parchment decorating cone. Place the cocoa in a small bowl. Set the pan of tempered chocolate on the heating pad. Dip the frozen centers, one at a time, into the chocolate and place on a baking sheet lined with foil.

Fill the cone with about ¼ cup of tempered chocolate. Cut a ¹⁄₁₆-inch tip on the cone. Pipe a delicate striping back and forth in one continuous line on each truffle going slightly beyond the truffle with each pass. Allow the pattern to set, about 3 minutes, then roll each truffle in cocoa. Refrigerate for 5 minutes to set the chocolate.

····•———◆———•····

JAMAICAN TRUFFLES

Caramel cream and rum are blended with dark chocolate in this ganache, and the whole enrobed in bittersweet chocolate textured with crunchy hazelnut praline and cookie crumbs. Because of the intricate timing, I recommend this to experienced truffle makers only!

Caramel:

¼ cup sugar
2 tablespoons water
½ teaspoon lemon juice

Filling:

¾ cup heavy cream
1 vanilla bean, cut in half
A few grains of salt
8 ounces bittersweet chocolate, in 1-inch pieces
1 egg yolk
1 tablespoon dark rum
½ tablespoon butter, cut in half, at room temperature

Confectioners' sugar, for shaping centers

Coating:

1½ pounds bittersweet chocolate couverture
1 recipe Hazelnut Praline (Page 12)
6 Pepperidge Farm Bordeaux cookies

To prepare the caramel, combine the ingredients in a small saucepan over medium-low heat, stirring to dissolve the sugar. Increase the heat to medium and bring to a boil. Wash down the sides of the pan with a pastry brush dipped in cold water to dissolve any remaining sugar crystals. Allow the syrup to boil, swirling the pan occasionally, until it begins to darken, about 8 minutes. While the syrup is cooking, fill a bowl with ice water. As soon as the syrup begins to darken, swirl constantly until it becomes a dark brown. When it begins to smoke, remove immediately from the heat and place the bottom of the pan in ice water for 30 seconds to prevent the caramel from burning.

While the syrup is cooking, prepare the other ingredients for the filling. Combine the cream, vanilla, and salt in a small saucepan over medium heat. Bring to a gentle boil, then remove from heat and allow to cool for 5 minutes. While the cream is heating, melt the chocolate in a heavy 2-quart saucepan, stirring frequently. Set aside.

Strain the hot cream through a fine sieve into the caramel. Cook over medium-low heat, stirring constantly, until the caramel has dissolved into the cream, about 3 minutes. Return the pan to the ice water to cool the mixture to 110°, stirring constantly. Pour the cream into a mixing bowl. Whisk in the egg yolk and the chocolate. Stir in the rum and butter and blend well. Allow to cool to room temperature, cover with plastic wrap, and freeze overnight.

To shape the centers, use a melon baller to scoop the filling and roll into ⅞-inch balls. Dust the melon baller and your hands with confectioners' sugar if necessary. Place the centers in pie tins, cover with plastic wrap, and freeze until firm, about 2 hours.

To coat the truffles, temper the bittersweet chocolate couverture. Pulverize the hazelnut praline and set aside. Finely crush the cookies with a rolling pin and combine with the praline. Set the pan of tempered chocolate on a heating pad and stir in the praline and cookies. Bring the couverture to dipping temperature. Dip the frozen centers one at a time and place on a baking sheet lined with foil. Refrigerate for 5 minutes to set the chocolate.

SARONNO TRUFFLES

To add variety, I suggest two ways of coating this coffee Amaretto ganache, to make two distinctively different looking results. For a charming gift, pack the truffles in the bright red Amaretti tin.

Filling:

⅔ cup heavy cream
1 vanilla bean, cut in half
1 teaspoon coarsely ground espresso coffee beans
A few grains of salt
8 ounces bittersweet chocolate, in 1-inch pieces
1 ounce milk chocolate, in 1-inch pieces
1½ tablespoons Amaretto
1 teaspoon Cognac
½ tablespoon butter, cut in half, at
   room temperature
Confectioners' sugar, for shaping centers

Coating:

1½ pounds bittersweet chocolate couverture
1 4½-ounce tin Amaretti di Saronno

To prepare the filling, combine the heavy cream, vanilla bean, espresso, and salt in a small saucepan over medium heat. Bring to a gentle boil. Remove from the heat and allow to cool for 5 minutes. While the cream is heating, melt the chocolate in a heavy 2-quart saucepan, stirring constantly with a rubber spatula. Set aside.

   Strain the hot cream through a fine sieve into a small mixing bowl.

Whisk in the chocolate. Stir in the Amaretto and Cognac. Add the butter and blend until smooth. Allow to come to room temperature, cover with plastic wrap, and freeze overnight.

To shape the centers, use a melon baller to scoop the filling and roll into ⅞-inch balls. Dust the melon baller and your hands with confectioners' sugar if necessary. Place the centers in pie tins and cover with plastic wrap. Place one tin in the refrigerator and the other in the freezer; chill for 2 hours.

To coat the truffles, temper the bittersweet couverture. With a rolling pin, crush the Amaretti cookies into fine crumbs. Set aside in a small mixing bowl. Place the pan of tempered chocolate on a heating pad. Dip the refrigerated centers, one at a time, into the chocolate. Immediately after dipping, roll each truffle in the crumbs until it is completely coated. Transfer to a plate and refrigerate for 5 minutes to set the chocolate.

Pour the remaining crumbs into the tempered chocolate; stir until blended. Bring the chocolate to dipping temperature by returning the pan to the hot tray for a few seconds. Dip the frozen centers, one at a time, into the chocolate and set on a baking sheet lined with foil. Refrigerate for 5 minutes to set the chocolate.

W·ALNUT PRALINE TRUFFLES

Walnut praline and Nocello, a walnut flavored liqueur, bring a rich warmth to this ganache which is enclosed in a bittersweet couverture studded with finely-chopped walnuts and cookie crumbs.

Filling:

1 recipe Walnut Praline (Page 12), pulverized
⅔ cup heavy cream
1 vanilla bean, cut in half
A few grains of salt
8 ounces bittersweet chocolate, in 1-inch pieces
2 tablespoons Nocello
1 teaspoon dark rum
Confectioners' sugar, for shaping centers

Coating:

1½ pounds bittersweet chocolate couverture
6 Pepperidge Farm Bordeaux cookies
¾ cup finely chopped walnuts
1 cup unsweetened cocoa

To make the filling, combine the praline, heavy cream, vanilla bean, and salt in a small saucepan over medium heat. Bring to a gentle boil. Remove from the heat and allow to cool for 5 minutes. While the cream is heating, melt the chocolate in a heavy, 2-quart saucepan, stirring frequently with a rubber spatula. Set aside.

Pour the hot cream into a small mixing bowl and remove the vanilla bean. Whisk in the melted chocolate. Add the Nocello and dark rum and blend until smooth. Allow the mixture to cool to room temperature, cover with plastic wrap, and freeze overnight.

To shape the centers, use a melon baller to scoop the filling and roll into $7/8$-inch balls. Dust the melon baller and your hands with confectioners' sugar if necessary. Place the centers in pie tins, cover with plastic wrap, and freeze until firm, about 2 hours.

To coat the truffles, temper the bittersweet chocolate couverture. Crush the cookies with a rolling pin and combine with the walnuts in a small bowl. Put the cocoa in another small bowl.

Place the pan of tempered chocolate on a heating pad. Stir in the nuts and cookies. Bring the couverture to dipping temperature by returning it to the hot tray for a few seconds. Dip the frozen centers, one at a time, into the chocolate and place on a baking sheet lined with foil. When the truffles have been dipped, roll each in cocoa. Refrigerate for 5 minutes to set the chocolate.

ORANGINE TRUFFLES

Candied fresh orange zest captures the tart flavor of the fruit which is often missing in store-bought candied peel. Here its flavor is intensified by maceration in Grand Marnier and Cognac. The bittersweet coated truffle is rolled in confectioners' sugar.

Candied Orange Zest:

1 large navel orange
1½ cups sugar
2 cups water
½ teaspoon lemon juice
1 tablespoon Cognac
2 teaspoons Grand Marnier

Filling:

⅔ cup heavy cream
1 vanilla bean, cut in half
A few grains of salt
8 ounces bittersweet chocolate, in 1-inch pieces
½ tablespoon butter, cut in half, at room temperature
Confectioners' sugar, for shaping centers

Coating:

1½ pounds bittersweet chocolate couverture
3½ cups confectioners' sugar

To make the candied orange zest, remove the zest from the orange with a vegetable peeler in 1-inch wide strips, removing as little of the bitter white pith as possible. Blanch the zest in 3 successive pots of boiling water for 3 minutes each. Drain and rinse under cold water between each blanching.

Meanwhile, dissolve the sugar, water, and lemon juice in a small heavy saucepan over medium-low heat and bring to a boil. Dissolve any sugar crystals on the side of the pan with a pastry brush dipped in cold water. Add the blanched zest. Cook at a gentle simmer until the zest is translucent, about 1½ hours. Drain and reserve the flavored syrup for another use, such as a soaking syrup for cake. Finely chop the zest and put it into a small bowl with the Cognac and Grand Marnier. Cover and allow to sit overnight.

To prepare the filling, combine the heavy cream, vanilla bean, and salt in a small saucepan over medium heat. Bring to a gentle boil, then remove from the heat and allow to cool for 5 minutes. While the cream is heating, melt the chocolate in a heavy 2-quart saucepan, stirring frequently with a rubber spatula. Set aside.

Strain the hot cream through a fine sieve into a small mixing bowl. Whisk in the chocolate. Stir in the chopped zest and liqueur. Add the butter and blend until smooth. Allow to cool to room temperature, cover with plastic wrap, and freeze overnight.

To shape the centers, use a melon baller to scoop the filling and roll into irregularly-shaped 1-inch balls. Dust the melon baller and your hands with confectioners' sugar if necessary. Place the centers in pie tins, cover with plastic wrap, and freeze until firm, about 2 hours.

To coat the truffles, temper the bittersweet couverture. Sift the confectioners' sugar if it is lumpy and place in an 8-inch square dish. Make 1-inch troughs in the sugar the length of the pan. Place the tempered chocolate on a heating pad. Dip the frozen centers one at a time and place in the sugar. Cover with sugar and transfer to pie tins. Refrigerate for 5 minutes to set the chocolate.

BITTERMINT TRUFFLES

I recommend peppermint oil for this recipe as it generally has a much fresher flavor than extract. Unsweetened chocolate contributes a slightly bitter flavor to this dark chocolate ganache.

Filling:

⅔ cup heavy cream
1 vanilla bean, cut in half
A few grains of salt
8 ounces bittersweet chocolate, in 1-inch pieces
½ ounce unsweetened chocolate
1 egg yolk
1 tablespoon Cognac
¼ teaspoon peppermint oil or extract
½ tablespoon butter, cut in half, at
    room temperature
Confectioners' sugar, for shaping centers

Coating:

1½ pounds bittersweet chocolate couverture

To make the filling, combine the cream, vanilla bean, and salt in a small saucepan over medium heat. Bring to a gentle boil, then remove from the heat and allow to cool for 5 minutes. While the cream is heating, melt the chocolates in a heavy 2-quart saucepan, stirring frequently with a rubber spatula. Set aside.

Strain the hot cream through a fine sieve into a small mixing bowl. Whisk in the egg yolk and the chocolate. Add the Cognac and peppermint. Stir in the butter and blend well. Allow to cool to room temperature, then cover with plastic wrap, and freeze overnight.

To shape the centers, use a melon baller to scoop the filling and roll into 1-inch balls. Dust the melon baller and your hands with confectioners' sugar if necessary. Arrange the centers in pie tins, cover with plastic wrap, and freeze until firm, about 2 hours.

To coat the truffles, temper the bittersweet couverture. Make a parchment cone. Place the saucepan of tempered chocolate on a heating pad. Dip the frozen centers, one at a time, into the chocolate and set in rows on a baking sheet lined with foil. When all the truffles have been coated, fill the cone with about ¼ cup of tempered chocolate. Cut a ¹⁄₁₆-inch tip in the cone. Pipe delicate striping back and forth in one continuous line over the truffle, going slightly beyond the truffle with each pass. Refrigerate for 5 minutes to set the chocolate.

HAZELNUT PRALINE TRUFFLES

Ground hazelnut praline adds an interesting texture to this ganache, and its flavor is enhanced by orange zest and hazelnut-flavored Frangelico liqueur. Cognac can be substituted for this liqueur, though the truffles will not taste as nutty.

Filling:

1 recipe Hazelnut Praline (Page 12)
2/3 cup heavy cream
1 vanilla bean, cut in half
4 strips orange zest, 1/2 by 4-inches
A few grains of salt
8 ounces bittersweet chocolate, in 1-inch pieces
2 tablespoons Frangelico
1 teaspoon dark rum
1/2 tablespoon butter, cut in half, at
    room temperature

Coating:

1 1/2 pounds milk chocolate couverture
1 1/2 tablespoons reserved hazelnut praline

Pulverize the hazelnut praline and reserve 1 1/2 tablespoons for topping the coated truffles. Combine the remaining praline powder with the heavy cream, vanilla, orange zest, and salt in a small saucepan over medium heat. Bring to a gentle boil. Remove from the heat and allow to cool for 5 minutes. While the cream is heating, melt the chocolate in a heavy 2-quart saucepan, stirring frequently with a spatula. Set aside.

Strain the hot cream through a fine sieve into a small mixing bowl. Whisk in the chocolate. Add the Frangelico, dark rum, and butter and stir to blend well. Allow to cool to room temperature, cover with plastic wrap, and freeze overnight.

To shape the centers, use a melon baller to scoop out the filling and roll into 1-inch balls. Dust the melon baller and your hands with confectioners' sugar if necessary. Place the centers in pie tins, cover with plastic wrap, and freeze until firm, about 2 hours.

To coat the truffles, temper the milk chocolate couverture. Set the pan of couverture on a heating pad. Dip the frozen centers one at a time into the chocolate and transfer to a baking sheet lined with foil. Immediately after placing each truffle on the baking sheet, sprinkle it with a pinch of praline powder. Refrigerate for 5 minutes to set the chocolate.

VIENNESE TRUFFLES

The coffee, rum, and walnuts frequently combined in Viennese pastries provide a sophisticated blend for this dark ganache. The creamy milk chocolate couverture is textured with finely-ground praline.

Filling:

1 recipe Walnut Praline (Page 12), pulverized
⅔ cup heavy cream
1 vanilla bean, cut in half
2 teaspoons coarsely ground coffee beans,
   preferably Mocha
A few grains of salt
7 ounces bittersweet chocolate, in 1-inch pieces
1 ounce milk chocolate, in 1-inch pieces
2 tablespoons Nocello
2 teaspoons dark rum
Confectioners' sugar, for shaping centers

Coating:

1½ pounds milk chocolate couverture

Overleaf, left: A Valentine's Day selection of molded chocolate and golden Saronno truffles, with a plate of dark Hawaiian and milk Yucatan truffles, accompanied in the basket by white Madagascar.

Opposite: Three irresistible Christmas baskets in dark chocolate containing Summer truffles (left), Bittersweet truffles (center), and an assortment of dark Bittermint, golden Saronno, nubbly milk Yucatan, white Pistachio, and praline topped Hazelnut Praline.

Combine the praline powder with the heavy cream, vanilla bean, coffee, and salt in a small saucepan over medium heat. Bring to a gentle boil, remove from heat, and allow to cool for 5 minutes. While the cream is heating, melt the chocolate in a heavy 2-quart saucepan, stirring frequently with a rubber spatula. Set aside.

Strain the hot cream through a fine sieve into a small mixing bowl. Whisk in the melted chocolate. Stir in the Nocello and rum. Allow to cool to room temperature, then cover with plastic and freeze overnight.

To shape the centers, use a melon baller to scoop the filling and roll into 1-inch balls. Dust the melon baller and your hands with confectioners' sugar if necessary. Place the centers in pie tins, cover with plastic wrap, and freeze until firm, about 2 hours.

To coat the truffles, temper the milk chocolate couverture. Make a parchment decorating cone. Set the pan of tempered chocolate on a heating pad. Dip the frozen centers, one at a time, into the chocolate and transfer to a baking sheet lined with foil.

Fill the cone with about ¼ cup of couverture and cut a ¹⁄₁₆-inch tip on it. Pipe a delicate striping back and forth in one continuous line over each truffle, going slightly beyond the truffle with each pass. Refrigerate for 5 minutes to set the chocolate.

Previous page, right: A dark chocolate Easter egg containing a selection of dark Hawaiian, milk Yucatan, and white Coconut Lime truffles.

Opposite: A chocolate basket of miniature madeleines accompanies a plate of filled madeleines and milk, white, and dark chocolate tuiles.

YUCATAN TRUFFLES

Named for the region where chocolate, vanilla, and cinnamon were first married with other spices in a native Indian drink, the Yucatan also uses vanilla seeds to give a subtle texture to this classic combination.

Filling:

3 vanilla beans
⅔ cup heavy cream
2 teaspoons coarsely ground coffee beans,
  preferably Mocha
A few grains of salt
8 ounces bittersweet chocolate, in 1-inch pieces
1 ounce milk chocolate, in 1-inch pieces
1½ tablespoons Kahlua
1 teaspoon Cognac
A pinch of cinnamon
½ tablespoon butter, cut in half, at
  room temperature
Confectioners' sugar, for shaping centers

Coating:

¾ cup slivered almonds
1½ pounds milk chocolate couverture
6 Pepperidge Farm Bordeaux cookies

Trim the ends from the vanilla beans, then cut them in half. Split the halves lengthwise. In a small saucepan, combine the beans (ends included), the heavy cream, coffee, and salt over medium heat. Bring to a gentle boil. Remove from the heat and allow to cool 5 minutes. While the cream is heating, melt the chocolate in a heavy 2-quart saucepan, stirring frequently with a rubber spatula. Set aside.

Strain the hot cream through a fine sieve into a small mixing bowl. Using a paring knife, scrape the tiny black seeds from inside the beans and add them to the hot cream. Strain the cream back into the pan to remove any pieces of coffee bean that may have stuck to the vanilla.

Reheat the cream to 110° and return to the mixing bowl. Whisk in the melted chocolate. Add the Kahlua, Cognac, and cinnamon. Stir in the butter and blend until smooth. Allow to cool to room temperature, cover with plastic wrap, and freeze overnight.

To shape the centers, use a melon baller to scoop the filling and roll into ⅞-inch balls. Dust the melon baller and your hands with confectioners' sugar if necessary. Place the centers in pie tins, cover with plastic wrap, and freeze until firm, about 2 hours.

To prepare the coating for the truffles, preheat the oven to 350°. Spread the almonds in a cake pan and bake until golden brown, about 8 minutes. Swirl the pan occasionally for even browning. As soon as the almonds have browned, immediately dump them in a cool cake pan to stop cooking. Cool completely, then finely chop. Crush the cookies with a rolling pin. Combine the crumbs and almonds and set aside.

Temper the milk chocolate couverture and place the saucepan of tempered chocolate on a heating pad. Add the cookies and almonds and stir just to blend. Return the couverture to dipping temperature. Dip the frozen centers one at a time and place on a baking sheet lined with foil. Refrigerate for 5 minutes to set the chocolate.

HAWAIIAN TRUFFLES

Macadamia nuts and coconut cream give this truffle a distinctly Hawaiian flavor. If you're unable to find unsalted macadamia nuts, remove the salt by blanching the nuts in boiling water before toasting.

Filling:

⅓ cup heavy cream
⅓ cup coconut cream
1 vanilla bean, cut in half
A few grains of salt
8 ounces white chocolate, in 1-inch pieces
1 egg yolk
2 teaspoons dark rum
Confectioners' sugar, for shaping centers

Coating:

⅓ cup unsalted macadamia nuts
1 cup sweetened shredded coconut
1½ pounds bittersweet chocolate couverture

To make the filling, combine the heavy cream, coconut cream, vanilla bean, and salt in a small saucepan over medium heat. Bring to a gentle boil. Remove from the heat and allow to cool for 5 minutes. While the cream is heating, melt the white chocolate in a heavy 2-quart saucepan, stirring constantly with a rubber spatula. Set aside.

Strain the hot cream through a fine sieve into a small mixing bowl. Whisk in the egg yolk and the melted chocolate. Stir in the rum. Allow to cool to room temperature, cover with plastic wrap, and refrigerate until it thickens to the consistency of pudding, about 2 hours.

Whip in an electric mixer, using the paddle attachment if you have one, until the filling lightens in color and forms peaks, about 30 seconds. Spoon into a small bowl, cover with plastic wrap, and freeze overnight.

To shape the centers, use a melon baller to scoop the filling and roll into ⅞-inch balls. Dust the melon baller and your hands with confectioners' sugar if necessary. Place the centers in pie tins, cover with plastic wrap, and freeze until firm, about 2 hours.

To prepare the coating, preheat the oven to 325°. Spread the macadamia nuts in a cake pan and toast until lightly browned, about 10 minutes, swirling the pan from time to time to ensure even browning. As soon as the nuts are toasted, remove from the oven and transfer to a cool pan to prevent further browning. When the nuts have completely cooled, chop finely. Toast the coconut until lightly brown in the same way. Combine the chopped nuts and coconut in a small bowl.

Temper the bittersweet couverture. Place the pan of tempered chocolate on a heating pad and stir in the coconut and nuts. Bring the couverture to dipping temperature by returning it to the hot tray for a few seconds. Dip the frozen centers, one at a time, into the chocolate and transfer to a baking sheet lined with foil. Refrigerate for 5 minutes to set the chocolate.

Summer Truffles

The refreshing flavors of orange and lemon permeate this white chocolate ganache, while the white chocolate couverture is sparked with an almond Amaretti crunch.

Filling:

½ cup heavy cream
1 vanilla bean, cut in half
1 tablespoon grated lemon zest
1 tablespoon grated orange zest
A few grains of salt
8 ounces white chocolate, in 1-inch pieces
1 egg yolk
Confectioners' sugar, for shaping centers

Coating:

¾ cup sliced unblanched almonds
¼ cup Amaretti crumbs
1½ pounds white chocolate couverture

To make the filling, combine the heavy cream, vanilla bean, lemon and orange zest, and salt in a small saucepan over medium heat. Bring to a gentle boil. Remove from heat and allow to sit for 10 minutes. While the cream is heating, melt the chocolate in a heavy, 2-quart saucepan, stirring constantly with a rubber spatula. Set aside.

Strain the cream through a fine sieve into a small mixing bowl. Whisk in the egg yolk and melted chocolate. Blend until smooth. Allow to cool to room temperature, cover with plastic wrap, and refrigerate until it thickens to the consistency of pudding, about 2 hours.

Whip the filling in an electric mixer, using the paddle attachment if you have one, until it lightens in color and forms peaks, about 30 seconds. Spoon into a small bowl, cover with plastic wrap, and freeze overnight.

To shape the centers, use a melon baller to scoop the filling and roll into ⅞-inch balls. Dust the melon baller and your hands with confectioners' sugar if necessary. Place the centers in pie tins, cover with plastic wrap, and freeze until firm, about 2 hours.

To coat the truffles, preheat the oven to 350°. Toast the almonds on a baking sheet until lightly browned, about 8 minutes. Halfway through baking, turn the sheet and stir the nuts to ensure even browning. Pour the almonds onto a cool baking sheet to stop browning and cool to room temperature. Crush the almonds with a rolling pin and combine with the Amaretti crumbs in a small bowl.

Temper the white chocolate couverture. Place the pan of tempered chocolate on a heating pad. Pour in the almond and Amaretti crumbs and stir to blend. Bring the couverture to dipping temperature by returning it to the hot tray for a few seconds. Dip the frozen centers, one at a time, into the chocolate and place on a baking sheet lined with foil. Refrigerate for 5 minutes to set the chocolate.

MADAGASCAR TRUFFLES

Madagascar is the source of most of the vanilla we use today, and this truffle uses both the pod and the tiny seeds it contains. Vanilla is of course the dominant flavor (the seeds also add texture to the ganache) which is further heightened by the Cognac, while the egg yolk contributes a richness to the ganache. The white chocolate couverture is textured with a cashew crunch.

Filling:

3 vanilla beans
½ cup heavy cream
A few grains of salt
8 ounces white chocolate, in 1-inch pieces
1 egg yolk
1 tablespoon Cognac or Crème de Cacao
Confectioners' sugar, for shaping centers

Coating:

1½ pounds white chocolate couverture
6 Pepperidge Farm Bordeaux cookies
¾ cup finely chopped roasted, unsalted cashews

Trim the ends from the vanilla beans, then cut them in half. Split the halves lengthwise. Combine the beans (ends included), the heavy cream, and salt in a small saucepan over medium heat. Bring to a gentle boil. Remove from the heat and allow to cool 5 minutes. While the cream is heating, melt the chocolate in a heavy 2-quart saucepan, stirring constantly with a rubber spatula. Set aside.

Strain the hot cream through a fine sieve into a small mixing bowl. Using a paring knife, scrape the tiny seeds from the vanilla beans and add them to the hot cream. Discard the scraped beans. Whisk in the egg yolk and melted chocolate. Blend in the Cognac or Crème de Cacao. Allow to cool to room temperature, then cover with plastic wrap and refrigerate until the filling thickens to the consistency of pudding, about 2 hours.

Whip in an electric mixer, using the paddle attachment if you have one, until the mixture becomes lighter in color and forms peaks, about 30 seconds. Spoon into a small bowl, cover with plastic wrap, and freeze overnight.

To shape the centers, use a melon baller to scoop the filling and roll into 7/8-inch balls. Dust the melon baller and your hands with confectioners' sugar if necessary. Place the centers in pie tins, cover with plastic wrap, and freeze until firm, about 2 hours.

To coat the truffles, temper the white chocolate couverture. Finely crush the cookies with a rolling pin and combine the crumbs with chopped cashews in a small bowl. Place the pan of tempered chocolate on a heating pad. Blend in the cookie crumbs and cashews. Bring the couverture to dipping temperature by returning to the hot tray for a few seconds. Dip the frozen centers, one at a time, into the chocolate and place on a baking sheet lined with foil. Refrigerate for 5 minutes to set the chocolate.

Coconut Lime Truffles

Coconut cream and lime zest give this all-white truffle a tropical flavor. The coconut cream, so popular in summer cocktails, should be stirred well before measuring.

Filling:

1/3 cup heavy cream
1/3 cup coconut cream
1 vanilla bean, cut in half
2 teaspoons grated lime zest
A few grains of salt
8 ounces white chocolate, in 1-inch pieces
1 egg yolk
2 teaspoons dark rum
Confectioners' sugar, for shaping centers

Coating:

1 cup sweetened shredded coconut
6 Pepperidge Farm Bordeaux cookies
1½ pounds white chocolate couverture

To make the filling, combine the heavy cream, coconut cream, vanilla bean, lime zest, and salt in a small saucepan over medium heat. Bring to a gentle boil, then remove from the heat and allow to cool for 10 minutes. While the cream is heating, melt the white chocolate in a heavy, 2-quart saucepan, stirring constantly with a spatula. Set aside.

Strain the warm cream through a fine sieve into a small mixing bowl. Whisk in the egg yolk and melted chocolate; add the rum and blend until smooth. Allow to cool to room temperature, then cover with plastic wrap and refrigerate until the filling thickens to the consistency of pudding, about 2 hours.

Whip the filling in an electric mixer, using the paddle attachment if you have one, until it becomes lighter in color and forms peaks, about 30 seconds. Spoon into a small bowl, cover with plastic wrap, and freeze overnight.

To shape the centers, use a melon baller to scoop the filling and roll into ⅞-inch balls. Dust the melon baller and your hands with confectioners' sugar if necessary. Place the centers in pie tins, cover with plastic wrap, and freeze until firm, about 2 hours.

To prepare the coating for the truffles, preheat the oven to 325°. Toast the coconut in a cake pan until lightly browned, about 10 minutes, swirling the pan from time to time to ensure even browning. Remove from the oven and immediately pour the coconut into a cool cake pan to prevent further browning. Allow to cool to room temperature. Finely crush the cookies with a rolling pin and combine with the coconut. Set aside.

Temper the white chocolate couverture. Place the pan of tempered chocolate on a heating pad. Add the coconut and cookie mixture and stir to blend well. Bring the couverture to dipping temperature by returning it to the hot tray for a few seconds. Dip the frozen centers, one at a time, into the chocolate and set in rows on a baking sheet lined with foil. Refrigerate for 5 minutes to set the chocolate.

CAPUCCINO TRUFFLES

The freshly ground coffee beans and Tia Maria, together with a hint of cinnamon, give a rich yet delicate flavor to this ganache. I sprinkle the white chocolate couverture with a pinch of cocoa to finish this truffle.

Filling:

½ cup heavy cream
1 vanilla bean, cut in half
2 tablespoons coarsely ground coffee beans,
    preferably Mocha
A few grains of salt
A pinch of cinnamon
8 ounces white chocolate, in 1-inch pieces
1 egg yolk
1½ tablespoons Tia Maria
Confectioners' sugar, for shaping centers

Coating:

1½ pounds white chocolate couverture
1 tablespoon unsweetened cocoa

To make the filling, combine the heavy cream, vanilla bean, coffee, and salt in a small saucepan over medium heat. Bring to a gentle boil. Remove from the heat, stir in the cinnamon, and allow to cool 5 minutes. While the cream is heating, melt the chocolate in a heavy 2-quart saucepan, stirring constantly with a rubber spatula. Set aside.

Strain the hot cream through a fine sieve into a small mixing bowl.

Whisk in the egg yolk and chocolate. Add the Tia Maria and blend until smooth. Allow to cool to room temperature, then cover with plastic wrap and refrigerate until the mixture thickens to the consistency of pudding, about 2 hours.

Whip in an electric mixer, using the paddle attachment if you have one, until the mixture becomes lighter in color and forms peaks, about 30 seconds. Spoon into a small bowl, cover with plastic wrap, and freeze overnight.

To shape the centers, use a melon baller to scoop the filling and roll into 1-inch balls. Dust the melon baller and your hands with confectioners' sugar if necessary. Place the centers in pie tins, cover with plastic, and freeze until firm, about 2 hours.

To coat the truffles, temper the white chocolate couverture. Place the cocoa in a small bowl. Set the pan of tempered chocolate on a heating pad. Dip the frozen centers, one at a time, into the chocolate and transfer to a baking sheet lined with foil. Sprinkle each truffle with a pinch of cocoa immediately after placing it on the baking sheet. Refrigerate for 5 minutes to set the chocolate.

PISTACHIO TRUFFLES

This all-white chocolate truffle is lightly-textured with ground pistachios. Pistasha liqueur fills out the flavor of the nuts but can be substituted with Cognac for a milder pistachio taste.

Filling:

½ cup heavy cream
⅓ cup blanched unsalted natural pistachio nuts
1 vanilla bean, cut in half
A few grains of salt
8 ounces white chocolate, in 1-inch pieces
1 egg yolk
1 tablespoon Pistasha
1 teaspoon Cognac
Confectioners' sugar, for shaping centers

Coating:

1½ pounds white chocolate couverture

To make the filling, combine the heavy cream, pistachios, vanilla bean, and salt in a small saucepan over medium heat. Bring to a gentle boil. Remove from the heat and allow to cool for 5 minutes. While the cream is heating, melt the chocolate in a heavy 2-quart saucepan, stirring constantly with a rubber spatula. Set aside.

When the cream has cooled, remove the vanilla bean. Combine the cream and pistachio nuts in a food processor or blender until the nuts are finely ground. Pour the mixture back into the saucepan and gently reheat. When the cream has heated, pour into a small mixing bowl.

Whisk in the egg yolk and melted chocolate. Add the Pistasha and Cognac and blend until smooth. Allow to cool to room temperature, cover with plastic wrap, and refrigerate until the mixture thickens to the consistency of pudding, about 2 hours.

Whip the filling in an electric mixer, with the paddle attachment if you have one, until it lightens in color and forms peaks, about 30 seconds. Spoon into a small bowl and wrap with plastic. Freeze overnight.

To shape the centers, use a melon baller to scoop the filling and roll into 1-inch balls. Dust the melon baller and your hands with confectioners' sugar if necessary. Place the centers in pie tins, cover with plastic wrap, and freeze until firm, about 2 hours.

To coat the truffles, temper the white chocolate couverture. Make a parchment decorating cone. Set the pan of tempered chocolate on a heating pad. Dip the frozen centers, one at a time, into the chocolate and transfer to a baking sheet lined with foil.

Fill the cone with about ¼ cup of chocolate. Cut a ¹⁄₁₆-inch tip in the cone. Pipe a delicate striping back and forth in one continuous line on each truffle, going slightly beyond the truffle with each pass. Refrigerate for 5 minutes to set the chocolate.

4

MORE SWEET SEDUCTIONS

····———◆▶———·····

One of the extravagances of truffles is that there is always couverture left after dipping. The easiest way to put this to good use is to add an ingredient such as nuts or dried fruits for texture, and spread it to set as bark. Chocolate Tuiles are a light and crisp balance to the truffles. The ganache-filled Madeleines and Woven Chocolate Basket are more ambitious projects, while the cake is a spectacular finale to any meal.

CHOCOLATE ALMOND BARK

Any combination of nuts, fruits, coconut, or cookie crumbs can be added to the couverture in a ratio of about 2 cups to 1½ cups of couverture to make bark. Textured couvertures add an extra interest to chocolate bark; try adding almonds to the Amaretti Saronno or chopped macadamia nuts to the Hawaiian.

The nuts or fruit should be dry and as close in temperature to the couverture as possible; chilled nuts or fruit should be spread in a cake pan and set on the hot tray to warm.

2 cups toasted whole almonds
1½ cups tempered dark, milk, or white couverture

Line a baking sheet with foil. Add the nuts into the chocolate and stir gently to blend. Pour the mixture onto the sheet, spreading it evenly with a palette knife or spatula to ⅛-inch thickness. Refrigerate for 10 minutes to set the chocolate, turning the sheet after 5 minutes for even cooling. Allow the chocolate to set on a rack for at least 2 hours. Holding the bark with wax paper to prevent finger marks, break the bark into 3-inch pieces. Store between layers of wax paper in an airtight container in a cool, dry place.

CHOCOLATE TUILES

A chocolate version of the classic French almond cookie, tuiles are draped over a rolling pin just before setting to give the shape of curved roof tiles from which they get their name. If you have less than about 1¼ pounds of chocolate, use a smaller quantity of almonds. These quantities will yield about 30 tuiles and 6 ounces of bark.

1¼ pounds dark, milk, or white couverture
2 cups sliced toasted unblanched almonds

Make patterns for the tuiles. On foil, trace 30 circles 2¼-inches in diameter. Cut out the circles, leaving about a ½-inch border around the tracing for handling the tuiles. Secure a 1¼-inch diameter rolling pin to a work surface with tape.

Temper the chocolate in a heavy 1-quart saucepan. Place the pan of tempered chocolate on a heating pad. Lightly crush the almonds, then add them to the chocolate by the handful, gently stirring after each addition. Check the temperature of the couverture and allow to reheat if necessary. Stir the couverture frequently while making the tuiles, and check the temperature at regular intervals.

Place a generous teaspoon of couverture on each foil circle, working with a few circles each time. Quickly spread the chocolate to the edges of the tracing with a palette knife. Allow to sit until almost set, about 2 minutes. Drape the chocolate covered foil over the rolling pin and allow to set completely, about 3 minutes. Transfer the tuiles to a baking sheet; place in a cool spot with good air circulation and allow to sit one hour. Do not refrigerate.

Continue making the tuiles until three-quarters of the mixture has been used. Use the remainder to make almond bark: spread the chocolate on a foil-lined baking sheet and allow to sit at least two hours.

Remove the foil from the tuiles. Store between layers of wax paper.

MOCHA-FILLED MADELEINES

These thin madeleine shells are filled with a light mocha ganache and capped with couverture. There are a variety of madeleine molds in different shapes and sizes, so to be sure you'll have enough chocolate, measure a single mold with water beforehand. Multiply this by the number of sections and use 8 ounces of chocolate for each ¾ cup of water. These quantities yield 12 3-inch madeleines. Before beginning this recipe, read the instructions for molding.

For Shells:

1½ pounds dark, milk, or white chocolate couverture

Filling:

½ cup heavy cream
1 vanilla bean, cut in half
1 teaspoon grated orange zest
1 teaspoon coarsely ground coffee beans, preferably
   Mocha
A few grains of salt
9 ounces bittersweet chocolate, in 1-inch pieces
1 ounce milk chocolate, in 1-inch pieces
1 egg yolk
2 teaspoons Cognac

Temper the couverture in a heavy 1-quart saucepan. Meanwhile, prepare the filling. Combine the heavy cream, vanilla bean, orange zest,
coffee beans, and salt in a small saucepan over medium heat. Bring to a
gentle boil. Remove from the heat and allow to cool for 5 minutes.
While the cream is heating, melt the chocolate in a heavy 2-quart
saucepan, stirring frequently with a rubber spatula. Set aside.

Strain the hot cream through a fine sieve into a small mixing bowl.
Whisk in the egg yolk and the melted chocolate, then stir in the
Cognac. Set aside, stirring from time to time. Clean the mold with a
lint-free cloth or cotton balls.

Set the pan of tempered chocolate on a heating pad. The temperature
of the molds should be about 80°; if necessary, warm them with a hair
dryer. Using a soup spoon, fill half the molds with chocolate to just
below the top. Tap the molds to release air bubbles. Fill the remaining
molds and tap again. Refrigerate the chocolate until the edges have set
to ¹⁄₁₆ to ⅛-inch, about 2 or 3 minutes. Invert the mold over a sheet of

foil and shake vigorously in a circular motion to remove the excess chocolate. Return the mold, raised on tartlet pans and inverted over a baking sheet, to the refrigerator. Allow the chocolate to set for 30 seconds to 1 minute. Remove from the refrigerator and, using a baker's scraper, smooth the edges. Remove any scraps of chocolate in the shells with a dry pastry brush.

Make two parchment decorating cones. Place the filling on the hot tray and heat to 85°. Fill and cut a ¼-inch tip in each cone. Pipe the filling into the shells to just below the edge, about seven-eighths full. Smooth slightly with a small spoon and refrigerate until the filling is firm, about 10 minutes.

Remove the molds from the refrigerator. Check the temperature of the chocolate. Cap each with chocolate, spreading across the entire surface of the mold with a palette knife to ensure even coating. Chill 1 hour, until the madeleines are completely set, when they will have contracted slightly from the sides of the molds.

To unmold, invert the pan over a surface padded with 2 or 3 clean kitchen towels, lightly tapping the edge of the mold on the work surface if necessary. Store in an airtight container, packed between layers of wax paper. Stored at 65°, they will keep two to four days.

Woven Chocolate Baskets

Perhaps the most dramatic presentation for chocolate truffles is this exquisite woven basket. Tempered chocolate is piped over molds, building up layers of delicate threads, and the finished baskets look like miniature French grapevine baskets. Woven lids cover the truffles after the basket has been filled. Try to make the baskets on a cool, dry day, and allow about two hours working time.

1½ pounds tempered dark, milk, or white chocolate
   couverture

Special Equipment:

2 1-cup metal timbale molds
6 parchment decorating cones

Wrap the outside of the timbale molds with foil, leaving a 1-inch
border overlapping the top. Tuck this inside the mold. Invert one mold
on a baking sheet lined with foil and trace two circles onto the foil.
These tracings will be the patterns for the lids.

Set the pan of tempered chocolate on a heating pad. While making
the baskets, stir the chocolate regularly and check the temperature from
time to time.

Ladle chocolate into a parchment cone. Cut a ¹⁄₁₆-inch tip. Invert one
mold on your fingertips and pipe four evenly spaced 'warp' threads
along the length of the mold. Place the mold upright on the baking
sheet and repeat for the second mold. Allow to set, about 3 minutes.

To begin the basket lids, pipe two lines in the shape of a cross,
intersecting at the center, using the traced circles as guides. Allow to
set.

Replace a mold over your fingertips. Holding it horizontally, pipe
closely-spaced zigzag lines across the warp threads around the mold,
turning the mold as you pipe. These lines are 'weft' threads. Replace
the mold on the baking sheet and repeat with the second mold.

Return to the lids. Starting in the center of the first circle, pipe a
closely spaced spiral to the edge of the tracing. Repeat for the second
lid and allow to set.

Pipe a second series of warp threads on both molds, evenly spaced
between the original threads. (Each mold will now have eight warp

threads.) Allow to set. Similarly, pipe a second cross on each lid, evenly spaced between the first. Each lid will have two crosses.

Returning to the molds, pipe a second layer of weft threads. Allow to set. Pipe another spiral on the basket lids. Pipe a set of warp threads along the original warps on each basket. Pipe a cross over the original cross lines on each lid. Pipe a third series of weft threads around each mold. Pipe a third spiral on each lid. Pipe over the second set of warp threads on the molds and allow to set.

Continue to pipe warp and weft threads on the baskets in this manner until each warp thread has been piped four times and the weft threads eight times. (Allow the chocolate to set after each addition.) End the piping with weft threads.

Pipe over the second cross on the lids. Continue piping until you have gone over each cross four times and have eight layers of spirals. (Again, allow the chocolate to set after each addition.) End the piping with a spiral. When the chocolate has completely set, carefully lift the finished basket lids off the foil and set aside on a rack.

To unmold the baskets, bring 1½ cups of water to a simmer. Peel back the 1-inch border of foil inside the molds. Pour ¾ cup of simmering water into the first mold, being careful not to splash the chocolate. Loosen the mold and lift it out of the chocolate basket. Work quickly so that the basket does not melt from the heat of the hot water. Repeat for the second basket. Peel off the foil. Set the baskets upright on a baking sheet lined with foil.

Check the temperature of the chocolate and adjust if necessary. To form the bottoms of the baskets, ladle ⅛ cup of chocolate into each. Spread it evenly using the back of a small spoon. Allow the bottoms to set completely before removing from the baking sheets, about 20 minutes. Trim any blobs of chocolate with a sharp knife. Store the baskets in a cool, dry, dark place. Each will hold ten truffles.

TRUFFLE CAKE

This incredibly rich, chocolatey cake looks like a giant truffle. A delicate layer of chocolate spongecake is molded in a round bowl and filled with a delicious hazelnut praline chocolate mousse. After chilling several hours, the cake is spread with an airy chocolate ganache, spiked with a covering of hazelnut meringue chips, and lightly dusted with cocoa. The preparation is elaborate, but it can be separated into several stages. This cake will serve 12 to 16 generously.

CHOCOLATE SPONGECAKE

1 teaspoon butter, at room temperature
1 tablespoon sifted flour
6 eggs, separated, at room temperature
⅔ cup sugar
⅛ teaspoon salt
2 teaspoons vanilla extract
¼ teaspoon cream of tartar
6 tablespoons sifted unsweetened cocoa
1 tablespoon confectioners' sugar

Preheat the oven to 350°. Lightly butter a 12 × 18-inch jelly roll pan and line with parchment paper. Butter and flour the paper; set aside.

Beat the egg yolks with ⅓ cup of sugar, adding it 1 tablespoon at a time, in an electric mixer on medium-high speed. Add the salt and vanilla. Beat until the mixture becomes light and lemon-colored, about 5 minutes.

In a clean bowl, beat the egg whites to soft peaks. While beating, add the cream of tartar and the remaining ⅓ cup sugar one teaspoon at a time, and continue to beat until the mixture forms a soft meringue. Fold one quarter of the meringue into the yolks to lighten them. Gently fold in another quarter of the meringue. Sift 2 tablespoons of the cocoa over the mixture and fold in. Alternately fold in the remaining meringue and cocoa in two batches of each. Pour the batter into the prepared pan and spread evenly.

Bake for about 25 minutes, turning the pan after 15 minutes for even baking. The cake is done when a toothpick inserted in the center comes out clean. Cool the pan on a cake rack for 15 minutes. Sprinkle the cake with confectioners' sugar. Remove the cake by covering it with a baking sheet and inverting. Gently peel off the paper and allow the cake to cool completely.

To mold the cake, use a round 2-quart bowl about 4½-inches deep. Line the bowl with two long strips of plastic wrap crossing them in the center and leaving enough over the edge of the bowl so that it can be brought up to cover the cake. Cut a lengthwise strip of the cake 1-inch wider than the depth of the bowl. Cut this strip of cake in half crosswise. Line both sides of the bowl with the two strips, gently molding them to the sides. The cake should extend about 1-inch over the top of the bowl. This will leave the bottom and 2 triangular areas of the bowl uncovered. Cut pieces from the remaining cake to fit these areas, reserving enough cake to cover the bowl when the mousse has been added. Fit the strips as closely together as possible, overlapping slightly if necessary. Cover the cake and the bowl and set aside.

HAZELNUT PRALINE CHOCOLATE MOUSSE

When toasting the hazelnuts for the praline, double the quantity and reserve half for the hazelnut meringue.

1 recipe Hazelnut Praline (Page 12)

14 ounces bittersweet chocolate, in 1-inch pieces
6 tablespoons butter
3 eggs, separated
A pinch of salt
3 tablespoons dark rum
2 tablespoons strong coffee, at room temperature
2 teaspoons vanilla extract
1 tablespoon sugar
¾ cup heavy cream

Chop and pulverize the praline. Melt the chocolate and butter in a heavy 2-quart saucepan, stirring frequently. Set aside. While the chocolate is cooling, combine the praline powder, egg yolks, and salt in a mixing bowl. Set the bowl over a pan of barely simmering water, making sure that the bowl does not touch the water. Whisk the praline and yolks constantly until they feel warm to the touch, about 2 minutes.

Remove from the pan and beat the yolks in an electric mixer on medium-high speed for 3 minutes. Combine the rum, coffee, and vanilla in a measuring cup. Add half the rum and coffee flavorings to the yolks, one teaspoon at a time, blending well after each addition. Reserve the remaining flavorings. Continue to beat until the yolks lighten in color and fall from the beaters in a thin ribbon, about 8 minutes. Set aside.

In a clean bowl, whisk the egg whites into soft peaks. Add the sugar one teaspoon at a time, whisking constantly until the whites are just shy of the stiff peak stage. Set aside.

Fold the melted chocolate and butter into the yolks. Gradually fold in the remaining rum and coffee, then fold in the egg whites. Set aside.

Whip the cream in a clean bowl to the soft peak stage. Fold this into the chocolate mixture. Pour the mousse into the cake-lined bowl, smoothing over the top. Cut the remaining cake to fit over the mousse and set into place. Trim the edge of the cake with scissors to make it level. Bring up the plastic wrap to seal and refrigerate 12 hours.

HAZELNUT MERINGUE

2 teaspoons butter, at room temperature
1½ tablespoons sifted flour
⅓ cup toasted hazelnuts
½ cup plus 1 tablespoon sugar
A pinch of salt
2 egg whites, at room temperature (reserve
    yolks for ganache)
⅛ teaspoon cream of tartar
2 teaspoons sifted unsweetened cocoa
½ teaspoon vanilla extract

Preheat the oven to 300°. Lightly butter two baking sheets or jelly roll pans. Line with parchment, and butter and flour the parchment.

Pulverize the hazelnuts with 1 tablespoon of sugar and the salt in a food processor or blender. Set aside.

Beat the egg whites in an electric mixer at low speed until frothy. Add the cream of tartar, increase speed to medium, and beat to soft peak stage. Increase speed to high and carefully add the ½ cup sugar one teaspoon at a time. Beat to a stiff meringue. Sprinkle the toasted nuts over the meringue and sift the cocoa on top. Fold in gently. When the cocoa is almost incorporated, fold in the vanilla.

Spoon half the meringue into a pastry bag fitted with a #4 round tube. Pipe the meringue into strips ¾-inch apart running across the width of the sheet. Repeat for the remaining meringue. Bake each sheet

30 minutes, refrigerating one while the first is baking. Turn halfway through baking for even browning. Allow to cool completely on cake racks, then cut the meringue into ¼-inch pieces. On humid days, store the meringue pieces in a plastic bag.

CHOCOLATE GANACHE

Make the ganache at least 2 hours before assembling the cake. To unmold the cake, peel back the plastic wrap, cover the cake with a cardboard circle or serving plate and invert. Remove the bowl and lift off the plastic wrap. Gently press in the bottom edge of the cake with your fingers to give it a more rounded look. Set aside.

⅔ cup heavy cream
A pinch of salt
1 vanilla bean, cut in half
3 ounces bittersweet chocolate, in 1-inch pieces
2 egg yolks, chilled
2 teaspoons dark rum

1½ tablespoons sifted unsweetened
  cocoa, for decoration

Combine the heavy cream, salt, and vanilla in a small saucepan over medium heat and bring to a gentle boil. Remove from the heat and allow to cool 5 minutes. While the cream is heating, melt the chocolate in a heavy 2-quart saucepan, stirring frequently with a rubber spatula. Set aside.

Strain the cream through a fine sieve into a small mixing bowl. Whisk in the egg yolks and the melted chocolate. Allow to cool to room temperature, cover with plastic wrap, and refrigerate at least 2 hours.

Beat the ganache in an electric mixer on medium speed. When it starts to thicken, add the rum one teaspoon at a time. Increase the speed to medium-high and beat to soft peak stage, about 3 minutes.

To complete the cake, use a palette knife to spread an even coating of ganache over the surface. Gently press handfuls of chopped meringue into the ganache, covering evenly. Dust the cake with sifted cocoa.

The truffle cake should be refrigerated and cut when chilled.

Molding Chocolate

Molding is a practical (and elegant) way to use leftover tempered couverture before it sets. Tiny and delicate or large and dramatic, solid or hollow, molded chocolate is special indeed. As you have tempered chocolate on hand, all you will need is the mold itself. If you're lucky enough to have unusual antique molds that are in good condition, by all means use them. Otherwise, there are a wide variety of metal and plastic molds available in stores and through some of the mail order sources at the back of this book. With care metal molds will last indefinitely.

Ideally the chocolate should be cooled gradually at about 55° until completely set. On a cool, dry day chocolate can be set in an open window (out of sunlight) or in front of an air conditioner. As the chocolate will mirror the surface of the mold, use a shiny, unblemished, mold and clean carefully with a lint-free cloth or cotton ball before use. If you plan to mold couverture regularly, use your molds for chocolate only. Don't wash them afterwards, but melt leftover chocolate with a hair dryer and wipe clean with a lint-free cloth. This will build up a thin coating of cocoa butter on the surface of the mold, making unmolding easier.

SOLID MOLDING

The techniques of solid molding are fairly straightforward. Choose a mold that is the right size for the amount of couverture you have; measure the capacity of your mold with water. (On average, about 1 pound of couverture is left after dipping. Each pound is 1½ cups.)

Heat the clean, dry mold with a hair dryer to a temperature close to the couverture before filling. Ladle or spoon couverture to just below the edge of the mold. Tap the lip of the mold against the work surface several times to release any air bubbles in the chocolate (you will see them rise to the surface and pop). If you are using a tray of molds such as madeleines fill half, then tap against the work surface and repeat for the second half. Wipe any chocolate drips from the top of the mold with a cotton ball.

Refrigerate the mold for 1 hour to set the chocolate, turning halfway through for even cooling. When the chocolate is completely set, it will have contracted slightly from the sides of the mold and will unmold easily. (If not, return to the refrigerator for several minutes.)

To unmold, invert the mold over a surface padded with clean tea towels. Allow to sit for one hour, then store in a cool, dry, dark place.

HOLLOW MOLDING

If solid molding is easy, hollow molding is not. There are however, endless wonderful ways to enjoy these chocolates—filled with fresh raspberries and cream, a light mousse, ice cream or sherbet, and certainly truffles.

Hollow molding initially follows the same techniques as solid: scrupulously clean dry molds are slightly warmed, then filled to just below the edge with tempered chocolate.

Tap the mold to release air bubbles and refrigerate until a thin border of set chocolate forms, about 2 to 5 minutes. Take the mold from the refrigerator. To remove the excess chocolate and produce a hollow shape, invert the mold and shake vigorously in a circular motion over a foil lined baking sheet. (This excess chocolate, if it has no additional ingredients, can be reused but must be retempered. First allow it to cool completely. Wrap well in foil and plastic wrap. Temper it with an equal amount of new chocolate.)

Chill the molds to harden the chocolate by refrigerating them, inverted and raised over a baking sheet until the drips are just beginning to set, about 1 or 2 minutes. Scrape the top of the mold with a baker's scraper to make smooth edges. Remove any scraps of chocolate from the shells with a dry pastry brush.

Return the mold to the refrigerator until the chocolate is completely set and has contracted slightly from the sides of the pan. Carefully unmold the shells onto a padded surface. If you wish to fill the shells, follow the directions for Mocha-filled Madeleines in the previous chapter.

To avoid finger marks on molded chocolate, handle it with wax paper. Properly stored in a cool, dry place, unfilled molded chocolate will keep at least one week.

ACKNOWLEDGEMENTS: I'd like to thank Wolfman Gold & Good Company, Tiffany & Co., Dean and DeLuca, and Somethin' Else Antiques, who supplied props, and Dimitri Levas, who styled the photographs. Too many chocolate manufacturers and importers provided samples for this book to mention individually, but I'd like to give special thanks to Rudy Sprungli of Lindt.

SOURCES OF SUPPLY

Chef's Catalog
3915 Commercial Avenue
Northbrook, IL 60062

The Chocolate Factory
P.O. Box 3053
Department CN
Stony Creek, CT 06471

Madame Chocolate
1940-C Lehigh Avenue
Glenview, IL 60025

Maid of Scandinavia
3244 Raleigh Avenue
Minneapolis, MN 55416

CHOCOLATE:

Albert Uster Imports, Inc.
9845 Kitty Lane
Oakland, CA 94603

Chocolate Collection from Nestlé
Department 350
Ronks, PA 17573

Christopher Stephens Importer
P.O. Box 114
Carversville, PA 18916

Confection Connection
18660 Ventura Boulevard
Tarzana, CA 95113

De Choix Specialty Foods
58-25 52nd Avenue
Woodside, NY 11377

Edelweiss Candy Kitchen
444 North Cañon Drive
Beverly Hills, CA 90210

Fowlers of Durham
Brightleaf Square
905 W. Main St.
Durham, NC 27701

Krön Chocolatier
506 Madison Avenue
New York, NY 10022

Simply Chocolate
P.O. Box 16037
St. Paul, MN 55116

A Southern Season
East Gate
Chapel Hill, NC 27514

EQUIPMENT:

The Broadway Panhandler
520 Broadway
New York, NY 10012

Brooklyn Thermometer Co.
90 Verdi St.
Farmingdale, NY 11735

Dean & DeLuca
121 Prince St.
New York, NY 10012

Lekvar-by-the-Barrel
1577 First Avenue
New York, NY 10028

ANTIQUE MOLDS:

Spencer K. House
Mail Order
100K Waldon Road
Abingdon, MD 21009

INDEX

THE AUTHOR: Adrienne Welch has worked as a professional chef for over ten years. Before moving to New York City, she apprenticed with Madeleine Kamman and worked as a pastry chef in a number of restaurants and stores. From 1979 to 1981 she was with Dean & DeLuca in New York, where she developed a line of truffles, cakes, and pastries. Currently, Bloomingdale's sells Adrienne's truffles exclusively through their New York store.